Neptune Noir

Unauthorized Investigations
into *Veronica Mars*

EDITED BY

Rob Thomas

WITH LEAH WILSON

BENBELLA BOOKS, INC.
Dallas, Texas

"Welcome to Camp Noir" © 2006 by Lani Diane Rich
"Story Structure and *Veronica Mars*" © 2006 by Geoff Klock
"Veronica Mars: Girl. Detective." © 2006 by Yvonne Jocks
"Daddy's Girl" © 2006 by Joyce Millman
"Daddy Dualities" © 2006 by Amy Berner
"On the Down-Low: How a *Buffy* Fan Fell in Love with *Veronica Mars*" © 2006 by Lynne Edwards
"The Noir of Neptune" © 2006 by Amanda Ann Klein
"Reality on *Mars* and Neptune" © 2006 by Jesse Hassenger
"'I Cannot Tell a Lie. And If You Believe That . . .'" © 2006 by John Ramos
"Lawless Neptune" © 2006 by Alafair Burke
"The New Normal: Breaking the Boundaries of Vigilantism in *Veronica Mars*"
    © 2006 by Kristen Kidder
"The Duck and the Detective" © 2006 by Chris McCubbin
"The United States of Veronica: Teen Noir as America's New Zeitgeist" © 2006 by Deanna Carlyle
"I'm in Love with My Car: Automotive Symbolism on *Veronica Mars*"
    © 2006 by Lawrence Watt-Evans
"Boom Goes the Dynamite: Why I Love Veronica and Logan" © 2006 by Misty Hook
"Innocence Lost: The Third Wave of Teen Girl Drama" © 2006 by Samantha Bornemann
"From Golden Girl to Rich Dude Kryptonite: Why Veronica Mars Is in with the Out-Crowd"
    © 2006 by Judy Fitzwater
"The Importance of Not Being Earnest" © 2006 by Heather Havrilesky
Additional Materials © 2006 by Rob Thomas

BenBella Books, Inc.
6440 N. Central Expressway, Suite 503
Dallas, TX 75206
www.benbellabooks.com
Send feedback to feedback@benbellabooks.com

Printed in the United States of America
10 9 8 7 6 5 4 3

Library of Congress Cataloging-in-Publication Data

Neptune noir : unauthorized investigations into Veronica Mars / edited by Rob Thomas with Leah
Wilson.
    p. cm.
    ISBN 1-933771-13-5
    1. Veronica Mars (Television program) I. Thomas, Rob. II. Wilson, Leah.

    PN1992.77.V47N46 2007
    791.45'72—dc22

                                                                                    2006039330

Proofreading by Lynn Hess and Jennifer Canzoneri
Cover illustration © 2006 by Clint Scism
Cover design by Laura Watkins
Text design and composition by John Reinhardt Book Design
Printed by Bang Printing

Distributed by Independent Publishers Group
To order call (800) 888-4741
www.ipgbook.com

For special sales contact Robyn White at robyn@benbellabooks.com

Table of Contents

Rob Thomas

Digressions on How *Veronica Mars* Saved My Career and, Less Importantly, My Soul

I TAUGHT HIGH SCHOOL during my mid-twenties in Austin, Texas. I have clear memories of sitting in my living room watching TV and wondering how clearly god-awful programming made it on the air. Unfunny comedies. Cheesy dramas. Why can't every show be *Seinfeld* or *Northern Exposure* or *Moonlighting? Surely there are smart, well-paid, well-intentioned people involved in the process of creating these shows,* I'd say to myself. *And even if there aren't, doesn't someone at the network watch the show and say, "This is bad television; let's fix it or get it off the air!"?*

They're spending tens of millions of dollars on something that is by almost any measurable standard *bad. Do they know? How can they not know? Do they care? How can something this bad happen?*

I moved to Los Angeles for good nine years ago at age thirty-two, and here's what I learned in the TV/film business: It's a minor miracle when any finished product *doesn't* suck.

I learned this particular lesson the hard way. It's possible to have a collection of talented people all working together on a project, all with the best intentions, working hard, and it still be far, far easier to fail than to succeed. It doesn't take much to destroy a project: one bad piece of casting; the wrong director interpreting it; a "gotcha" ending that doesn't "getcha"; one belligerent person in a test screening; one bad network "note."

The list is a long one. A television show is a house of cards, and if you place one of those cards wrong, the show will collapse.

Does this seem obvious? Perhaps, but it wasn't to me.

I spent nine years playing in a rock band trying to *make it*. I never came close. Of course, I was at a bit of a disadvantage as a musician as I wasn't a very good one. So, after I quit the band, I turned to writing to fill this "artistic void" I felt in my life. To my surprise, after I finished my first novel, things happened extraordinarily quickly for me. I found an agent. I got a book deal. It was the beginning of a seven-year ride where everything I wrote was published or produced. I wrote four novels and a short story collection. Simon & Schuster published all of them. I wrote two feature films, an independent and a studio film—both went into production. And in the biggest miracle of all, I wrote a television pilot that went on to become a well-received if ratings-starved series. While I was writing and producing that series, *Cupid*, David Kelley called me. He was going to do a new series, and he wanted to know if I'd be interested in running it for him. It was going to be the first time he created a new show and immediately handed it off to another writer. I felt as though I were being anointed crown prince of Television Land. Competing studios offered me millions of dollars for my services. I'd only moved to Los Angeles eighteen months earlier. It's safe to say I was ripe to get smacked around.

Which, unfortunately, I did.

I left the David Kelley series *Snoops* before we even began shooting episodes. David and I didn't see the series in the same way, and it was his show, so I left. But that's not the hard lesson. That came later. I didn't realize at the time but the day I quit *Snoops* was the first day of a five-year period that would see my career cool, cool some more, then freeze over. For the next five years it felt as though I were typing directly into a trashcan. I probably wrote a dozen pilots in that time, and nothing made it on air.

Soon after quitting *Snoops*, I wrote a pilot for Fox about a minor league hockey team in South Texas. I was proud of the script, and the pilot was given a green light. I was attempting to get something akin to *Northern Exposure* on the air—smart, fish-out-of-water stuff, mixing in my own experiences moving to small-town Texas when I was a kid. I wanted Paula Marshall, one of the leads from *Cupid*, as the lead. She agreed to do it, but didn't like the way her character was introduced. She was playing a girl who grew up in Texas, moved to New York, dropped her accent, and found success in the business world. In the first draft of the script, it was the death of her mother that brought her home to Texas. Paula was afraid that the show opened on too much of a downer. I wrote out the mother's death. Instead, she came home because her brother, who was supposed to take over the family business, came out of the closet and moved to West Hollywood. It was less of a downer but, in retrospect, it lessened the emotional weight. The network president who had signed me to my big deal asked me to add a character to the show. He said I should give the "Fox audience" something a bit more familiar. Melrose Place was going off the air, and he thought I should add a "bitch" character to mix it up a bit with the Paula Marshall character. In came the saucy blonde sister-in-law.

When you're already on the air, you have some leverage with a network. They've spent millions of dollars promoting your show. They're invested. In development, the network holds all the cards. If they say they want a cute six-year-old in the show, you say, "Can it be an orphan?!?" So you make compromises. And I certainly made *these* compromises. It's possible the show could have survived all that, but the biggest mistake was all mine, and it doomed us.

There was a two-season trend during the late nineties of doing pilot presentations. Rather than doing a full forty-two-minute pilot episode, networks were ordering twenty-minute "presentations." I was forced to cut my sixty-page pilot script into a thirty-page presentation script. Smart writers, when given the order for a presentation, threw out their original script and reconceived it as a thirty-page story. I didn't do that. I attempted to tell my original story in half the pages. The end result was a mess. I remember sitting in the editing room tinkering for hours and then having it dawn on me: *This doesn't work. It will never work. It's bad. We've spent a couple million dollars to make it. And there's nothing I can do now to save it.* Good, talented people with fantastic credits and best intentions had worked hard to make the show a success. I had believed in it absolutely when I wrote it.

It was a terrible, sobering epiphany. I can put all my energy into a project, and it can still end up not working. I remembered my days sitting on my couch in Texas wondering how bad shows happen. Easily, it turns out.

A couple years later, I did a pilot for ABC based on a British series. I rewrote the pilot, and despite loving the British version, I changed one plot point around. Rather than having the bad guy deliver a solo declaration of his evil intentions in the first act, I decided to hold off on that reveal until after he had actually committed a nefarious act. I thought my way was smarter. (I have an aversion to monologues. Who actually speaks out loud to oneself?) It was a big mistake. The climax in the British version is terrifying. The climax in my version? Not terrifying. It probably cost me getting the show on the air.

To set the stage for *Veronica Mars* and what the show has done for me, it's important to understand my frame of mind at the time I wrote it. My initial seven years of success had given way to nearly five years of failure. I felt like I was spending my prime writing years on the sidelines. I love producing a show. I love going to work. I love having my work out there for public consumption. Each fruitless development season put me further down an emotional well.

Every writer in development makes a decision about how to proceed in development. There's an easy way that becomes difficult, and there's a difficult way that becomes easier. Networks have agendas during each development season. Generally they are chasing the success of a show on some other network. In the wake of *CSI*, every network went chasing procedural shows involving some sort of science. In the wake of *Lost*, every network wanted "outside the box" (read: non-cop, non-doctor, non-lawyer) shows with an ongoing unsolvable mystery. *ER* begat a dozen high-incident procedural dramas. The easy path for a writer in development is to find out what kind of show a network *wants* to put on, then give them exactly what they drew up on a dry-erase board on one of their many retreats. When you go down this path, the networks *want* you to succeed. Executives feel ownership of a show that they can truthfully say they helped with the creation of. The difficulty is that, when it's their notion, they become very proprietary with the show. If you're not careful, you become the hired gun executing their vision. Also, when network executives come up with ideas, they're almost never what one would call "fresh."

They're rehashing of someone else's success, so you're generally stuck writing "a *male* Sex and the City" or "ER—*in space!*"

If you take the other route—writing something you find inspiring or truly original—you face a longer road to get it ordered to script, ordered to pilot, ordered to series. You don't necessarily have a champion at the network. No executive is saying, "That's my horse in the race." The reward is that if you succeed in getting this show ordered, it's a personal vision. It's usually smarter and fresher. And the network is generally more apt to let you do your own thing.

I'd like to be able to claim that throughout the dark days of my career that I consistently stuck to my guns and only worked on projects that were inspiring personal visions, but that would be untrue. The hockey pilot was certainly a personal, out-of-the-box vision, and I'd gotten my ass handed to me on it. Over the next few years, I did more than my share of network-generated ideas.

With my high school teaching background as well as my start in young adult fiction, I'd long wanted to do a teen drama. The trouble was, my favorite teen drama ever, *Freaks and Geeks*, was already on the air, and it was failing. There weren't many networks clamoring to put another teen drama in primetime—unless it was a soap opera about sexy kids doing sexy things.

Years before, I'd sold Simon & Schuster two titles that were supposed to be my next two novels. The first, *Seattle and Back*, was going to be about a band on tour. The second, "Untitled Rob Thomas Teen Detective," was going to be about a boy who becomes ostracized by his peers when his sheriff father botches a murder investigation of one of his classmates. This boy was going to start working in his father's private detective agency after school. I'd named the boy Keith Mars.

I started thinking about marrying a teen "coming of age" show with an anthological case-driven show. Strangely, during my brief stint at *Snoops*, I'd enjoyed breaking mystery stories. I kept coming back to my "teen detective" idea. Somewhere in the thought process, the boy became a girl and Keith became her father. I pitched the show at a couple networks including the WB, but no one was interested. I decided to write it anyway. Since becoming a professional writer, I hadn't written anything "on spec." ("On spec" is synonymous with "for free.") There's a thrill to writing on spec. You're simply writing what you want to write. No studio or network executive has spelled out any parameters. You haven't had to get an outline approved before writing. For better or worse, it's all you. I can guarantee that, had I sold the pitch to a network, there is absolutely no way Veronica would've been a rape victim. There's no way she would've been allowed to plant a bong in her antagonist's locker. She would not have been allowed to steal evidence out of a police locker.

Honestly, I never thought I'd be able to sell *Veronica Mars* to a broadcast network. It seemed too dark. The character was too edgy. I hoped to convince someone at FX to give it a chance, or HBO, or Showtime. I had an informal, get-to-know-the-new-network-executives meeting at UPN. These are usually fruitless, but the head of drama, Maggie Murphy, said they were looking to skew young and female. I thought, "What the hell?" I told her I had this script about a seventeen-year-old female detective lying around in a drawer. She asked to take a look at it. That was on a Friday. On Monday, Maggie bought the script. (Of note: The show wouldn't exist without Maggie's championing of it. She's an executive who believes in writers' visions.)

We shot the pilot with almost no script notes from the network and none from the studio, but during process there were a couple of crossroads where, had we gone a different direction, it would've spelled disaster.

I find it almost impossible to imagine Veronica Mars played by anyone other than Kristen Bell. We had some fantastic actresses audition for the part, but Kristen was in another league. As producers, we audition scores of people for series regular roles, then we bring our finalists to the studio for approval, and the actors who get approved by studio then audition for the network. After Kristen auditioned at studio, the first comment from an executive was that "she might be good in the best friend role, but not as a lead." It almost seems ludicrous now, but we had to fight to convince our studio to let us take Kristen to the network audition. Had we lost that argument, there would be no show today.

Then, after the pilot was shot, the network began having second thoughts about not cutting the references to Veronica being raped. At the end of the day, they let us keep the rape story line, but had it been excised from the pilot, Veronica's motivations would have all become fuzzy. The pilot wouldn't have made sense.

I suppose that, in summary, in the process of writing, casting, shooting, and editing the pilot into a TV show, there are a couple hundred important decisions, and it's possible to botch any one of them and ruin the show. To quote Nigel Tufnel, "There's a fine line between clever and stupid."

After we finished the *Veronica Mars* pilot, I took my girlfriend on a cruise from Athens to Istanbul. I proposed on the first night in Athens. We were scheduled to fly back from Istanbul to New York in time for the announcement of the UPN fall schedule. At the time, I didn't know if we'd make the schedule. There was one slot available and five pilots vying for it. What I did know, and I explained this to my fiancé, was that *Veronica Mars* was my best work, and that if it didn't make the fall schedule, I was done in the television business. I was frustrated and worn out, and I couldn't take another year of being a writer whose work was never seen. I was very, very close to moving back to Texas and returning to the world of young adult fiction.

Thankfully, we were on the schedule.

I certainly appreciated my good fortune when I got *Cupid* on the air so quickly in my career, but I don't think I appreciated it *enough*. So many things have to go right. Every year a typical network drama department will hear 100 drama pitches, order forty scripts, make ten pilots, order three pilots to series, and just one of those will see a second season. We're in the middle of our third season, so we've defied the odds, and I can say with absolute certainty, there's nothing about *Veronica Mars* that I take for granted. Sure, we don't do well in the ratings, but our fans are fervent, and they pay attention to detail. I loved reading the essays in this collection. The fact that people care enough about this piece of pop culture to invest this level of critical thinking blows my mind, and makes it all worth it.

In some ways this was a difficult essay for me to read. I hate camp. With few exceptions I dislike almost anything that's described as "campy." I'm never going for an ironic appreciation of the work. When something on Veronica Mars *feels campy, it means we (read: I) have failed. Reading Lani's essay, however, I see that she has both a wider net of what she considers camp than I, and a greater appreciation for it when she sees it.*

Here's the thing . . .

We are faced with this conundrum when breaking stories for the show: like Murder, She Wrote, *each episode requires a crime of some sort. (Thank God we don't require a murder.) I feel like we land in what I feel is uncomfortably campy territory when we bite off more than we can chew story-wise. My personal least favorite episodes—or if not episodes, storylines—are when the stories feel too big for Veronica's world. (See the E-String Strangler, see season three's bone marrow transplant story, see Meg's coma.) When I think of quintessential VM MOWs, I think of a story like, "My boyfriend took a dirty video of me. Help me get it back." It's not lightweight and fluffy like a Nancy Drew mystery or something you might find on a family friendly network. It's noir and edgy, but it feels solvable by a seventeen-year-old girl with skills.*

Clearly, we're not trying to do a little art-house film each week. We want to be the thinking-man's (or -woman's) popcorn show. It's fun. Stuff happens. When we get too campy, it means we dropped the "thinking-man's" part. In those cases, we just cross our fingers and hope the show works on some other (read: funny) level.

Lani Diane Rich

Welcome to Camp Noir

H I. MY NAME is Lani, and I'm a TV junkie.

I formed my addiction in the seventies, when I took my first hit off shows like *The Love Boat, Fantasy Island, The Partridge Family*, and *The Brady Bunch*. (Hey, give me a break. Out of all the shameful skeletons people have locked away in their seventies closets, I think I did pretty well.) In the eighties, I refined my palate a touch. *Moonlighting* was my drug of choice, with its ace dialogue and, sadly, unparalleled shark jumping. *Cheers* was my Thursday Night Special, and is to this day one of the hands-down funniest shows ever written. And *Growing Pains* was...well. It was *Growing Pains*. (Yeah, yeah, I know. But I was a teenage girl, and it was Kirk Cameron. I never stood a chance.) By the time *Northern Exposure, Seinfeld*, and *The X-Files* hit the scene, there was no hope for me; I was on the juice but good. (Hey, it beat a crack addiction by a country mile. Although crack does come with that awesome weight loss. Eh. Everything's a tradeoff.)

Anyway, all this to say that, when it comes to TV, I'm your basic whore with a heart of gold: I've been around. If the fifties were seen as television's Golden Age, right now we're smack in the middle of a platinum one—thank you, Joss Whedon, for kicking that off—and my TiVo and I are *likethis*. Every year I get my list of new shows and make my predictions like a college bookie before March Madness: which ones will make it, which ones will tank, and how long it will take FOX to kill this season's most promising new show. (I still haven't forgiven them for canceling *Firefly* and *Wonderfalls*. Two very bitter pills, my friends.) Not to toot my own horn, but usually, I'm fairly close with my calls.

With *Veronica Mars*, though, I was miles off target. Modern-day Nancy Drew? UPN? Pfft. I gave it a half-season only because, unlike some other networks that shall remain nameless (Damn you, FOX! Damn you!), UPN wasn't quite as quick to Kevorkian an investment. I had no idea *Veronica* would turn into what it is: one of the defining shows of the Platinum Age.

So, where were we? Oh, yeah. When the 2004 season rolled out, I watched maybe two episodes of *Veronica Mars*, and decided, "Meh." I didn't really think about it again, allowing Tuesday after Tuesday to slip by celebrated only by *Gilmore Girls* and *House*.

Then, the buzz started. The unbelievable, unrelenting hype. People I hugely respected were calling it genius. Stephen King gave it high praise in an *Entertainment Weekly* article. Kristin Vietch at E!, whose TV tastes run pretty square with mine, raved every week. Joss Whedon acknowledged and embraced the *Buffy* comparisons.

Me? Big doof that I was, I *still* didn't get it. The writing seemed. ..well...clunky to me. I didn't get the characters. The verbal quips were too crisp, the teenagers too clever and in charge, the flashbacks too flashy, the storylines too outrageous. It was all too *too* for me. I pretty much figured I was going to have to sit this particular cultural zeitgeist out.

Then, one day, I ran across a person who described the show as "camp noir." (I can't find this person, or I'd credit him or her with it; a thorough e-mail and Google search has yielded nothing. So if you're that person, out there reading this...hey. Go, you.) Anyway, as soon as this person put the ideas together for me, it was like the skies opened and angels sang; suddenly, all became clear. (Okay, I might be overdramatizing a tad. But it was sunny.)

Camp Noir. *Of course.* Camp, referring to over-the-top storytelling with a hint of kitsch that's not even trying for reality; noir, French for "black," used to describe storytelling with a dark edge, expressed visually by shadowy lighting and the classic Venetian blind stripes on any wall that'll have 'em. The two styles of storytelling are like Reese's, two great tastes that taste great together, and to the best of my knowledge, a television show has never combined them before. You could argue that films have touched on it (the Tarantino oeuvre comes to mind immediately, and I hear *Sin City* would also qualify, although I personally haven't seen it) but it's fairly uncharted territory for television.

So, with this new perspective, I hurried out, got the season one DVD of *Veronica Mars*, and had myself a lost weekend. (Oh, don't judge. You know you've done it, too.) Finally, it all made sense. *Finally*, I got it. No longer was *Veronica* too *too*; it was just plain brilliant television. The thing I loved the most was that the camp and the noir, rather than being evenly mixed, were instead dolloped in like ingredients in a pint of Ben & Jerry's. (Mmm... Ben & Jerry's.) Just when you'd finished with a big chunk of Lilly-Kane's-death-scene noir, you could follow it up with Paris Hilton's acting? Seriously? Camp.[1] Sometimes the two mix evenly—I think camp and noir were in a dead heat when that freshman showed his tape of Lynn Echolls taking her swan dive off the Coronado Bridge ("Mars vs. Mars," 1-14[2])—but at any given moment, with characters and storylines, it tends to be more one than the other. Let's start sorting the dark from the you've-got-to-be-freaking-kidding-me, and feel free to play along. Camp Noir is officially in session.

Veronica. There's no better place to start than with the teenage detective with the mostest, and at first glance, we're coming in firmly on the noir side. Veronica has all the necessary noir elements. She's missing a parent. She's been ostracized from her peers. Her best friend has been brutally murdered. She's a rape victim. No, wait, she's *not* a rape victim. Noooo...wait...*yes*, a rape victim.[3] She has a long-lost love who might-could-have-been her brother (bummer) but then wasn't (yay!) but then knocked up another girl and escaped the country

---

[1] And Paris does act. But not seriously.

[2] Did anyone else laugh when the Lynn Echolls doll hit the water? Does that say something bad about me?

[3] With a side of chlamydia. Ew.

with their baby (bummer again). Basically, this babe is some black eyeliner and two angry lesbian poems away from taking a dive off the Coronado Bridge herself.

But luckily, the you've-gotta-be-kidding-me superhero kitsch swoops in to save her. More clever than her dad, a highly skilled private eye who used to be sheriff? *Sure.* Able to break into the sheriff's office/principal's office and obtain whatever she wants whenever she wants without ever getting caught or grounded? *You betcha.* Able to ward off a motorcycle gang with nothing more than a pit bull, a Taser, and a smile? Oh, hell. Why not? Combined with the occasional dropping of an ironic, funky-white-girl *fo' shizzle*,[4] all this camp mixes smoothly with the noir, creating a gentle balance between elements which, left to their own devices, would probably grate like a Taser on a chalkboard. As it is, I'm a little bitter about Kristen Bell's lack of Emmy nominations. Get on it, Academy.

Veronica's Final Tally: 80% noir, 20% camp

Keith Mars. Aw, the schlubby private eye with a surprising streak of tough-guy: what girl wouldn't dream of having this guy for a dad? (I mean, aside from the girls who would mind him doing background checks on all their boyfriends, then dropping not-so-subtle reminders that he owns a gun.) Keith Mars is probably about as balanced a mix of camp and noir as we're gonna see on this show. Sure, he's lost his job, his reputation, and his wife, and is one repossessed pickup truck away from being a country song cliché, but he's also...kinda crazy. From buying a ten-dollar garage sale waterbed on a whim to out-crazying Alicia Fennel's craaaaaazy tenant, when the camp quotient needs a hike, Keith's your guy.

On the other side, though, he's good for a heady shot of noir when it's needed, too. When Veronica meddled in the screwed-up pregnant neighbor's screwed-up life, Keith was the one shooting bad guys through windows and saving the day ("The Girl Next Door," 1-7). When Veronica got locked in a refrigerator and set on fire by a homicidal maniac,[5] it was Keith who risked life, limb, and skin grafts to save her ("Leave It to Beaver," 1-22). He's got the noir *flava*, baby. (It just doesn't work as well when I do it, does it? Fo' shizzle.)

---

[4] Hand to God, the girl said it (in "Like a Virgin," 1-8). Even stranger, it kinda worked.

[5] And they say there's no such thing as an original plot!

Anyway, while the noir and the camp are pretty much in a dead heat at this point, it's Keith's sad, sad love life that earns him a slight nudge toward the noir. His alcoholic wife cheated on him, left him twice, and stole his money. His brief fling with the school counselor ended when Veronica couldn't deal. And he can't seem to hold on to Alicia Fennel, Wallace's maternal unit, either; she lied about her ex, he invaded her privacy, and—shocker—the relationship fell to pieces. However, there is hope these two crazy kids will make it work in season three.[6] Until he gets him some sweet, sweet lovin', though, Keith Mars is going down as slightly more noir than camp.

Keith's Final Tally: 55% noir, 45% camp

Duncan Kane. Oh, holy mother of all that is holy, this is one dude-de-noir. He found out his one true love might be his sister. Yugh. His real sister got brutally murdered. Yargh. He's prone to violent epileptic fits that leave him totally blacked out and provide a smidge of doubt as to whether he's innocent of his sister's murder. Gak. He discovered Veronica wasn't his sister (yay!) and then lost her to his slightly psychotic (although sooooooo very yummy) best friend.[7] He got girl, lost girl, got her back, lost her again. He knocked up another girl, who went into a coma after a bus crash, only to die from a blood clot (luckily, Baby Noir survives).[8] He escaped the country with Baby Noir, but was still close enough to order a hit on his sorta-best-friend's homicidal maniac of an old man.[9]

In two seasons, the closest this guy got to a lighthearted moment was when he was pretending to be drunk during a poker game so his friends would underestimate him and lose the money that doesn't mean anything to anyone anyway because they've all got more money than God ("An Echolls Family Christmas," 1-10[10]) He did get into funny-crazy camp when he jumped off the bleachers and cracked his head open, but, alas, he did it to distract Veronica from kissing Troy, and he also, you know, cracked his head open ("Meet John Smith,"

---

[6] As of this writing, season three has not yet aired. But for now, indulge me, huh? A girl can dream.

[7] It's wrong, wrong, *wrong* that Veronica ended up with Duncan in "Normal is the Watchword" (2-1). Discuss amongst yourselves the wrongness.

[8] The episode was "One Angry Veronica" (2-10). And who can blame her, really?

[9] It takes a really dark soul to order a murder hit while building sandcastles with his infant daughter. I'm just saying.

[10] Kinda like the Charlie Brown special, only infinitely more disturbing.

1-3). Kinda put a damper on the camp. Despite the fact that Duncan was set up to be Veronica's One True, I think the total lack of camp in his character just killed it. After all, how could Veronica possibly be with a guy who couldn't even pull off an ironic fo' shizzle? Noir-boy was doomed from the start.

Duncan's Final Tally: 99.9% noir, .1% camp

Logan Echolls. Heavy in the camp, the school's "obligatory psychotic jackass"[11] has surprisingly separated from the pack and become quite the leading man. Always living at one end or the other of the camp-noir continuum—usually on the camp side—Logan is all pooling brown puppy-dog eyes and perpetual heat on a slow simmer. (Yes, I have a *slight* Jason Dohring thing. Your point?) He starts out as sort of a Dick Casablancas v1.0 (perfected with the final version, the real Dick), a Quippy McCamperson with a pimped-out yellow SUV and a trust fund that would bring a sentimental tear to Bill Gates's eye. But somehow, through that thick sheen of campy jackass, a fascinating noir-rimmed character emerges. Alternately a total jerk and a sensitive soul, Logan keeps us on our toes. He beat out Veronica's headlights with a tire iron, then soulfully created a tear-jerking-yet-bird-flipping video homage to his dead girlfriend.[12] He rushed to Veronica's rescue when she was in danger from a teenage undercover cop, then made her his by planting one of TV's best kisses *ever* on her ("Weapons of Class Destruction," 1-18). Then he became a drunken, wallowing, anti-hero jerkface when he lost her.[13] He's a hero, he's a jerk, he's a hero, he's a jerk...but whenever he's a hero again, we're ready to take him back. As is Veronica. Cut her some slack; she's only human, and have you seen those eyes? I'm with Logan on this one; these two are epic.

Logan's Final Tally: 20% noir, 80% camp

Weevil. Eli Navarro, for such a cute guy, is among the most contradictory—and most interesting—characters to hit the small screen in a long time. He duct-taped poor, sweet Wallace to a flagpole, then

---

[11] As Veronica describes Logan the first time we see him, in the pilot. Ah. Young love.

[12] Oh, come on. Admit it. You know you fell for Logan the second he took those video tapes from Duncan.

[13] See: most of season two.

repeatedly came to Veronica's rescue at the beep of a text message. He beat up Logan on the bluff in the pilot, but also took the rap for a crime he didn't commit to spring his grandma from jail. He set Thumper up to be killed by the Fitzpatricks to avenge Felix's death, and then got all repentant in confession about it.[14] He heads a drug-running motorcycle gang, but stays in school because of a promise he made to Grandma. He's tough and he's cuddly and he might be Frank Capra's great-grandson. He is an enigma; he is the heart of noir... except when he and his gang go to boutiques and try on the fashions to intimidate the owner, or when he uses his six-year-old niece and her fuzzy pink backpack to steal the senior class trip money.

Whatever. Love the tattoos, Weevil. Don't ever change.

Weevil's Final Tally: 95% noir, 5% camp

Okay, with the main characters figured out, let's not forget the fine, fine set of secondary characters at play in Neptune.

The Echolls Family. Oh, holy kitsch, Batman, the Camp Quotient is off the charts with this bunch.

Aaron Echolls. The abusive, philandering, aging A-lister with a slight homicide problem gets bonus camp points for the show's use of clips from Harry Hamlin's early career "B"-buster, *Clash of the Titans*, as an exhibit of the fictional Echolls's Hollywood icon status.[15] **Most campified moment:** Beating up Trina's boyfriend with a tiki torch.[16]

Lynn Echolls. Here we have the buxom, collagen-lipped trophy wife who, despite having a full bottle of prescription pills, took a dive off a bridge anyway. Why? Because she's a big drama queen. **Most campified moment:** Doesn't matter. Pick one. They're all winners. Although I'd have to say the bridge jump does slightly edge out the carolers-while-her-husband-lay-bleeding-from-an-icepick-wound scene.[17]

---

[14] And what kind of killer Mafioso name is Fitzpatrick supposed to be, anyway? Maybe I've known too many jolly Irishmen, but Fitzpatrick just doesn't strike fear in my heart. Thumper's a scarier name than Fitzpatrick.

[15] They use the scene where he stabs the big monster-looking thing. Oh, wait. That kinda describes all the scenes in that movie, doesn't it?

[16] To this day, I think this is one of my favorite *Veronica Mars* moments, coming up close against any time Logan is onscreen.

[17] In "An Echolls Family Christmas" (1-10). Told you it was disturbing.

Trina Echolls. Totally unlikable as written, and yet, when played by the über-lovable Alyson Hannigan, you can't help but just adore her. She's snarky and heartless and just wants a man like good ol' Dad—meaning cute, crazy, and violent as a Category Five hurricane. I have to admit to secretly wanting Hannigan's full-time gig, *How I Met Your Mother*, to tank in the ratings so she can come back to Neptune full-time. (Alyson, if you're reading this, I'm sorry, it's just the way I feel.) **Most campified moment:** Although watching her boyfriend get beat to a pulp with a tiki torch runs a very tight second, I'd have to say it was when she happily pretended to be dying in order to smoke out the wealthy Kanes, who she thought were her birth parents ("My Mother the Fiend," 2-9). Now *that's* class. Come back, Trina. Come back.

The Echolls Family Final Tally: 0% noir, 100% camp

The Kane Clan. Oh. Dear. Turns out that Duncan apple didn't fall far from the noir family tree.

Jake Kane. Fairly nice for a gazillionaire, and he only cheats on his wife a little. Of course, he did try to cover up his daughter's murder, but only because he thought the killer might be his son. **Biggest Noir Queen Moment:** Well, finding Lilly's beaten, bloodied body is definitely a black moment, but also in the running are "You killed your sister, son," and the crazy, "You killed my daughter" switcharoo tune he sang when he found out about Aaron Echolls being a homicidal maniac ("Leave It to Beaver").[18]

Celeste Kane. The long-suffering wife who really only exists to complain about her life and shoot Veronica dirty looks. **Biggest Noir Queen Moment:** When she told Veronica that she couldn't stand to look at her because she represented everything that was wrong in Celeste's life ("Hot Dogs," 1-19).[19]

Lilly Kane. A breath of camp air in the Kane mansion! From bopping around in the pool house with her boyfriend's homicidal maniac of a dad to making ghostly cameos in her pep squad uniform while bleeding profusely from the head.[20] Lilly never had a moment that

---

[18] And since it has to be said—what a shame they didn't save that bon mot for the season two finale title, no?

[19] And yes, sadly, this is the most interesting thing they gave her to do all season.

[20] Seriously, they couldn't give her a Kleenex or something?

wasn't pure camp. **Most Campified Moment:** Impossible to pick just one. I'm going with the pep-squad-bleeding-from-the-head scenes. All of 'em.

The Kane Clan Final Tally: 66.6% noir, 33.3% camp

The Shameful Casablancases. The lovely thing about secondary characters is that you can really camp 'em up without serious consequences, and while just having two kids named Dick and Beaver alone seemed about ready to blow the top off the Camp-O-Meter, the Casablancases had hardly gotten started.

Richard "Big Dick" Casablancas. Let's see; he swindled investors out of billions then hopped in a helicopter to presumably escape to places south, where the extradition laws are as loose as the women. Unlike his stock, his Camp Quotient (or CQ) went through the roof. **Most Campified Moment:** The helicopter, baby.

Kendall Casablancas. She engaged in an affair with her stepsons' buddy Logan, then later, when she realized her CQ was dropping, she hopped in the sack with Logan's dad, the homicidal maniac everyone loves to hate, Aaron Echolls. **Most Campified Moment:** Headboard bopping with Aaron Echolls. Hands down.

Dick Casablancas. This mop-haired, soulless rich boy might be as murderous as his little brother if only he had a little more ambition. **Most Campified Moment:** Making out with a transvestite hooker at the school carnival.[21]

Beaver-um-the-name's-Cassidy Casablancas. Can't forget the bus-bombing, chlamydia-spreading, clothes-stealing, skyscraper-jumping Beaver-um-the-name's-Cassidy. Any guy who ever lets himself be called Beaver in the first place pretty much defines camp. Go, Beaver! (Um. Sorry. Cassidy.) **Most Campified Moment:** Trying to look like a killer on the roof with Veronica ("Not Pictured," 2-22). Smart enough to rig a bus bomb, I'll buy. At all able to shoot someone point blank without losing his aim or wetting himself? I don't think so.

The Shameful Casablancases Final Tally: 0% noir, 100% camp

---

[21] Was I the only one who felt bad for the hooker?

The Rare Exceptions. The thing about tearing something apart in an academic manner (or, in my case, pseudo-academic) is that somewhere along the line, something comes in to bust up your theory, and then you have to do all this work to monkey-wrench them in. In this grand tradition of intellectual (or, in my case, pseudo-intellectual) muscling, we have:

Wallace Fennel. Wallace is a charming, funny, handsome, fairly unscarred, seemingly well-adjusted young man who has never been victim of, nor party to, murder, rape, or incest. (As of this writing, anyway.) The only unbelievable element to Wallace is that Veronica hasn't jumped him. Now that their parents have dated it's a little easier to grasp, because there's a brother-sister element and we really don't need to go down that particular incestual alley again. But in the pre-Keith-hearts-Alicia days, I thought it was completely unpardonable for Veronica to not at least *try* to snatch her some Fennel flava. (Yeah, I still can't pull it off, can I? Sadly, neither can I resist a good alliteration.) **How I'm Making It Fit:** Wallace is a foil, the normal character who gives highlight and contrast to the insanity around him. Sound good? Sure. Moving on.

Cindy "Mac" Mackenzie. Despite the fact that she was the victim of clothes-stealing from her cutesy-yet-murderous boy toy Beaver-um-the-name's-Cassidy Casablancas, and she was switched at birth with the heinous Madison Sinclair, I maintain that there's something about Mac that's seductively... normal. From the rebellious but standard streak of blue hair to the *Rain Man*-ish computer wizardry to the achingly bad taste in men, Mac remains only slightly camp-of-center on the noir-camp continuum. Truthfully, she's just a normal girl... living in a seriously screwed-up town. **How I'm Making It Fit:** Mac is a foil, the... uh... normal character who gives highlight and contrast to the insanity around her. Pay no attention to that academic (or, you know, pseudo-academic) behind the curtain.

In conclusion, I could be totally full of crap (now, where else in pseudo-academia are you going to get that kind of honesty, huh?) but I really think there's something to this Camp Noir thing. At any rate, the revelation made a convert out of me and for that, even if it's all in my head, I'm grateful. *Veronica Mars*, for all its carefully constructed insanity, combines outrageous scenarios with fascinating characters and is one of the most cleverly written shows to hit the small screen in a long while. And, since it's not on FOX, I think we can look forward to more coma babies, slutty gold-digging step-moms, and teenage super-sleuthing action for years to come.

(Oh. And let's not forget those puppy-dog eyes. Ah, Logan. *Sigh.*)

LANI DIANE RICH is a wife, mother, and novelist living in central New York. You can get more information about her novels at http://www.lanidianerich.com, or find her blogging with her friends at http://www.literarychicks.com. Feel free to e-mail her with comments at lani@lanidianerich. com...just don't expect a response on Tuesday nights.

Geoff mentions in his essay that Joss Whedon calls a good act break "a thing of beauty forever." It is. And I'm sure Joss would tell you the vast amounts of time a writing staff gives to considering its act breaks. In the VM writers' room, we usually start with the question, "What are our act breaks?" As I write this, we're currently breaking an episode in season three about Wallace's murdered basketball coach. After a day of story-breaking, all we have to show for it are our first four act breaks....

> Cold Open Out—Coach's family hires Mars Investigations to save them.
> Act One Out—Coach's son, who Veronica has befriended, arrested for crime.
> Act Two Out—Coach's son escapes from jail.
> Act Three Out—Coach's son, who Veronica has begun to doubt, shows up in Veronica's car.

Here's the irony. A studio executive, who will remain anonymous, told me once that his studio did a study on the importance of act breaks, believing that they could use the evidence the study provided to goad writers into bigger act breaks. The results actually showed that act breaks meant almost nothing in terms of audience retention. People don't switch channels because of weak act breaks. And yet, we all still think in terms of old serial movies. We need the damsel tied to the railroad tracks, the train steaming towards her and our hero galloping in to save her. That's an act break!

Geoff makes an important point about VM finales that holds true for our season two finale and the rape mystery finale from season three that I just finished directing last week. We're a mystery show, that's our stock in trade, but our finales turn into thrillers. For better or worse, we break form.

Geoff Klock

Story Structure and
Veronica Mars

VERY TIME WE read a book or watch a movie we bring our experiences to bear on what we are reading or watching. Someone with an aversion to violent imagery, for instance, is likely to declare *Kill Bill* a bad movie without a thought to any aspect of the film beyond the dismemberment. For those of us with an education in the humanities, assumptions may be more explicit, and come with philosophical backing: gender theory, Marxism, psychoanalysis, feminism, formalism, reader response theory, structuralism, deconstruction, post-colonialism, new historicism. For many years my own hobby-horse has been Harold Bloom's poetics of influence, and it still serves me well. These theories, and ones like them, claim to tell us more about our experience of books and movies and music. You thought you knew what *Wuthering Heights* was about, they say, but let me tell you what it's *really* about (class, gender, language, and so on).

Academic ways of looking at literature often add to the sum total of our knowledge, but only rarely (and even then, often accidentally) give us a deeper appreciation of the book we are reading, or the film we are watching. Even worse, many academic approaches lead us to overvalue terribly written but theoretically interesting work. Cultural studies may explain how Allen Ginsburg's *Howl* can tell us a lot about the climate of the 1960s, but it is nevertheless a very bad poem. One approach to film and television that can affect our appreciation for the better—that can actually offer us what we need, which is better taste—is the lesson in story structure found in any good guide to screenwriting. Because these guides are aimed solely at the burgeoning screenwriter, they don't often find their way into the hands of fans, critics, and academics, in spite of the good they would do. An understanding of character arcs, exposition through conflict, dangling causes, pacing, retardation, beats, scenes, open and closing values in scenes, inciting incidents, acts, act breaks, plot points, sequences, and the classical screenplay structure are vital parts of the aesthetic appreciation of film and television. This understanding should not be solely possessed by those in, or trying to get into, the industry. When Joss Whedon discusses his favorite *Buffy* episodes in the booklet included in the complete *Buffy the Vampire Slayer* box set, he singles out the season two episode "Ted," and says, "A good act break is a thing of beauty forever." We should all know enough to be able to agree with him.

That Whedon quote got me talking to a filmmaker friend of mine, Brad Winderbaum, who pointed me toward Robert McKee's *Story: Substance, Style, and the Principles of Screenwriting*, David Howard's *How to Build a Great Screenplay*, Syd Field's *Screenwriting* (and related books), and Paul Joseph Gulino's *Screenwriting: The Sequence Approach*. As a fan of *Veronica Mars*, I want to pass on what I learned by going through "Leave It to Beaver" (1-22), story by Rob Thomas and teleplay by Rob Thomas and Diane Ruggiero, the final episode of season one, with the eye of a screenwriter but the mind of a critic. I want to use screenwriting tools—primarily the idea of act structure—to say why the episode is good, but I want to avoid reducing it to merely a model for young writers. Television has gotten so good in recent years—*Firefly, Lost, 24, Unscripted, Scrubs*—we owe it to ourselves to be better viewers, and Derrida isn't the place to go. My look at "Leave It to Beaver" will not touch on every screenplay concept in the books. My more modest hope is to point toward what is missing in our appreciation of film and television.

Story Structure

In film and television, stories are said to have a structure of at least three parts: a character wants something, there is an obstacle to getting it, and then the tension is resolved. This "ending" often involves the creation of a new tension that sets in motion the next part of the story. As Gulino points out, this story structure is like a fractal, iterated at different levels (11): it organizes series, seasons, episodes, acts, and scenes. The structure of *Veronica Mars* as a whole might be Veronica's simple quest for safety and happiness. The structure of season one is the attempt to solve the murder of Lilly Kane. Weevil finds out that Veronica suspects Logan, and this sets up a new conflict for season two. A major structure in "Leave It to Beaver"—as I will show—has to do with trying to achieve domestic happiness with biological parents. Veronica learns to accept life without her mother, but this has new consequences that will be dealt with in future episodes. The structure of the first act of "Leave It to Beaver" is organized around capturing Logan and healing Veronica's family, but these are only temporary solutions (because they are false ones) and lead into new problems in act two. In a single scene in act one of "Leave It to Beaver," Weevil attempts to kill Logan but Logan is arrested by the police; Weevil attacks because Veronica made him suspect Logan; Veronica (inadvertently) solves the problem by having Logan arrested, but this causes problems that generate the scenes that follow. Like boxes nested in boxes, story structure is inescapable.

The most important structure in a television show is the act structure. After the teaser (the pre-credits sequence), a one-hour cable-television drama is divided into four roughly even-length acts—labelled as such in the script—that are divided by commercial breaks. A typical feature-length movie has three acts: the first act is usually the first thirty minutes, the second is usually the middle hour, and the third is usually the final thirty minutes. (The difference between a three- and four-act structure is minimal, and should not concern us here.) The act structure in a film is further subdivided into several ten- to fifteen-minute sequences (essentially mini-acts each with their own beginning, middle, and end): two sequences in the first and third acts and four sequences in the second act. Without these little "movies within movies" the audience becomes bored and restless.

Film sequences have their origin in the old Hollywood reels, which could only hold ten to fifteen minutes of material before they had to be changed for fresh film (Gulino 3-4). Once films got longer than fifteen minutes, they consisted of reels strung together. Story structure emerged from this physical limitation, and stayed with us even after reels became obsolete. Though in film acts are subdivided into sequences, in television acts and sequences are one and the same. Acts are thus especially important in the appreciation of cable television, because the demands of commercials make the old Hollywood reel structure indispensable.

To follow the structure of "Leave It to Beaver" closely we must break it into its component parts and summarize its acts, just as Paul Gulino analyzes sequences in his screenwriting book.

The Teaser: Establishing the Status Quo

The purpose of a teaser is obvious: it hooks the audience into the coming show. But it also serves as the starting point that the episode will disrupt. If the show is the same at the end as is was at the beginning, why would we watch it? (The exception to this rule is a show where lack of change is the point, as it was in *Seinfeld*.) *Veronica Mars* has unusually long teasers, and "Leave It to Beaver" is no exception. Six of its eight scenes all establish the status quo. The remaining two scenes are the hook, the inciting incident for the plot of the episode.

It begins at a newspaper office, where Keith Mars is trying to convince someone to run a story about how Abel Koontz is innocent of the murder of Lilly Kane. (Pretentious naming—such as "Cain" and "Abel" in a murder investigation—is one of the few weak points of *Veronica Mars*.) Rob Thomas re-establishes the season one plot arc that will be resolved in this episode: Who killed Lilly Kane?

In the second scene, Keith Mars picks up the envelope containing the results of his paternity test before entering into the domestic scene of Veronica and her newly returned mother cooking. This establishes the second season-long plot arc: Can Veronica Mars's family stay together? The water bottle her mother drinks out of is planted in this scene—it will be important in act two—and the family banter reinforces the show's structure on the level of theme: the discussion of how to chop onions without crying points to the real tears between mother and daughter that have been and will be shed, and the discussion of the relevant theme music for a meal (e.g., Creedence Clearwater for hot dogs) points to the relevancy of the theme song for *Veronica Mars*, the Dandy Warhols's "We Used to Be Friends." The lyrics of the song retool its opening line: "A long time ago, we used to be friends, but I haven't thought of you lately at all." The song can be read in a number of ways: because of her father's investigation into the death of Lilly Kane, Veronica became an outcast at school, and her old friends haven't thought of her lately at all; likewise, Lilly Kane has also not been able to think of her friend Veronica (because Lilly is dead). In the context of this episode, however, the song has a new, ironic dimension: Veronica is obsessed with Lilly; she cannot stop thinking about Lilly. It will be otherwise at the end.

In the third scene, Keith Mars opens the paternity test and meets with a lawyer about suing the Kane family for the $50,000 they owe him but are refusing to pay. This re-establishes the antagonism between the two families, which will change in the course of the episode.

In the fourth scene, two minor characters, Dick and Beaver (cf. Kane and Abel, above), read the newspaper article Keith Mars set in motion and remark that they were supposed to keep secret about something. This scene seems especially important at this moment, since the episode is called "Leave It to Beaver." This is the first half of the show's inciting incident, the thing that will set the plot in motion.

In the fifth scene, Veronica Mars and Wallace discuss the newspaper article. Veronica's pride in her father is re-established, and she gets Wallace to help her avoid Logan Echolls (she found secret video recording equipment in his pool house in the previous episode). Wallace appears here only because he has nothing else to do in the episode, and a season finale would be incomplete without all of the show's main characters.

In the next scene Keith Mars breaks up with Wallace's mother, Alicia Fennel, because his estranged wife, Veronica's mother, has returned. This break-up parallels the Logan-Veronica split that also occurs in this episode. Both Alicia Fennel and Logan are potential new members of the Mars household, and they have both been rejected. At this point in the episode family unity is what is wanted by both Keith and Veronica.

We then cut to the Kane house, where Duncan Kane's father tells him that he murdered his sister in an epileptic fit. This is the answer we have been searching for all season, and Duncan has been a major suspect, but it is delivered so suddenly at the top of the finale that we know it is a false answer. The domestic scene at the Kanes'— mother, father, and son—parallels Veronica's home life. The sitcom *Leave It to Beaver* is emblematic of the perfect family, and thus it makes sense that domestic life is at the heart of an episode that is named after it.

The last scene of the teaser undercuts the "discovery" of the murderer by setting up a new suspect. Beaver arrives to tell Veronica that Logan was jealous of a new lover he discovered Lilly had and that he was not in Mexico as the police thought. The teaser is long, but a lot of information needs to be set up for the episode to work. The scenes are relatively isolated because they either establish or re-establish the status quo before the show gets its inciting incident: Logan killed Lilly and he must be caught and punished. Now the show is in motion.

Act One: Arresting Logan Echolls

If each act is a miniature plot, the plot of act one is "Arresting Logan Echolls." It begins as Veronica and her father discuss Logan as a possible suspect. Veronica calls her father and confirms over the phone that she thinks Logan killed Lilly (Logan suspiciously pointed to Duncan as the killer) but is overheard by Weevil, another of Lilly's lovers. Keith meets with the Kanes, who offer to settle with him for $50,000 if Veronica waives all further claims on the Kane fortune.

The show has hinted that Veronica is Jake Kane's illegitimate daughter; the next scene ends the question once and for all. Veronica agrees to never sue the Kane family and is told by Keith that she gave away nothing, because the paternity test he has proves that he is her real father. The show, through Keith, immediately suggests that they can go after Logan now. As a major part of the Veronica-Duncan conflict is resolved, a new tension is established: Veronica's brother didn't kill Lilly (she doesn't have a brother); her boyfriend, Logan, did.

In the next scene, Aaron Echolls answers the door as the police come to search Logan's room, and the air vents in particular. It sets

Aaron on the search for the tapes in the air vents in Lilly's room, and thus on a collision course with Veronica. But this scene serves a second important purpose: it re-establishes Aaron's existence in the show. When he is revealed to be Lilly's killer, the more we have seen him, and the more recently we have seen him, the more powerful the effect will be. (If, for example, the killer turned out to be a minor character not seen since the pilot, we would feel we had been cheated of a satisfying ending.)

Weevil goes to attack Logan, but Logan is arrested before he gets the chance. Veronica, responsible for both events, has both put Logan in danger and saved his life. As the police interrogate him, Logan learns it is Veronica who turned him in. This is the end of the show's first act. Acts always end with a plot point that hooks the audience into the next act by changing the direction of the show. This act break is a key point of no return. No matter what happens, no matter who killed Lilly, Veronica has betrayed Logan and he knows it. (In season two we see that this betrayal has not prevented them from getting back together, but at this point we don't know that.) Act one closes with a false ending: Veronica Mars has her family back, and Lilly Kane's killer, with motive and opportunity, is in the hands of the police. Act two will take that false ending apart.

Act Two: Clearing Logan Echolls

The second act of "Leave It to Beaver" is comparatively short, and it consists of Veronica's attempt to clear Logan. The sheriff talks to Keith Mars over the phone and lets him know they had to let Logan go. At the beach Logan confronts Veronica and everything changes: Logan insists he is innocent and Veronica believes him. The proof, he says, is in a letter he wrote to Lilly the night she died. Veronica believes the letter is hidden in an air vent in Lilly's room. Because the Kanes are hosting a party for the governor, Veronica goes to the house undercover as a waitress. While preparing her disguise Veronica takes a sip from her mother's water bottle—the bottle it was established that her mother was drinking out of in the teaser—spits it out, and calls the rehab center. Once at the Kane house Veronica sneaks into Lilly's bedroom and begins to unscrew the vent. At the act break, someone is about to come in on her.

The act break seems, at first, to be quite minor, but because season finales are the biggest moments in a television show, the person on the other side of the door is likely to be someone important; it is likely to be the killer. In any case, the false ending of the first act is already ruined before the second act break: Veronica's mother is still drinking—the domestic scene is ruined—and our heroine now believes Logan is innocent.

Act Three: Revealing Aaron Echolls

The through line of the third act is the discovery of Lilly's real killer, and that discovery's consequences. (This can, however, be difficult to see, as the episode veers off to tie up a season-long loose end, and to set up a new tension for the new season.) It begins as Duncan Kane catches Veronica and confronts her. We expected Lilly's killer to open the door; Duncan was told he was Lilly's killer in the teaser. Veronica, in the process of explaining herself, recaps the show thus far. Veronica is about to discover Lilly's killer, and the effect will be more powerful if the full context of the discovery is expressed in a few sentences and if the climatic discovery is held back a moment longer.

The second act began with a mini "teaser" (in which Keith Mars finds out the police let Logan go) before getting to the aim of the act in the second scene (Veronica thinks Logan might be innocent). The movement of the third act, its change of direction, is also set up in its second scene: the killer and what happened is immediately revealed, and the rest of the act is spent attempting to apprehend him. Veronica has discovered not the note she expected would clear Logan, but video tapes. One tape shows Lilly having sex with Aaron Echolls— her boyfriend's father—the day she died. Veronica says she knows what happened and a full flashback reveals that Lilly was killed because she was blackmailing Aaron, a movie star with a penchant for violence. Duncan discovered her after she was dead, and that was the scene his parents walked in on. The Kane cover-up of the murder resulted from the mistaken impression that their son killed their daughter. Veronica tells Duncan that Aaron is a psychopath: he beats Logan, and Veronica saw him savagely beat a man and then calmly ask Logan about his day at school.

This beating occurred in episode nineteen and is an excellent example of satisfying misdirection: the scene in which Aaron beats up the man who beat his daughter is scored with Dean Martin's "That's

Amore." In that episode the show is preparing evidence that Aaron is Lilly's killer, but doesn't want us to figure it out before this moment in "Leave It to Beaver." Intellectually we see Aaron's savagery, but emotionally we don't connect him with a murder, because the song keeps the tone of the beating and the tone of the murder separate. The tone is further separated by the status of the victims: we feel Lilly should not be dead, but we find poetic justice in seeing a man who beats women beaten himself. We don't connect the evidence as we should, and when we realize we should have, the effect is more powerful, because it feels both inevitable and surprising.

Discovering Aaron Echolls is the killer is also the payoff set up by both the domestic scenes in the teaser and the episode's title. It is satisfying both in narrative terms and in thematic ones: Lilly Kane's killer broke up Veronica's family and exposed the corruption of the Kane family; the murder of Lilly Kane should therefore have something to do with bad families, and it does, as Lilly was killed by her boyfriend's father to cover up their affair.

At the end of this scene, after Veronica tells Duncan to keep an eye on Aaron while she takes the tapes, she tells him that they are not brother and sister. This is not strictly part of the act structure of the episode; it could be cut without damaging the integrity of "Leave It to Beaver." It serves instead to tie up a loose plot thread from the season as a whole, which would be unsatisfying without the scene; the incest plot has been with us from the pilot, from the beginning of the Lilly Kane plot, and it needs to be dealt with in some way by the end of the season. The show has suggested that its title character has been the victim of both rape and incest. Ultimately, however, the teeth are removed from both: we learn in the previous episode that although Veronica was drugged when she had sex, Duncan was drugged as well and had sex with her because he loved her. She woke up alone and assumed she had been raped, but he fled because he believed he had committed incest. Now everyone is clear neither rape nor incest occurred. (At least for now; the season two finale will give us new information, but that is not relevant to the structure of this episode.)

As she leaves, Veronica calls her dad immediately to tell him Aaron is the killer, a minor subversion of what usually happens in such films (the only person who knows is incapacitated, leaving the killer to do more damage in the meantime). *Veronica Mars* is out to reinvig-orate the noir genre, and avoiding this cliché is one of its tactics.

We next cut to Logan, drunk and teetering on the edge of a bridge when Weevil and his gang show up. Veronica's phone call to Logan is the only point of transition. This scene, which will not be resolved, is also not crucial to the structure of the episode. It instead serves to create tension between seasons one and two, since the main tension will be resolved in this episode. The first two acts were about Lo-gan Echolls, while acts three and four focus on his father; something must be done to Logan so he is not completely forgotten about as the show makes this massive shift of focus. The murder of Lilly Kane will be solved, but the consequences of this scene on the bridge will di-rect season two.

The act break occurs as Veronica calls Duncan while driving and finds out that Aaron is missing. Aaron appears behind Veronica, in the back seat of the car, and seizes the tapes. Veronica crashes the car, and the act ends. Again we have a false ending as the show plays—just for a moment—with the possibility that Veronica's discovery of Lilly's killer at the top of the act has lead to both of their deaths at the bottom—that her quest for justice set up in the pilot has lead to trag-edy in the finale. But television's four-act structure means however much we are startled, we know there is more to come.

The third act is mystery. The fourth act is a thriller.

Act Four: Capturing Aaron Echolls

Act four is the apprehension of Aaron Echolls. Though she is un-able to answer it, Veronica's phone rings and brings her to conscious-ness before Aaron. Veronica grabs the tapes and rushes to the nearest house for help, ditching the tapes along the way. Aaron escapes from the car and enters the house so that when someone hears her at the back door and comes to help her, Aaron knocks them both out. Though it is a small detail, the show has once again pointed to a do-mestic scene: the battle occurs at someone's home.

Veronica awakes in an abandoned refrigerator, the perfect domes-tic appliance.[1] Here a battle ensues in which Keith, who has gone

---

[1] The fact that Veronica Mars is locked in a refrigerator may be much more significant than it might at first appear. In a 1994 issue of the comic book *Green Lantern* (No. 54), the writer, Ron Marz (note the name), wrote a story in which the title character comes home to discover his girlfriend killed by a supervillain and stuffed in a refrigerator. In 1999, Gail Simone, one of only

looking for her since she did not pick up her phone, is burned saving Veronica, and Aaron appears to escape, before being attacked by Veronica's dog "Backup" (fulfilling his name) and hit by a flower truck. In a nod to both the show's creator and the name of Aaron's victim, the truck has the name Thomas and an image of a lily on it. Veronica shows up with a gun and tells the truck driver to call a fire engine, an ambulance, and the police.

In the aftermath of the battle Duncan shows up with his father to establish that his father knows who the real killer is. Implicitly the main tension between the Kane family and the Mars family has been resolved (Keith Mars believed someone in the Kane family was responsible for Lilly Kane's death). The tension resolved here is a complement to the smaller tension (the issue of incest) between Duncan Kane and Veronica Mars resolved in act three. But a new tension has been set up, as the Kane-Mars tension of season one becomes the Kane-Echolls tension of season two.

At the hospital Veronica waits by her father, and a nurse asks if there is anyone she can call. We transition to Veronica's mother, at home, since her mother is the expected answer to the nurse's question. Veronica tells her mother that she knows her mom checked herself out of rehab early and kicks her out of the house. At the hospital Keith wakes up to see Alicia watching over him. Veronica called her, because she knows they really care about each other. In the course of the episode Veronica has learned to accept someone other than her biological mother in her family, because biological families, as seen in this episode, are not necessarily paradise. While Veronica sleeps, her mother steals the check from the Kane family and leaves. This is the point of no return for Veronica's mother: her lapse can be forgiven, but stealing cannot. The domestic scene established in the teaser, and the dream that finding Lilly's killer will restore her family (explicitly stated at the end of the pilot), ends

---

a handful of women working in superhero comics, coined the term "women in refrigerators" to refer to the fact that powerful women are often destroyed in comics in order to spur their male counterparts on to greater heights. She created a "Women in Refrigerators" Web site (reconstructed on http://www.unheardtaunts.com/wir/women.html), an infamous list of women destroyed in comics. Once our heroine is in the refrigerator, the men of *Veronica Mars* get down to fighting, but not at Veronica's expense. That she survives may be a revision of a trend, and Aaron Echolls's comparison of Veronica to Joan of Arc in this scene–Joan of Arc is of course another powerful woman destroyed–may point to this revision.

here, as Veronica's mother leaves their lives as a villain. In the same episode in which she gains (metaphorically) her biological father, she loses her biological mother. And interestingly, just as the Keith-Alicia split paralleled the Veronica-Logan split at the beginning of the episode, the Keith-Alicia reunion parallels the Veronica-Logan reunion that we will learn about in a series of flashbacks at the beginning of season two.

The penultimate scene is a dream sequence in which Veronica and Lilly Kane relax in the pool together, at peace. Duncan's hallucinations of Lilly walking around with a head wound have been replaced by Veronica's idyll. Lilly tells Veronica never to forget her, invoking the show's theme song in a new way: for the first time there is a danger Veronica will let Lilly pass out of her memory. This is the proper ending of the episode. The final scene—a knock at the door wakes her up, and she answers, pleased, but we don't see who she sees—is the transition to next season. The episode and the season resolve, but the conflicts involved set a new structure for a new season in motion.

GEOFF KLOCK is the author of *How to Read Superhero Comics and Why* (Continuum 2002) and the upcoming *Imaginary Biographies: Misreading the Lives of the Poets* (Continuum 2007), based off his doctoral thesis at Balliol College, Oxford. The first book applies Harold Bloom's poetics of influence to comic books; the second argues that the bizarre portrayal of historical writers in nineteenth and twentieth century poetry constitutes a genre (and will be followed by a companion book on film). His blog—*Remarkable: Short Appreciations of Poetry, Comics, Film, Television and Music*—can be found at geoffklock. blogspot.com. He lives in New York City.

References

Field, Syd. *Screenwriting: The Foundations of Screenwriting.* New York: Dell, 1994.

Gulino, Paul Joseph. *Screenwriting: The Sequence Approach.* New York: Continuum, 2005.

Howard, David. *How to Build a Great Screenplay.* New York: Souvenir Press, 2004.

Marz, Ron (w), Darryl Banks (p), Romeo Tanghal (i). *Green Lantern* No. 54. New York: (DC Comics): 1994.

McKee, Robert. *Story: Substance, Structure, Style, and the Principles of Screenwriting.* London: Methuen, 1999.

Buffy the Vampire Slayer: The Complete DVD Collection. Dir. Joss Whedon et al. Fox, 2004.

I believe that in film schools across the country, film students are being taught that first-person narration is, inherently, a flaw. "Narration isn't cinematic. It's a crutch." It's a blanket statement that I think has seeped into public consciousness. (Of course, I wouldn't know this for sure as USC, NYU, UCLA, and UT all rejected my film school application.)

The truth is, we've used first person narration in ways of which I'm proud, and we've used it, at times, badly. Our "bad" voiceovers are often the result of budgetary conflicts. How so? Let's say we've written a script that includes Veronica breaking into Jake Kane's office and stealing a document out of a desk drawer. Shooting off-stage is expensive. Shooting "action" sequences is expensive. (Lots of short shots requiring many lighting setups. You can shoot six pages of two people talking easier than you can shoot one page of "action.") So, our budget comes in and we have to cut $25,000 out of an episode; what happens?

INT. VERONICA'S BEDROOM – NIGHT

Veronica enters her room clutching a file folder.

VERONICA (V.O.): I can't believe I didn't get caught breaking into Jake Kane's office. Fortunately, the night watchman was drunk, etc., etc.

It's gross, I know.

One of the things I hate in television is "emotional exposition." It's used all the time. People, particularly all the teens on the WB, talk about their feelings. Though we're not always successful, I want Veronica Mars writers to have "action" define character rather than dialogue or monologue. I like it when our voiceovers reveal Veronica's attitude, but don't reveal, and often "deflect," her feelings. Even in internal dialogue, I think we—and this we definitely includes Veronica—delude ourselves.

I was pleased to see Evelyn list, "You want to know how I lost my virginity? So do I," as the moment she was sold on Veronica Mars. That line of voiceover was the first thing written for the show. It was part of my pitch for the show. In my original notes, I jotted down that line and circled it.

In the first scene of the pilot, I tried to write the most Chandler-esque voice over I could to reflect the spirit of Veronica.

VERONICA (V.O.): I'm never getting married. You want an absolute? A sure thing? Well, there it is. Veronica Mars, spinster…old maid. Carve it in stone. I mean, come on. What's the point? Sure, there's that initial primal drive…hormonal surge…whatever you want to call it. Ride it out. Better yet, ignore it. Sooner or later, the people you love let you down…betray you. And here's where it ends up—fat men, cocktail waitresses, cheap motels on the wrong side of town. And a soon-to-be ex-spouse wanting a bigger piece of the settlement pie.

But of course, the network demanded the scene be cut (as I've bitched about elsewhere). I'll spare you the many, many examples of Veronica voiceovers of which I'm less proud.

Evelyn Vaughn

Veronica Mars:
Girl. Detective.

DO ME A FAVOR. Read this, the opening voiceover from the pilot episode of *Veronica Mars*:

> VERONICA (V.O.): This is my school. If you go here, your parents are either millionaires, or your parents work for millionaires. Neptune, California: a town without a middle class. If you're in the second group, you get a job: fast food, movie theaters, mini-marts. Or you could be me. My after-school job means tailing philandering spouses or investigating false injury claims.

Now—read it again, and imagine it being spoken by Humphrey Bogart.

If you immediately started thinking about cigarette smoke, men in fedoras, and femmes fatale with great gams, then clearly it's working—Rob Thomas (a TV God, along with the likes of Joss Whedon and Aaron Sorkin) has created a hard-boiled detective protagonist out of a little blonde California girl.

Cool, huh?

The fact that the series is neo-noir isn't particularly earth-shattering. What's notable about its success in this arena, though, is the importance words play in creating that effect. More specifically, Veronica's words.

The power of the voiceover narration in *Veronica Mars* to capture the hard-boiled detective feel, however, is only half of the equation. The narration also captures—bear with me, here—a completely unexpected but unmistakably girly vibe.

Don't believe me?

Do me a favor. Read the following voiceover, from a lunch-period scene in the pilot:

> VERONICA (V.O.): It's not like my family met the minimum net worth requirement. My dad didn't own his own airline like John Enbom's, or serve as ambassador to Belgium like Shelly Pomroy's, but my dad used to be the sheriff and that had a certain cachet. Let's be honest, though. The only reason I was allowed past the velvet ropes was Duncan Kane, son of software billionaire Jake Kane. He used to be my boyfriend.

Now: Read it again, and imagine it being spoken by Sarah Jessica Parker as Carrie Bradshaw in *Sex and the City*.

Wait—I can hear your howls of protest from here. I'm not saying that Veronica is anything like Carrie Bradshaw. One of the reasons I love Veronica is that she's almost the anti-Carrie...the idea of Veronica spending rent money on a pair of fashionable Manolo Blahniks is ludicrous. I'm talking about the voiceover technique. So please. Go back and give it a try.

Not as farfetched as you would have thought, huh?

Here's my theory about the perfection of the voiceover narration in *Veronica Mars*. By using a voiceover with short, cynical sentences, the writers are indeed harkening back to the days of the hard-boiled detective thrillers. This certainly fits, because Veronica is almost as much a professional detective as her dad—just ask lawyer Cliff McCormack. But keep in mind that this technique, so popular in the early twentieth century, long ago became almost mockable, the venue of sitcom dream sequences and Flonase nasal spray commercials. So why does it still work so well for Veronica?

Because more recently, voiceover narration for anything but comedy has become increasingly *feminine*.

And here's why. . . .

Girl Talk

Yes, okay, so voiceovers really became popular in film noir. That's because the filmmakers were trying desperately to capture the cynical first-person viewpoints of the great hard-boiled detectives like Dashiell Hammett's Continental Op (his later and more famous Sam Spade was written in third person) and Raymond Chandler's Philip Marlowe. I'm going to talk a bit more about these guys later, but what you most need to know about them for now is this:

The hard-boiled detective is one of two distinctly American fictional archetypes.

Oh sure, the British arguably popularized detectives first—Sherlock Holmes, for example. But as Raymond Chandler himself points out in "The Simple Art of Murder," neither Holmes nor the other British detectives (think Miss Marple) were exactly action heroes: "The English may not always be the best writers in the world, but they are incomparably the best dull writers" (56). The British generally wrote about armchair detectives solving cozy mysteries. British detectives were generally middle- or upper-class, rarely had to rub elbows with the criminals, and certainly tried to avoid violence themselves. Violence is so terribly boorish, after all. In contrast, American mystery writers like Dashiell Hammett "took murder out of the Venetian vase and dropped it into the alley" (Chandler, "Simple" 58).

The American hard-boiled detective, in contrast to the British, was tough, poor, urban, gritty, rebellious, and adamantly independent. Basically? American. We're a country that came into existence through rebellion and guerilla fighting. A country of rugged individualism. A country where what you can do is (allegedly) more important than who you are or how much money you have or what class you're born into. We proudly count among our heroes the not-particularly-polished frontiersmen Davy Crockett and Daniel Boone, and create tall tales about Paul Bunyan and Pecos Bill.

In case you hadn't noticed, we Americans aren't known for our fine manners or passivity. And the brilliant writing of Hammett, Chandler, and Mickey Spillane captures that. It's not just famous for its use of first person—Mark Twain and Edgar Allan Poe did excellent first-person as well. Where hard-boiled detective first-person goes the extra mile is that in almost every sentence, the reader is submerged into a world of action and, sometimes, justice—even if that justice comes not from a jury but from the business end of a bullet. A struggling schmuck may need to work for the haves, but in true democratic fashion, he speaks to them with the same frankness that he does his friends, the have-nots. It's a world of brawls, not fisticuffs. Not British.

So—in an attempt to capture this tough-guy American voice, film-noir incorporated the now-famous voiceovers about a detective sitting in his empty office, hung over, until the aforementioned femme fatale with great gams walks in.

It worked. For a while.

Back during Grampa's time.

Why did this technique fall out of esteem to the point that the Aflac duck now uses it to sell insurance? Here's my theory—and don't worry, I'll get back to Veronica as soon as possible. The increasing unpopularity of voiceovers probably had something to do with the second distinctly American fictional archetype: the cowboy.

Yes, I know—the cowboy as we know him is actually based on Mexican heritage, the word buckaroo coming from *vaquero* and the word lariat coming from *la riata*. But it's American pop culture that combined these details with the independent woodsman character of James Fenimore Cooper's *Leatherstocking Tales* and ended up with an archetype that filled countless dime novels, chapter plays, and radio shows about *The Lone Ranger*. The TV cowboy, a rule-follower who generally did believe in law and order, hit his stride in the fifties and sixties—about the time that the hardboiled detective was falling *out* of popularity. In fact, in the 1958–59 TV season, four of the top-five-rated TV shows were Westerns: *Gunsmoke*, *Wagon Train*, *Have Gun Will Travel*, and *The Rifleman* ("October").

This is notable because, with only a few exceptions, cowboys weren't a talkative lot. Cowboys were defined by how *little* they talked. In fact, Jane Tompkins's essay "Women and the Language of Men" (from *West of Everything: The Inner Life of Westerns*) makes a pretty good argument that Western stories distrust language. A cowboy's manhood is determined by his taciturnity, and it is women, not men, who "shatter into words" in a crunch: "When Joey asks Shane if he knows how to use a rifle, Shane answers, and we can barely hear him, 'Little bit'" (42, 31).

In case you hadn't heard of the definitive Western *Shane*, the Alan Ladd movie based on the Jack Schaefer novel, Shane is very, very good with all forms of guns. But the tougher a cowboy is, the more he leans toward understatement.

And all of this applies to *Veronica Mars* how?

Because ever since the height of cowboy shows, men who talk a lot are not generally portrayed as, well, manly. On *The O.C.* we've got nerdy Seth, who never says in two words what he can say in twenty, versus tough-guy Ryan, who can communicate a great deal with raised eyebrows and silence. On *Buffy the Vampire Slayer* we had Xander, whose dialogue sped up the more nervous he got, and Angel, who simply...brooded.

A man who narrates directly to the audience via voiceover is equally suspect. True, we had a few good examples of voiceover narration in the late eighties, with the movie *Stand by Me* and the TV show *The Wonder Years*. But neither of these reminiscing protagonists—Gordie Lachance, voiced by Richard Dreyfuss, or Kevin Arnold, voiced by Daniel Stern—are exactly what you'd call tough. Hard-boiled heroes like Mike Hammer and Philip Marlowe could take Gordie or Kevin pretty handily, if it came to a fight. Also, *Stand by Me* came out twenty years ago, and *The Wonder Years* ran only to '93. Pop culture has moved on and, for the most part, not in the direction of male narrators.

Also true, voiceovers have seen a recent comeback on television, with the likes of *Everybody Hates Chris*, *My Name is Earl*, and *How I Met Your Mother*. But you'll notice that almost all recent examples are used for comic effect. Neither Chris, Earl, nor Ted are meant to be seen as particularly manly. No offense.

Veronica Mars, however, is tough. And she gets away with voiceovers all the same. Why? Because she's a girl, and girls are allowed to talk. In fact, as surely as with hard-boiled detectives, it's the "voice" that distinguishes the currently popular subgenre of woman's fiction known as "Chick Lit," based loosely on a combination of *Sex and the City* and *Bridget Jones's Diary*.

Never fear—I'm still not equating Veronica with Carrie Bradshaw or Bridget Jones, neither in her character nor her priorities. But one thing she does have in common with them—that she *must* have in common with them—is that second X chromosome. Maybe you noticed? Veronica's no man, manly or otherwise. And because of this, she's allowed to talk.

For what it's worth, this same bias helps us to accept other more serious female narrators like Mary Alice Young (Brenda Strong) on *Desperate Housewives* and Dr. Meredith Grey (Ellen Pompeo) on *Grey's Anatomy*. And how are the vocal introductions and conclusions of Mary Alice, Meredith, and the dearly departed-to-syndication Carrie Bradshaw of *Sex and the City* similar? Because all three of them, along with musing about medical superstitions or the universality of secrets, often talk about girl things. Veronica, for example, narrates about clothes...and boys:

> J. Geils was right: love stinks. You can dress it up with sequins and shoulder pads but one way or another you're just gonna end up alone at the spring dance strapped into uncomfortable underwear. ("Ruskie Business," 1-15)

She narrates about girl magazines...and boys:

> Dear *Seventeen* magazine. How can I tell if the super cute boy in my class likes me? No. Scratch that. Dear *Seventeen*. How can I tell if the super cute boy in my class killed his own sister? ("Weapons of Class Destruction," 1-18)

Yes, okay, and murder. She narrates about social embarrassment and (surprise!) boys:

> There are a million things Duncan could have written about me that I'd sooner impale myself on a rusty spike than have someone else read. I must get that computer back. ("An Echolls Family Christmas," 1-10)

But more than just her romantic musings, Veronica discusses relationships. In general, women openly prioritize their relationships very highly. Veronica does, too. Her narration, as well as her actions, shows how she values her relationship with her father, like in "Drinking the Kool-Aid" (1-9): "Jake Kane could be my father. But whether he is or isn't, would I really claim him as such and deny the man who raised me?"

Her voiceovers explore her lost relationships with her mother, with all the 09ers who turned against her, and with the late Lilly Kane. They relate her current friendship with Wallace Fennel and, later, Cindy "Mac" Mackenzie. Veronica's narration is filled with commentary that shows the priority she gives to the people in her life. As she muses in the first episode of season two, "Normal Is the Watchword" (2-1): "Senior year begins tomorrow and all appears hunky dory. Best friend? Check. Boyfriend? Check." You have to grant that in spending a decent amount of internal dialogue considering her various relationships, at least, Veronica is marginally girly.

Tough Talk

Of course, the very next line in "Normal Is the Watchword" is: "Lilly's killer behind bars? Check."

Because as surely as Veronica uses her feminine ease with words to keep her voiceovers natural, she really is far more than your average boy-happy, clothes-shopping "chick." While there's nothing wrong with being a girl, she's still not "just" a girl. She's a detective.

Which brings us back to the neo-noir.

The Wikipedia entry on "Hard Boiled American Crime Fiction Writing" lists several traits of the typical investigator. Included are that he's a private investigator. He's "both a loner and a tough guy." He's "certainly no family man and he does not associate with lots of friends." He's tough, hanging out at "shady all-night bars" and "shooting criminals if necessary." He's "always short of cash" and he "has an ambivalent attitude towards the police."

Sound like any girl detectives you know? Hint: I'm not talking Nancy Drew.

This was no coincidence. Rob Thomas himself has been quoted about the voiceover: "What attracted me originally was the whole idea of noir, and having the very Raymond Chandler-esque narration weaving through it" (Wharton).

Let's take a look at just how beautifully he succeeded in catching that hard-boiled voice for Veronica. You wanna know the moment at which I was truly sold on *Veronica Mars* as a series? It was in the pilot when, during a stakeout, Veronica—in voiceover—mused: "You wanna know how I lost my virginity? So do I." Until then, the episode had been good. But at that moment, it became stellar.

Why is that? Because that line was perfect tough-guy, with just an undercurrent of young, feminine vulnerability. After all, if a "tough" character hasn't suffered, then her attitude isn't all that tough in the first place, is it? What Veronica went through is horrible. Even worse was Sheriff Lamb's dismissal of the rape. In being able to forge on after this kind of treatment—much less to hide it from her father in order to protect him—Veronica proves herself to be tough indeed. She also, you might notice, reflects that "ambivalent attitude towards the police" that Wikipedia mentioned. It's an ambivalence that, in the continuing battle between Veronica and the clearly outgunned and outclassed Lamb, provides hours of viewer entertainment.

What I'm saying is that—girl or not—Veronica Mars's voiceovers *also* nail the tough detective narration, not in an over-exaggerated Flonase nasal spray satire but in its original earnestness.

A loner? As Veronica would say, "check." She's certainly that, which is why her theme song, "We Used to Be Friends," by the Dandy Warhols, is both so poignant and so apt. Her voiceovers capture the same loneliness, as in "A Trip to the Dentist" (1-21):

> As a rule, people that hate you aren't that helpful. There were about a hundred people at Shelly's party. Ninety-eight of them would walk over my corpse for free gum.

Tough? Again, check. In the episode "Drinking the Kool-Aid" (1-9), Veronica narrates of Jake Kane, whom she suspects sent threatening photos to her mother, "I'm taking this bastard down. Hard. I don't care whose father he is." She certainly mixes with the common and even criminal element, peppering her voiceovers with slang references to prostitutes, drugs, adultery, and combinations thereof: "Apparently I've pleasured the swim team while jacked up on goofballs" ("Like a Virgin," 1-8). And yes, with all her musings about how much she could rake in if she's Jake Kane's illegitimate daughter, how much she might earn from a case, and how much she dislikes cold showers, Veronica's voiceovers clarify that she's generally short on cash.

Her narration often uses clipped sentences or ironic observations, just like the first-person delivery in works by Hammett, Chandler, and

Spillane. As creator Rob Thomas admits, he prefers to keep Veronica's musings focused on "snarky commentary": "I don't want Veronica to share much with the audience in terms of her inner struggle" (Wharton). And yet, what even he may not recognize, and certainly what a lot of noir fans easily overlook, is that where Veronica truly captures the tough voice of the famous hard-boiled detectives, she is bringing on the vulnerability.

Consider Philip Marlowe's comment in Raymond Chandler's *The Long Goodbye*: "I'm supposed to be tough, but there was something about the guy that got me." Despite all his posing otherwise, the hard-boiled detective has a soft side, too. Let's do a little comparison. Take this Mike Hammer line from the first-person sequence at the start of Mickey Spillane's *I, The Jury*:

> There was my best friend lying on the floor dead. The body. Now I could call it that. Yesterday it was Jack Williams. The dead can't speak for themselves. They can't tell what happened. How could Jack tell a jury what it was like to have his insides ripped out?

Now compare it against Veronica's palpable loneliness for her murdered best friend, Lilly Kane, throughout season one:

> It's been a year and a half since I stood outside this door and watched my best friend's body carried away. A year and a half's worth of questions only I know and only someone in this house can answer. ("Kanes & Abel's," 1-17)

It's not that different, is it? Not despite the sense of loss, but *because of it*. Because, as Raymond Chandler explains about the tough American detective, his toughness is tempered by an incredible earnestness:

> He is a relatively poor man, or he would not be a detective at all. He is a common man or he could not go among common people; he has a sense of character, or he would not know his job. He will take no man's money dishonestly and no man's insolence without a due and dispassionate revenge; he is a lonely man and his pride is that you will treat him as a proud man or be very sorry you ever saw him. ("Simple" 59)

And this, *this* is where the sitcom dream sequences and Aflac commercials get it wrong, and *Veronica Mars* gets it right. The merely derivative versions of hard-boiled voiceovers focus only on the *tough*, and not on the *earnest*. The narrative technique employed by Veronica focuses on both. And in doing this, a petite California blonde, who can be compared to Nancy Drew as easily as she can be contrasted against her, may just save the concept of noir and raise it into legitimacy once more.

If anyone can do it, Veronica can.

Rita Award-winning author **EVELYN VAUGHN** has published fifteen romance and adventure novels (including *A.K.A. Goddess* and *Something Wicked*) and a dozen fantasy short stories in anthologies such as *Constellation of Cats*, *Vengeance Fantastic*, and *Familiars*. She also teaches literature and creative writing for Tarrant County College in Texas. When neither writing nor teaching...oh, who are we kidding? She's almost always writing and teaching. And watching TV (being an addict). It helps her rest up from the writing. And the teaching.

She loves to talk about what she writes, whether that's an attractive quality or not. Check out her Web site at www.evelynvaughn.com.

References

Chandler, Raymond. "The Simple Art of Murder." *The Atlantic Monthly*, Dec. 1944, 53–59.

Chandler, Raymond. *The Long Good-bye*. London: H. Hamilton, 1971. Orig. pub. 1953.

"Hard-Boiled American Crime Fiction Writing." History of Crime Fiction. *Wikipedia: The Free Encyclopedia* 12 Aug. 2006. <http://en.wikipedia.org/wiki/History_of_crime_fiction#Hard_boiled_American_crime_fiction_writing>.

"October 1958–April 1959." TV Ratings United States 12 Aug. 2006 <http://www.fiftiesweb.com/tv-ratings.htm>.

Spillane, Mickey. *I, the Jury*. Signet, 1947.

Tompkins, Jane. "Women and the Language of Men." *West of Everything: The Inner Life of Westerns*. USA: Oxford University Press, 1993.

Wharton, David Michael. "Hard-Boiled High School: Veronica Mars' Rob Thomas." *Creative Screenwriting*. 12 Aug. 2006 <http://www.creativescreenwriting.com/csdaily/trenches/05_05_06_Thomas.html>.

Here's the secret to having a great father/daughter relationship on television: hire actors as talented as Enrico Colantoni and Kristen Bell. Even when the material is uninspired, they give it heart. A perfect example is the scene in "Leave It to Beaver" when Keith tells Veronica he's her biological father. I've heard from so many people how much they loved the scene, but I can promise, it's not because of the dialogue.

I was single and childless when we shot the Veronica Mars pilot. I'm now married, and my daughter is nineteen months old. When I first wrote Keith, I decided to write him as the dad I'd hope to be. He still is that dad. We'll see how I do when Greta turns sixteen. I suspect it'll become more of a test.

Television writers complain loudly and often about the bad notes they get from their network and studio, and I've certainly had some of those, but credit where credit's due, the network gave me a note on the pilot episode for which I'm eternally grateful. Originally, Veronica was supposed to discover that Keith was keeping postcards from her mother hidden in his safe. At the conclusion of the pilot, Veronica and Keith were going to be estranged. The network wisely said, "Her best friend is dead. She's been raped. Her mom has deserted her. She's a pariah at school. You can't take her dad away, too."

And they were right.

Joyce Millman

Daddy's Girl

IKE GREAT TV series from *Buffy the Vampire Slayer* to *Lost*, *Veronica Mars* is a kaleidoscope for the imagination. It can be viewed as a coming-of-age drama, a private-eye spoof, a Southern California soap, or a mystery yarn. But when I lift the scope to my eye, what I see is a love story, about two people whose bond has withstood time, tragedy, and heartbreak—as well as potty-training, puberty, broken curfews, driving lessons, and college entrance exams. Yes, *Veronica Mars* is the love story of a father and a daughter, and any teen romance pales in comparison.

Until you actually have kids, it's hard to get your head around the bone-deep, scary-insane devotion and anxiety they can dredge up out of you. The writers of *Veronica Mars*, and actor Enrico Colantoni, who plays Veronica's father Keith Mars, perfectly convey the desperate humor of it all: parenthood gives you permission to fall madly in love with someone besides your spouse, but it wraps up this gift in a big box of shiny nightmares tied with knots of worry. "I'm thinking of getting you some sort of giant hamster ball, so you can roll everywhere in this protective sphere," Keith wearily told Veronica after she survived one of her frequent brushes with danger. "Nobody likes a blonde in a hamster ball," she snarked ("Happy Go Lucky," 2-21). Heh. Kids.

Veronica and Keith's relationship has been strengthened by shared ordeal. According to the backstory recounted in the series pilot, the Mars family—Keith, wife Lianne, and Veronica—was once comfortably settled in Neptune, an affluent (fictional) San Diego suburb. Keith's position as town sheriff brought them respectability, even if it didn't raise them into the true socio-economic elite. But it all ended the year before, when Keith bungled an investigation into the murder of Veronica's best friend, Lilly Kane. Keith was (mistakenly) convinced that Lilly was killed by her father, computer magnate Jake Kane. Keith was voted out of office in a Kane-backed special recall election, and he and his family became outcasts. Lianne began drinking heavily; she begged Keith to move them out of Neptune, and when he refused, she left home, abandoning her husband and daughter.

When we first see them in the series opener, Keith and Veronica are still living in Neptune, defiantly meeting public disgrace head-on. They've moved into a fifties-tacky apartment building (the bank took their house), Keith has hung out his shingle downtown as a private investigator, and Veronica works after school as his secretary, when she isn't doing some sleuthing of her own. Keith is the only constant left in Veronica's life. He blames himself for the fact that she is now motherless, but Veronica doesn't see it that way. "The hero is the one that stays," she told him succinctly in the first season episode "Meet John Smith" (1-3).

It's clear that Veronica is her father's daughter, and that she always was, even when her mother was around. Veronica shares Keith's sense of fairness and justice. In a humorous example of "like father, like daughter," Veronica found herself in the role of unofficial sheriff of Neptune High. Being a friendless pariah meant she had nothing to lose and nobody to alienate when she helped fellow outcasts and misfits fight back against bullies from the upper-class zip code ("09ers") and thugs from the wrong side of the tracks. Like Keith, Veronica is not impressed or intimidated by wealth or social status, or by people who throw their authority around. As father and daughter demonstrate in their jolly tag-team put-downs of Keith's successor, the arrogant and jerky Sheriff Don Lamb, they have no fear of speaking truth to power. They both know, from Keith's experience being hung out to dry over the Lilly Kane murder, that money and power corrupt.

Veronica and Keith share decidedly proletarian tastes—pizza and *The South Park Movie* on the DVD player is a perfect night for them. Their un-extravagant gifts to one another reflect the goofy face they put on their reduced circumstances; she baked him a lopsided birthday cake, he bought her a used waterbed at a yard sale ("Come on, you've wanted one of these things since you were, like, five years old!") ("Drinking the Kool-Aid," 1-9). Veronica and Keith are not ashamed of being almost poor in a place where wealth counts for everything, although Veronica does carry a grudge against the 09ers who were once her friends and who shunned her after her father's fall from grace. Still, when Keith fretted about how his mistakes have affected Veronica's life, she breezily reassured him, "Are you kidding me? You're the best father in the world! I mean, come on, look at me. I'm healthy, happy, good grades, all my own teeth, fancy shoes..." ("A Trip to the Dentist," 1-21).

A couple of episodes into the first season, just as Veronica was getting comfortable in her new identity as the anti-09er, the possibility was raised that Jake Kane, not Keith, was Veronica's biological father. This development dissolved what little fairy dust remained in Veronica's eyes after all that had happened to her family. Nothing was what it seemed, nothing could be taken for granted, and Veronica started to view her own life, her own identity, as a mystery to be solved. How did all the little pieces—feelings, memories, beliefs, actions—come to be arranged into the puzzle called Veronica Mars? She wondered what her life would be like if Jake really were her father. She re-examined her feelings about money and social class and about losing the modest social standing she once held with her peers. She questioned the meaning of family itself, of what the ties that bind are really made of. And she found her answers in the parental love and responsibility Keith has demonstrated every day of her life.

In the first season episode "Drinking the Kool-Aid," Veronica destroyed the results of the secret paternity test she ran on Keith without reading it. (It was later revealed that Keith took a paternity test, too, and he is, indeed, her father.) In voiceover, Veronica told us, "I sent off for those test results because I wanted the truth. But can a lab tech really see the shape of my soul in a drunken conga line of genes?

Jake Kane could be my father. But whether he is or isn't, would I really claim him as such and deny the man who raised me?" When Veronica decided to ignore the paternity test, she was not merely choosing to stick with the man who raised her. She was choosing to stick with the man who molded her, who taught her the meaning of family, loyalty, love. She was rejecting Jake Kane's values—he hid evidence incriminating his son Duncan in Lilly's murder and instead bribed a former employee to take the rap—in favor of Keith's values. *Her* values.

As the story of a girl detective living with her single father, *Veronica Mars* often recalls the Nancy Drew mysteries, but with a spiffy wit and nerve that puts an unmistakably modern edge on things. Oh, there are times when Keith goes all Old School Dad on Veronica, angrily reprimanding her for testing the limits of his trust and indulgence. But for the most part, Veronica and Keith's relationship is unusually harmonious, open, and relaxed for a TV depiction of a parent and teen. It's so open and relaxed that Keith's sometime-girlfriend, Alicia Fennell, suggested that he's too trusting and permissive. "She's not your average seventeen-year-old," Keith explained to Alicia, who replied incredulously, "How can she be, when you treat her like she's forty?" ("A Trip to the Dentist").

Alicia might have a point. Veronica and Keith's relationship is more like a partnership than a parent-child hierarchy. Their intimacy is apparent in the way they talk to each other, a peppy patter crackling with mock put-downs, inside jokes, and pop cultural references to everything from 1940s detective movies to Springsteen songs. In another measure of their closeness, Keith lets Veronica into his often seamy work world, showing her the ropes of investigation as if grooming her to take over the family business. He swallows his anxiety and lets her handle some cases on her own; they work side by side on others. On the home front, Veronica and Keith exhibit an earnest yet haphazard domesticity that reminds you of college roommates—or newlyweds. They take turns cooking dinner (if ice cream sundaes and canned chili can be considered cooking), and are fine-tuned to each other's moods, especially the lingering sadness of Lianne's betrayal and the family's public humiliation.

In Veronica and Keith's domestic cocoon, Lianne exists as a sort of feckless ghost, a specter of disappointment and lost promise for both father and daughter. Veronica, perhaps, feels this more acutely; after all, she tried to bring Lianne home, used her college savings to pay for rehab, and was let down a second time by Lianne's inability to commit to sobriety and her family. Veronica is determined to prove that she's a better woman than her mother. Unlike Lianne, who ran when things got tough, Veronica stands by her man. Indeed, it's almost as if father and daughter have created a kind of surrogate marriage to replace the failed one between husband and wife.

Not to imply anything icky, but there is sometimes an awkward sexual undercurrent to Veronica and Keith's self-consciously ironic banter. You won't find an exchange like this (from the second season opener "Normal Is the Watchword," 2-1) in any Nancy Drew book:

> KEITH: So, senior year. How was your first day of school, honey?
> VERONICA: Great! I beat up a freshman, stole his money, and then skipped out after lunch.
> KEITH: What, no premarital sex?
> VERONICA: Oh, yeah. . . . But don't worry, Dad. I swear you're gonna like these guys!
> KEITH: That's my girl!

Clearly, Veronica and Keith's wicked parody of an innocent father-daughter heart-to-heart is just their way of talking around the elephant in the room, Veronica's burgeoning maturity. Although he tries to be a cool, progressive dad, Keith is as uneasy about his daughter's sexuality as Mr. Drew must have been about Nancy's, back in the Dark Ages. But, let's face it, there is also something fascinatingly transgressive about Veronica and Keith joking about her implied promiscuity. And the vibe gets even stranger as the above exchange continues, and Veronica and Keith seamlessly shift into a housewife-and-breadwinner routine:

> VERONICA: I missed you.
> KEITH: Aw, I missed you too. Now, where's my turkey pot pie, woman?

Parent, child, husband, wife, partner, roommate, best friend—Veronica and Keith play a jumble of roles within their relationship.

They are all things to each other, much like lovers or spouses are in the intensely inward-focused first phase of their union.

Veronica and Keith's pantomime marriage is all subconscious, of course. But it sets in play very real actions and emotions. Jealousy arises when they begin to seek romantic partners; they have difficulty relinquishing ownership of each other's affections. Not that there's anything unusual about Keith flashing icily intimidating smiles at Veronica's various beaus, or opening the door to cut short front-porch goodnights—that's all pretty normal stuff, filed under the heading of Dads Who Can't Handle It When Their Daughters Start Dating. But there is something a bit weird about Keith and Veronica using their private eye skills to run background checks on each other's romantic interests; it calls to mind suspicious spouses checking up on one another for proof of infidelity. When Keith started dating Rebecca James, the Neptune High guidance counselor, a petulant Veronica dug up the woman's criminal record and threw it down in front of her father as if in triumph. Her refusal to share Keith with another woman suggests that she has been at least partly conscious of assuming Lianne's wifely role all along, probably in hopes of preventing Keith from seeking a real replacement and closing the door forever on a Mars family reconciliation.

There is an obvious, and amusing, Freudian element to Veronica's open hostility toward the idea of her father dating, and *Veronica Mars* delves deep into this fertile psychological terrain.The show provocatively acknowledges and explores the enduring theory that the quality of a girl's romantic attachment to her father sets the stage for all of her future relationships with the opposite sex. And Keith is going to be a tough act to follow. Throughout the first two seasons, Keith is depicted, much of the time through Veronica's perspective, as the perfect man. He is dependable, protective, loving, unselfish, strong, true. His virtues stand out even more sharply because he is pretty much the only morally upstanding adult in Neptune. (The town is a soap-operatic hotbed of murder, pedophilia, adultery, and child abuse that cuts across socio-economic lines.)

This idealized Keith fits the larger-than-life image girls form of their fathers in childhood. And Keith proved himself a father worthy of hero-worship in the climax of the first season finale, "Leave It to Beaver" (1-22). All hope seemed lost for Veronica as she lay trapped in a junked refrigerator that was about to be set ablaze by Lilly's killer, pervy movie star Aaron Echolls. She screamed for her father's help, and Keith came to the rescue, brawling with Echolls and then diving into the flames to free Veronica. "I love you so much!" Veronica cried as she cradled her injured father. "I knew you'd come! I knew you'd save me!"

Intriguingly, Veronica and Keith behave nothing like partners or pseudo-spouses during this climactic showdown with Aaron Echolls. We are starkly reminded of the real nature of their bond as they revert to the basic parent-child roles of protector and dependent—Keith unhesitatingly hurtled through fire to rescue Veronica, Veronica instinctively cried for his help. Veronica, too, seemed to emerge from this trauma with a new, more mature understanding of her relationship with her father. She realized that their bond as parent and child is something that stands apart from, and can't be destroyed by, the love they might feel for other people. She saw the foolishness of her childish illusions of keeping Keith all to herself. At the end of the episode, Veronica laid down her resistance to Keith having a romantic life and bestowed upon him an olive branch in the form of Alicia, his estranged girlfriend, letting Alicia take her place beside Keith's hospital bed.

Veronica then went home, only to receive a late-night visit from her troubled sometime-boyfriend, Logan Echolls (the son of Aaron Echolls). Logan showed up at Veronica's door beaten, scared, and disoriented; he was jumped by the Neptune High biker gang and it looked as if he might have killed one of them in the fray. In a striking parallel to the scenes we witnessed of Veronica tenderly ministering to the injured Keith, it was then an injured Logan whom Veronica cradled; he was stretched out in her lap, arms dangling to the floor, Pietà-like, while she soothed him. This was not the last time Keith and Logan would be linked by paralleling imagery. But it marked a crucial point in the series, where Veronica turned her romanticized focus away from her father and began looking (perhaps not even consciously) for the man who would take his place.

In the show's second season, set during senior year of high school, Veronica further embraced adulthood by having consensual sex for the first time (she was knocked out and date-raped in sophomore year). Her partner was not Logan, however, but her old boyfriend

Duncan Kane, whom she dated in the happy times before Lilly Kane's death, and with whom she briefly reunited. Asserting her independence from Keith even more, Veronica dug deep for self-knowledge by snooping into her mother's high school career. She discovered that she is more like Lianne than she knew—she has inherited her rebelliousness. And Veronica kept a monumental secret from Keith: she helped Duncan abduct his and the late Meg Manning's baby girl and flee the country rather than let Meg's abusive parents raise her. When Keith discovered Veronica's part in Duncan's drama, his candid, trembling anger and hurt came as a shock to his daughter (and viewers); it was the first major rift we've seen in their relationship.

But by far, the most telling clue that Veronica and Keith's relationship is changing comes in the second season finale, "Not Pictured" (2-22). In what was almost a replay of the first season's final episode, Veronica found herself at the mercy of the murderer she was tracking. But this time, Keith did not arrive to save the day. She was on a hotel rooftop, being held at gunpoint by Cassidy "Beaver" Casablancas, the classmate whom she had unmasked as the Neptune High bus-bomber. Keith, meanwhile, was on a plane escorting the mayor, a fugitive child molester, back to Neptune to face justice. And Beaver had placed a bomb on the plane. As the aircraft came into view, he detonated the bomb by remote control, and Veronica watched in agony as her world crumbled.

Just as Beaver was about to pull the trigger on Veronica, Logan (with whom she was in a shaky truce following their stormy fling) burst onto the scene and took the absent Keith's place in the rescue scenario. A few moments later, there was an interesting sequence of scenes, beginning with Veronica in her living room, sleeping Pietà-like in Logan's arms—a twin image of Logan's pose from the first season finale. Then we saw Veronica dreaming of being a little girl watching Keith put on a puppet show; Veronica in her bed, awakened from the dream by the smell of breakfast cooking; Veronica running into the kitchen expecting to find Keith at the stove, only to find Logan there instead. At that moment, the supposedly dead Keith walked in—he wasn't on the mayor's doomed plane after all.

The writers were doing a lot more here than just titillating fans of the Logan/Veronica pairing. The Great Logan/Keith Switcheroo depicted filial love and romantic/sexual love playing tug-of-war. Beginning with the rooftop rescue, these scenes traced Veronica's subconscious transferal of the primal affections she felt for her father over to the mercurial Logan.

On the surface, Neptune High's sarcastic, self-centered, poor-little-rich-boy seems to have nothing in common with Keith Mars, which is why it's such a shock when Logan borrows Keith's superhero cape to rescue Veronica. Veronica and Logan's on again/off again relationship seems to be one of attraction and repulsion. Veronica knows that Logan can be cruel, snobby, insincere, and a horndog. But he has also been abandoned by his mother, just like Veronica. And he loved Lilly—who was his girlfriend—as much as Veronica did. (And don't forget the possible, albeit debatable, soul-mate implications of those mirroring Pietà poses.)

Veronica tried not to care for Logan, but she was hooked. Part of that was her inability to turn away from someone in pain. It's her nature to want to fix what's broken, just as she tried unsuccessfully to fix her own family by bringing Lianne home for that disastrous, brief reunion. And there's no doubt that Logan is broken. You'd be, too, if your father beat you, slept with and murdered your girl, and drove your mother to (apparent) suicide.

When Logan replaced Keith as Veronica's savior in the second season finale, it was the fruition of that seed planted by the writers at the end of the first season, when they had Veronica leave her battered father's hospital bedside to comfort the equally battered Logan. It isn't just sympathy that draws Veronica to Logan, it's recognition: Logan eerily mirrors Keith's hidden but deep reserve of sadness, vulnerability, and anger. Logan is Veronica's irresistible mistake. He reminds her of Keith for all the wrong reasons.

Logan and Keith have both been abandoned by women they loved. Both "motherless" men fixate, sometimes to the point of over-protection and possessiveness, on the nurturing Veronica as a guiding light out of their personal darkness. And both Logan and Keith are terrific hot-heads. It's important to note that neither man has ever physically harmed Veronica. But the similarity in the way Keith and Logan express their anger—they adopt a fragile façade of jokey calm until their fuses blow with sudden fury—is too glaring to ignore. Keith's temper flared like a blowtorch when Veronica's morals were impugned during his cross-examination in the Aaron Echolls murder trial; he leaned out of the witness box and jerked the smarmy defense attorney down to face level by the necktie, threatening him with bodily harm. Logan displayed an explosive, even violent, streak when Veronica told him she was breaking up with him in the second season opener; he smashed a lamp while she cowered on the sofa. "My mom is dead!" he shouted, voicing his ever-present abandonment issues. "My girlfriend is dead! My dad is a murderer! And the only person I still care about is dumping me!" ("Normal Is the Watchword," 2-1).

Logan faced the prospect of losing Veronica with hurt, anger, and something approaching hysteria. But look how closely Logan's response was echoed by Keith when he learned that Veronica had deceived him and helped Duncan flee the country. His voice choked, eyes welling with tears, Keith could barely contain his panic when he told her urgently, "If they take you away, if you're sent to prison. . . . It's not just *your* life you're gambling with, Veronica. I would not survive without you!" Then, with a devastating glint of pain in his eyes, Keith lashes out at Veronica for her betrayal: "You played me, Veronica. . . . I love you. I will always love you. But I don't know how I'll ever trust you again" ("Donut Run," 2-11).

Even if Veronica doesn't realize that she is looking for a Keith substitute, we do. The writers reinforce this idea by rendering Keith AWOL not once but twice at key moments of the second season finale, first on the roof and then in the final moments of the episode. It was the day after Veronica's high school graduation, and Keith was taking her to New York City as a present. As they prepared to leave for the airport, Keith was delayed by a sudden visit from *femme fatale* Kendall Casablancas, who wanted to hire him for a P.I. job that couldn't wait. He sent Veronica ahead to the airport, promising to catch up. Instead, he took a look inside Kendall's briefcase, was seemingly tantalized by the (unseen) contents, and left Veronica waiting at the terminal.

The episode ended with Veronica standing alone at the gate as her flight was called for boarding, her face registering concern, confusion, and, finally, disappointment. We were left wondering how old, dependable Keith could have broken his promise. What did Kendall offer him? Was Keith corruptible after all? Was Veronica's notion of her father's perfection about to be shattered?

Perhaps. But then, isn't this just the natural course that most father and daughter relationships follow? Veronica's "abandonment" at the airport coincides with her high school graduation—symbolically the entrance into adulthood, the time of our lives when we begin to see our parents as flawed humans, not infallible gods. Keith can no longer be the center of her universe. Of course, viewed from the parental perspective, Keith's broken date with Veronica could be seen as merely a father's attempt to push his daughter out of the nest. But, whichever way you interpret this scene, the meaning is the same: Veronica's childhood is over. She is on her own. There will be grown-up romances and inappropriate men. And if she's lucky, somewhere along the way, she'll recapture the feelings of perfect love and security Keith once gave her. Here's hoping Veronica's skill at tracking down missing persons remains formidable, because she'll need it. She'll be looking for her father in every man she meets for a long, long time.

JOYCE MILLMAN is a freelance writer whose essays about television and pop culture have appeared in the *New York Times*, the *Boston Phoenix*, and *Variety*. She was a founding staff member and television critic for Salon.com, and a two-time finalist for the Pulitzer Prize in criticism for columns written while she was television critic for the *San Francisco Examiner*. She has contributed essays to several BenBella anthologies, including *Flirting with Pride & Prejudice*, *Mapping the World of Harry Potter*, and *Getting Lost*. She lives in the San Francisco area with her husband and son.

I always get *a wee bit defensive when asked why I paint (fill in the blank: moms, dads, the rich, the poor, the white, the non-white) as bad people. "Don't you get it?" I want to say. "I paint everyone as bad people!"*

It's noir. It's built on a culture of dirty little secrets. It's built on crime. In The Breakfast Club, all the kids end up blaming how screwed up they are on their parents. We just add murder, pedophilia, and infidelity to the equation.

But I'll admit, the fathers—save Keith—fare badly in the show. I'm pleased that Amy points out that, at the end of the day, Jake Kane isn't the worst father in the world. Jake does all he can to protect the surviving members of his family. If you had that much money and power, wouldn't you? Aaron's sins— beyond the obvious ones—of not knowing Logan's birthday or that he's allergic to shellfish almost seem more egregious.

But bad fathers also make for great characters—especially when they're played by actors as good as ours. By the end of the series, every writer wanted to write scenes for Aaron. Harry just became more and more interesting in the role. Among my favorite scenes from the series, I'd include Aaron and Keith discussing Russian lit in county jail, Aaron and Veronica in the Neptune Grand elevator, and Aaron having Trina's boyfriend sample his meat before he whips his ass. And whether it was, in fact, the Stonecutters who made Steve Guttenberg a star, the show doesn't get much better than when Woody Goodman finds Veronica on his computer and asks, "So, Veronica.... Are you as smart as you think you are?"

A sidenote: Bing Crosby was our inspiration for the Aaron Echolls character.

Amy's essay is a reminder that I do want to bring some powerful women into the show, be they good, evil, or somewhere in the middle. As I write this, we're searching for a new dean of Hearst College.

Amy Berner

Daddy Dualities

KEITH: Who's your daddy?
VERONICA: I hate it when you say that.

—"Pilot" (1-1) and "Leave It to Beaver" (1-22)

"D UALITY" IS ONE of the most important facets of characterization in noir, a film and literary style in which things are rarely what they seem. The conflicted anti-hero trying to walk a straight path, the corrupt authority figures, and the beautiful *femme fatale* are hallmarks of this genre in which victims become aggressors and predators become prey. Many primary characters in both noir and neo-noir (where elements of noir are mixed into other genres, as in *Veronica Mars*) are ambivalent, struggling with the coexistence of opposing attitudes, needs, or interests.

Veronica Mars regularly takes that concept and runs with it. From the primary conflict of the 09er "haves" versus the "have nots," to character placement (Veronica holding Logan on the couch in "Normal Is the Watchword" (2-1), and its reversal in "Not Pictured" [2-22]) and simple costuming color choices (remember Veronica's pale floral dress in her high school graduation dream versus reality's black dress in "Not Pictured"?), the entire show is built off of duality. It's in the setting, the plot structure, and the characters. The show takes this idea of duality even further by regularly creating parallels and reflections of those settings, plots, and characters, either foreshadowing or reminding us of major developments.

Take "Credit Where Credit's Due" (1-2), where Weevil's confession and willingness to serve jail time to save his grandmother stopped the investigation before the real perpetrator, his cousin Chardo, was ever investigated—much as Abel Koontz took the fall for the Kane family, bringing a halt to the official murder investigation and keeping Aaron Echolls from being found out. In "Meet John Smith" (1-3), we watched Veronica help a fellow student whose father had disappeared, giving us a backdrop for Veronica's absent mother and introducing the idea that Lianne's reasons might be more complicated than they initially seemed. In "The Girl Next Door" (1-7), the writers introduced the paternity issue with Sarah and her unborn child, an issue that haunted Veronica the entire season. In "Silence of the Lamb" (1-11), Keith found a kidnapped girl locked in a refrigerator, foreshadowing Aaron locking Veronica in a refrigerator in the season finale. Chlamydia came up in health class in "Nobody Puts Baby in a Corner" (2-7), but Veronica wasn't diagnosed until "Look Who's Stalking" (2-20). "My Mother, the Fiend" (2-9) featured not only faux babies for a lesson on parenthood in health class, but also the story of the Prom Baby, setting the stage for Meg's pregnancy. And the list goes on and on.

Just as many of these episode plots act in part as vehicles to explore the primary storylines of the seasons, some of the secondary characters on *Veronica Mars* become vehicles to examine the main characters and their relationships with each other. This is especially true of the primary relationship in the show.

Sit down, Logan fans, I'm not taking about *that* relationship. Logan is a fascinating character, but to my mind, his importance to the show doesn't quite equal that of another guy. No, Duncan fans, I'm not talking about him, either (although I will later). I'm not even talking about that type of relationship. I'm talking about Veronica's deep bond with her father.

As far as television dads go, you won't find many better than Keith Mars. This waterbed-buying, computer rebuild-arranging, ink bomb-setting dad is pretty darn close to what a perfect father could be in the real world. Yet all the while, he somehow stays within the realm of realism instead of reminding us of too-perfect television fathers like Howard Cunningham and Mike Brady. He's there for Veronica even while supporting her financially with a job he never willingly chose. He values his time with her and does whatever he can within his limited means to ensure her happiness and safety. Like any good dad, he protects his daughter as best he can while understanding that she needs space to grow and make mistakes, no matter how much it may pain him.

You've probably noticed that Keith has plenty of company in Neptune as far as fathers are concerned. From Richard "Big Dick" Casablancas to Terrence Cook, Stewart Manning to Nathan Woods, Dr. Tom Griffith to Van Clemmons, *Veronica Mars* is chock-full of fathers who far outnumber their female counterparts. In this age of single mother/wise daughter duos like Lorelai and Rory Gilmore on *Gilmore Girls* and Susan and Julie Mayer on *Desperate Housewives*, why does *Veronica Mars* choose to be so dad-heavy?

It's no accident. Although fans pay a great deal of attention to Veronica's various romantic interests, the key relationship in *Veronica Mars* isn't the one between our heroine and whichever guy she may be dating that week, but rather the all-important bond she shares with her father. Remember, it's the paternal relationship that set up the show's original premise following Lilly Kane's murder. Veronica chose to support her father rather than turn her back on him and side with the 09er crowd, even though she lost both her social circle and her mother in the process. If she hadn't, Veronica would be just another popular girl, and *Veronica Mars* would be just another clone of *Beverly Hills, 90210,* her life playing out much like we saw in her dream in "Not Pictured" (2-22).Veronica and Keith conflict on occasion, but not very often; their father-daughter relationship is one of the strongest on television. Normally, strong, healthy bonds aren't the compelling ones, but this show keeps the Mars family interesting by crafting other paternal or pseudo-paternal relationships that act as reflections of Keith and Veronica's relationship. These mirror images are always skewed or twisted, but each reflection still illuminates the show's central relationship in its own way, allowing us to better understand and appreciate Veronica and Keith's bond, and so we welcome that bond again and again.

There are plenty of fathers who appear in *Veronica Mars*'s first two seasons, but five of the fathers in (or formerly in) Neptune create the reflections that fascinate me most: Aaron Echolls, Abel Koontz, Jake Kane, Woody Goodman, and Duncan Kane.

Aaron Echolls

Imagine that you know nothing about the show. Got it? Okay, now ask yourself: Who would you rather have as your father, a handsome A-list movie star or a disgraced (not to mention short) former public servant? Silly question. Most teenagers would love to be the son or daughter of a movie superstar. Money, fame, cheesy television specials about your family... if you think about it outside the context of *Veronica Mars*, having Aaron as your daddy would sound very tempting (well, except for those cheesy television specials).

On paper, Aaron appears to be the coolest of cool dads. With a going rate of eight figures per picture, Aaron would hold a high place in our action movie star pantheon, somewhere between Harrison Ford and Bruce Willis. Cars drove by as part of celebrity homes tours, and he greeted them graciously, posing for photos and signing autographs. A pair of his old boots became the centerpiece of a school auction. Meanwhile, Keith remained nearly a pariah in Neptune society for much of the first season. All sorts of people wanted a piece of Aaron, and those people included much of the female population of Neptune.

With posters of himself on his walls and cameras installed to record his sexual exploits, Aaron had at least as inflated a view of himself as everyone else did. But while Keith's unflagging confidence stems from his expertise and belief in himself, Aaron's came from people paying him a great deal of money to look good and strut around on-screen making others believe in him (no offense meant to Harrison Ford or Bruce Willis, of course).

Here is where the primary twisted reflection of season one, the negative mirror image, comes into play. Keith and Veronica needed an opposite to balance the show, and while Jake and Lilly Kane certainly formed one reflection, they weren't as integral as we were led to believe at the beginning of the series. Instead, the violent, abusive, and domineering Aaron was the paternal half of that opposite reflection, the psychotic with (literally) movie-star good looks. But the other half wasn't his daughter Trina, or even his son, Logan; instead his victim, Lilly Kane, played that role.

While Veronica and her father have had many reflections as a pair, Veronica herself had one main reflection during that first season, who was her opposite yet the same: her best friend Lilly.[1] Before Lilly's death, she and Veronica were very different; Lilly was confident and brash, especially when compared to the more reticent Veronica. In fact, Lilly's death, while devastating, was what strengthened Veronica's individuality and allowed her to come into her own. Lilly's confidence and zest for life inspired Veronica after Lilly was gone. It was the combination of their better traits, the embracing of their duality, that created the Veronica we know today.

In addition to being self-confident, Lilly had a healthy sexual appetite and often cheated on her boyfriend Logan. Aaron Echolls was a movie star who regularly cheated on his wife with any available, willing, and beautiful woman. He was old enough to have been Lilly's father and, as her boyfriend's father, he should have served only in that capacity. Instead, he began a consensual affair with her.

We all know what happened. Lilly found the tapes he'd made of them in bed and threatened to make their affair public, and Aaron killed her in a rage, ensuring her silence. But look at it in the abstract: one father figure killed one daughter figure to create the mystery. Then, another father figure and another daughter figure solved that mystery. Within this framework, the climactic moment had to

---

[1] With Lilly's story complete, Kendall Casablancas took over as one of the Veronica reflections for the second season, albeit in a far more negative manner. Although she first appeared to be little more than the trophy wife of a successful (and corrupt) real-estate mogul, Kendall's abilities went far beyond just looking good. Like Veronica, Kendall came from a poor family, but while Veronica focused her efforts on her father's business and on her schoolwork in hopes of landing a scholarship, Kendall raised herself up by becoming a new person, and she continued to reinvent herself regularly. We know that Veronica has the knowledge necessary to create a new identity; Kendall actually did, becoming a rich and successful 09er all on her own. Though Kendall had the savvy and tenacity to get ahead, she didn't always display it, while Veronica proudly displays hers for all to see. Veronica occasionally does use her good looks and youth to obtain information and solve cases, but Kendall used her physical attributes as her primary weapon rather than a secondary one. They both know that it works. Kendall's sexual relationship with Logan in the second season cemented the parallel to Veronica, and came full circle to Veronica's first season reflection, Lilly, when we saw Kendall in Aaron's bed in "Not Pictured" (2-22).

involve a battle between the two father figures over the fate of the remaining daughter, and that is exactly the climax we received in the first season's finale, complete with blood and fire.

Aaron acted as Keith's reflection one more time when he was acquitted of Lilly's murder in season two. Despite everything that had happened, Aaron was released and cleared of all charges thanks to his shrewd lawyers, who knew how to take witnesses apart. Conversely, just for pursuing Jake Kane as a suspect, the population vilified Keith and recalled him from office, effectively convicting him of incompetence.

For a few moments, it seemed that both Aaron and Keith had died on the same day, both maliciously at the hands of others. But while Aaron's death may have felt like his just desserts, Keith's apparent death devastated Veronica (and nearly sent my little watching group into hysterics). No single event could affect Veronica more than the loss of her father, and no event could affect the audience more.

Luckily, Keith lived to investigate another day. Nobody cried when Aaron died.

Jake Kane and Abel Koontz

This biblically named pair did more than just create a huge neon-red herring signpost pointing to the idea that Duncan killed his own sibling. Jake Kane and his son Duncan, and Abel Koontz and his daughter Amelia DeLongpre, each formed another reflection of Keith and Veronica during season one that offered alternate meditations on how far a parent will go to protect their child.

First, let's get the Sunday school lesson out of the way: Abel was the son of Adam and Eve who was killed by his older brother Cain. Aside from the aforementioned red herring, the two also echo their Old Testament namesakes in that the dying "disgruntled former employee" Abel, in taking the fall for the Kane family, effectively lost his (remaining) life to them. Abel wasn't as simple or dumb as we might be tempted to believe of a man confessing to a crime he didn't commit; under the circumstances, his choice to confess and spend his last few months of life in prison in exchange for a hefty sum to be paid to his daughter Amelia seems smart.

But was his confession a noble act? It depends on your definition. The already-dying Abel thought he was ensuring Amelia's financial security and safe life with his confession, and he willingly sacrificed what little time he had left to do so. He lied to accomplish what he thought would be a greater good: supporting his daughter by providing her with 3 million dollars.

Conversely, Keith sacrificed his family's financial security in pursuit of the truth. Keith followed the evidence and found that it led to Jake. Despite the fact that his primary suspect happened to be the most powerful man in town, and even though his investigation ruined his law enforcement career and his marriage, Keith did what he believed to be the right thing to do: investigate the Kanes.

Although eventually released from prison and cleared of all charges thanks to Keith's efforts, Abel was still a dying man, and he wished to see Amelia one last time. But the money he'd earned, obtained in love in exchange for a lie, took his daughter out of his reach, and indirectly cost Amelia her life.

Jake and Abel, although originating from opposite sides of the class spectrum, are very much alike. Jake told Duncan in "Return of the Kane" (1-6) that "your happiness is all I've ever wanted," and that wasn't just a line (the way it would have been had Aaron said it). Everything Jake Kane did following his daughter's murder, he did out of love for his son. He didn't kill Lilly, but you can't fault Keith for suspecting him. After all, Jake did cover up the crime.

Jake isn't a perfect man (we learned of his long-time affair with his high school sweetheart, Veronica's mom Lianne, early on), but he loves his family. Remember, he is the father who lost his daughter. As he became the primary suspect and remained under suspicion from the Mars family (and the audience), it was easy to forget that important aspect of his character. He was genuinely devastated by Lilly's death, as his tears during Logan's video tribute to Lilly attested, and honestly tried to do right by Duncan, his remaining child. Although Jake was a smart and successful man with half the town loyal to him as the source of their high-tech fortunes, his world fell apart when Lilly died. He may not be the most ethical man but, thinking that his son was to blame, he did the best he could to save the family he had left using the resources that he had: his fortune and his loyal head of security.

Keith tried to save his family after their world fell apart as well. He continued to investigate the Lilly Kane murder even after removal from office, and he did so not to settle a score, but in an attempt to restore some normalcy to Veronica's teenage life. He was willing to give up his relationship with school counselor Rebecca James for Veronica's sake, and then broke things off with Alicia Fennel when Lianne returned, despite Lianne's secrecy, affair, and lack of support. And he went into battle to save Veronica from Aaron Echolls, suffering horrible injuries and burns. Keith doesn't have 3 million dollars, but he does have other currencies to work with, and he'd give them all for his daughter, just as Jake would do anything to save his son.

Woody Goodman

After the first season, Aaron, Jake, and Abel's stories had been largely played out; the show needed a slew of new fathers to use as comparison in season two. We saw quite a few over the course of the season, but right off the bat (pun intended), we met Woody Goodman at Shark Stadium, dressed in a baseball uniform (just as he might have been when he coached the boys he molested, but of course, we didn't learn about his evil deeds until much later).

Any character with a jolly name like "Woody Goodman" had to be more than he seemed, and the burger chain and baseball team owner, county supervisor, and nominal "Mayor" of Neptune certainly lived up to that expectation in perhaps the nastiest possible way. Unlike the real McDonald's owner who once owned the real San Diego baseball team, Woody Goodman was nowhere near the pillar of the community that he seemed to be. We didn't know the truth about Woody for quite some time, even with the suspicion both his name and the casting choice (the well-known Steve Guttenberg) automatically elicited from some viewers; like Harry Hamlin the season before, someone that well-known was unlikely to take on a role unless it was an important one. A good-guy character who was supportive of Keith, hoping to make him the chief of police in an incorporated city of Neptune, wouldn't have been enough.

Like Trina Echolls before her, Woody's daughter Gia didn't act as the other half of this reflection; Cassidy did. The younger Casablancas shared many of Veronica's more admirable traits: he was intelligent, he was thorough, and he was resourceful. Between those qualities and his drive to succeed after his father's departure, Cassidy seemed, on the surface, to be one of the characters most like Veronica on the show. His success with Phoenix Land Trust (and the lengths he went to in order to achieve it) was something Veronica herself would have been proud of, and his intricate plot to stop the truth about the past from getting out was equally ambitious; only Veronica's plot to get Duncan and his baby daughter out of the country equaled either in complexity or nerve. However, when Woody, Cassidy's coach and, as such, his stand-in father figure (from what we know of Cassidy's actual father, Woody's excuse that he was giving the boys the attention their fathers were not, however self-deluding, seems likely to also be true in this case), molested him, those potentially positive traits were warped, and he turned into a sociopath.

As a coach in a children's league, Woody's responsibility was to care for the children under his protection. Instead, he took advantage of them, abused them. Because of this, I consider Woody to be the official villain of the second season, and here we see parallels with Aaron. While Lilly was smart enough to take steps to protect herself—even if those steps got her killed—Cassidy and the other boys were too young and powerless to fight back.

While the fault for the season's main crime, the bus crash, still rests officially with Cassidy, Woody was the person who set that deadly plot in motion—along with everything else that Cassidy did, from raping the unconscious Veronica, to destroying his father, to killing Curly Moran, to Cassidy's own suicide—just as Aaron began the devastating series of events in season one (including the loss of status of the Mars family, Lianne's departure, Veronica's rape, and Abel Koontz's imprisonment) by engaging in a sexual relationship with someone much younger than himself (albeit a consensual one). Both men exhibited a similar pattern: they were both father figures who abused their position in society.

The second season revolved around information and how far one is willing to go to control it. Woody was willing to sabotage his own campaign for incorporation in order to keep his past deeds a secret when Cassidy threatened him with exposure. On the other hand, Keith sacrificed his bid for sheriff rather than jeopardize the bus crash investigation: he turned in evidence that would have cleared his just-sullied reputation to Lamb instead of going public. And while the season overflowed with acts like Woody's, where people hid information to improve or change their situation in some way (Richard

Casablancas's real estate fraud, Terrence Cook's gambling problems, Thumper's dealings with the Fitzpatricks), far fewer reminded us of Keith's, making his decision stand out in the crowd.

Duncan Kane

We know Duncan best as Veronica's ex-boyfriend (twice over), Lilly's younger brother, and, as the son of software billionaire Jake Kane, one of the crown princes of the 09er crowd. Duncan took on other roles during the first two seasons (such as murder suspect, and possible brother to Veronica), but by the middle of the second season, after the death of his ex-girlfriend Meg Manning, Duncan took on what would become his most pivotal role to date: single dad.

Early on, Duncan was a guy whose usual "way," according to Veronica, was to "stand idly by" ("The Return of the Kane," 1-6). He walked away from problems instead of dealing with them. He became student body president without actually entering the race himself. He didn't inform Veronica of their possible siblinghood, choosing instead to silently break off their first relationship by ignoring her, leaving her crushed and confused. Since it was easier than actually talking about it, he chose to believe that their tryst at Shelly Pomroy's party would be something they never spoke of, not knowing until much later that she had no memory of it and believed that she had been raped (of course, she really had been raped that night, but by someone else). His method of dealing with the suspicions against him regarding his sister's death was to run away to Cuba. Even his second courtship of Veronica after breaking off his relationship with Meg was fairly passive, consisting primarily of regular visits to Java the Hut.

The birth of his daughter changed Duncan's "way." He suddenly became proactive, his life centered on his child. Fellow father Keith has done his share of creative detective-work—as Veronica reminded him in "Like a Virgin" (1-8), "Overstepping is your main form of transportation"—but Duncan willingly took the law into his own hands to protect his daughter. In this, Duncan turned out to be more like his father than we would have suspected.

This previously unknown moral flexibility, a big part of what makes Duncan so fascinating as a father, was highlighted in "Donut Run" (2-11) as it directly affected the relationship between Keith and Veronica. Instead of bringing the audience in on the game from the start,

Veronica pulled the wool over our eyes, concealing her plot to help Duncan smuggle baby Lilly (formerly "Faith") out of the country until the second half of the episode. They began by faking a break-up, which took everyone's focus away from her actions while she helped arrange Duncan's escape. They succeeded brilliantly, of course, surprising us all with their tactics.

We weren't the only ones who were surprised. Veronica also deluded her own father completely, thus driving a wedge between them that had never existed before. Veronica has fooled a lot of people in her investigations, and she's quite good at it, but fooling her father is something else entirely. Although Veronica has no problem taking matters into her own hands without Keith's knowledge, this betrayal is different.

Most of the time, Keith can see through any ploy Veronica comes up with (think back to the aforementioned ink bomb from season one). However, in this instance, Veronica used his love for her against him, knowing that he would be too concerned about his broken-hearted daughter to question how she was spending her time. Veronica betrayed the one person who is there for her no matter what, and in helping one father, she lost the trust of her own.

But let's get back to our Man of the Moment. Duncan may have been created as the prototypical "sweet boyfriend," a symbol of the life Veronica had lost when Lilly died, but the finale of the second season showed exactly how much Duncan had changed since then. This supposedly sweet guy had Aaron Echolls assassinated from a comfortable sandcastle-side seat in Australia, again taking matters into his own hands (well, through Clarence Wiedman's gun, anyway). While a part of each of us may applaud Duncan for getting rid of such an awful man, someone who clearly deserved to be punished for his crimes, this cold-blooded act should disturb us. The original, passive Duncan we met in the pilot would never have been able to take such steps; the birth of his daughter—the responsibility he suddenly had for another human being, a responsibility Aaron Echolls failed to understand and Woody Goodman failed to live up to—changed him.

As you've probably noticed, dads in *Veronica Mars* fall into two categories: the dads whose actions are driven by doing what they think is best for their children and the dads, like Aaron and Woody, who do whatever they wish. Unsurprisingly, this exact dichotomy shows up within the Mars family as well, in the form of Keith and Lianne. Lianne took off rather than standing with her family, ostensibly to protect Veronica but just as much to protect herself from a situation she didn't know how to handle. She later accepted and subsequently squandered Veronica's life savings, and then, after returning home pretending to have been cured, stole the reward money from the Kanes, money that would have replenished Veronica's college fund. As much as Veronica has had to deal with others' villainous parents, we often forget that her mother falls in that category as well.

Yet again, it's all about duality, from the show's structure to its wardrobe details, to the way its plots are driven by the characters that embody that duality: the handsome movie star who is a murderer; the politician and business leader who shares the dirtiest of dirty secrets with an innocent-seeming boy who will go to the greatest lengths to keep those secrets hidden; and the good fathers who do bad things to protect their children. Those fathers have a lot to tell us about fatherhood, and a lot to show us about the main father of the piece, the one who does right because the deed is right, even if it hurts himself or his family in the short term—who does everything he can to help and protect his daughter without violating his own ethics. Keith and Veronica's exceptional bond is the result—and we appreciate it even more for seeing the alternatives.

> Freelance columnist **AMY BERNER** is obsessed with television. Although she spends much of her time as an event planner, she pops up in various places with reviews and essays, primarily covering genre television. She has appeared in several Smart Pop anthologies, including *Five Seasons of Angel*, *The Anthology at the End of the Universe*, *Alias Assumed*, *Farscape Forever!*, and *Getting Lost*. She lives in San Diego, California.

There are times when viewers pick out literary elements or devices from Veronica Mars of which I'm completely unaware. They uncover the "obvious" Christ imagery infused into the Wallace character or the underlying political message of the show. In many instances, I have to admit that the result is unintentional. In her essay, Lynne talks at length about a cornerstone of Veronica Mars of which I'm both aware and proud—the show's moral grayness.

It's not easy to get (and keep) a titular character on television who so often does as morally ambiguous things as Veronica Mars. She respects no one's privacy. She steals her ex-boyfriend's medical records and her classmates' permanent files. She is never satisfied with simple justice. She wants retribution. She's jealous and vindictive. She takes advantage of her friends' kindness as well as her enemies' weaknesses.

I remember a particularly frustrating experience on my first television-writing job at Dawson's Creek. In the episode I was writing, a football star was spreading rumors that he'd had sex with Joey. In my first draft, Joey was going to get even by spreading an equally mean-spirited rumor about the football star. The retribution got nixed, because, I was told, it would make Joey "look too mean." Perhaps. But the upside, to me, was that Joey became a character who wouldn't take shit from people. I hoped if the show were mine, Joey would go down swinging.

There's a sweet and cuddly core to Veronica (which Wallace points out in the pilot), but you have to go pretty far in there to find it. I want to make sure it stays that way.

Lynne Edwards

On the Down-Low
How a Buffy Fan Fell in Love
with Veronica Mars

A Long Time ago, We Used to Be Friends...

My guilt begins with the theme song: "A long time ago, we used to be friends, but I haven't thought of you lately at all...." It's the soundtrack to my shame, the rhythm of my secret agony at betraying Buffy, the Slayer, with Veronica, the bubble-gumshoe. As I gaze lovingly at my newly arrived *Veronica Mars* DVDs, I hear the Slayer whisper in my ear: "What about me?" After I turn the phones off and settle into my favorite chair on Tuesday night, I allow myself to finally face the ugly truth: I am on the down-low with Veronica Mars. I still love Buffy, the mythical slayer who battled vampires while looking for love and who empowered her posse, the Scoobies, to do the same. As a virtual Scooby, I reveled in our weekly triumphs, our loves and our losses—and our unrivaled kill-ratio. Yet, here I am, tiptoeing behind Buffy's back every week for some Neptune nookie. How did I let this happen?

Buffy and I go way back. We spent seven years fighting our inner and outer demons together, loving and hating the paths we were destined to follow. I've never known a program that made me so vividly remember the pain of lost love or imagine the horror of losing my mother. I've also never known a program that helped me connect with my students as much as *Buffy* did. From the intelligent dialogue infused with pop culture and literary references to the accessibility of its season-long story arcs, we "got" *Buffy*. The night I spent on speed-dial with a student, trying to figure out if Willow and Buffy would find the disk with the soul-restoration spell on it in time to save Angel, taught me that there was more to being a professor for me than just teaching—that connections didn't just happen in the classroom. Ultimately, however, it was the monsters and the mayhem that kept me coming back to Sunnydale. I found my inner demons much easier to face when their faces had fangs. There were few consequences when Buffy staked vampires—they turned to dust and then disappeared; it was all very black and white. Real life, of course, isn't so black and white. It's a pretty gray world in which we have to play nice with people who frequently aren't so nice, and we can't do a thing about it; I needed a place where I could vicariously slay the demons that I couldn't face in the real world. *Buffy*'s monsters were metaphoric beasties that provided a target for my frustration; Sunnydale gave me a place to hide while I slayed them.

Sunnydale wasn't perfect, of course. *Buffy the Vampire Slayer* was strict about "good" and "evil," but "bad" was sexy and redeemable. Redeemable monsters had both vampire and human faces to remind us why they were worth saving; evil, however, was ugly and neither sexy nor salvageable. Despite describing a world where good occasionally became evil and evil good, Buffy was clearly about the black and white: We all knew which monsters would not survive the episode and we knew why. It's that clarity that I love. In my weakest moments, I still retreat to the black-and-white world of Sunnydale until I'm ready to deal with the real one. It would take a special town to lure me from my Sunnydale haven and it would take a special heroine to make me cheat on my Slayer. Enter Veronica Mars of Neptune, California; a girl with a lot of sass from a town without a middle class. Wanna know how I lost my heart to Veronica? Yeah, so do I.

...But I Haven't Thought of You Lately at All...

Oddly enough, my relationship with *Veronica Mars* got off to a pretty rocky start. In fact, it's fair to say that my first nip into Neptune almost put me off television forever. Picture my pain for a moment—

I've finally decided to check out this program that my friends had been raving about for a year, and in the very first scene, I see Wallace taped naked to a flag pole in the center of the school parking lot with the word "snich" (*sic*) written in white paint on his chest. Surrounding him are laughing and jeering students; one even snaps a picture of himself next to the stoic Wallace. Lynching, Neptune-style. Why on earth was a Black man strung up (okay, taped up) on a pole in the middle of his high school parking lot in this day and age?

Things went downhill from there. It turned out that the unfortunate Wallace was taped to the flagpole by members of a Latino motorcycle gang for calling the cops when gang members stole beers from the convenience store where Wallace worked. This same gang menacingly surrounded Veronica while she sat on surveillance duty outside the Camelot motel trying to catch Jake Kane cheating on his wife. When Veronica offered to get the bikers off in court for robbing the convenience store in exchange for leaving Wallace alone for one week, Weevil agreed, but asked: "Why do you care so much for that skinny Negro? Things I heard about you, he must really lay the pipe right" ("Pilot," 1-1). "Negro"? "Lay the pipe right"? A racist, misogynistic, Latino motorcycle gang?

And it just kept getting worse. Rape and murder also appeared to be the norm in Neptune. Lilly Kane, Veronica's best friend and Logan's girlfriend, was murdered the previous year, resulting indirectly in the loss of Keith Mars's position as town sheriff and Veronica's loss of status among the 09ers after Keith accused Lilly's father of the crime. In the aftermath of the murder, as Veronica attempted to rebuild her life and re-assert her sense of self, she was drugged and raped at a party hosted by former friends. Rape, sadly, is not a big deal in Neptune, as evidenced by the sheriff's unwillingness to investigate; Veronica herself reduced the assault to a question of virginity and virtue: "Quite a reputation I've got, huh? You wanna know how I lost my virginity? Yeah, so do I" ("Pilot").

Let's recap: on my first date with Veronica Mars, I was treated to a modern-day lynching of a young Black man, a roving gang of misogynistic Latino thugs, and a sexual assault that was laughed off by the local sheriff and seemingly shrugged off by the victim. Neptune was a different world from my Sunnydale, one that didn't seem like a place where I'd want to hang out. And yet, I wanted more. Maybe it was Veronica's unapologetic style, the in-your-face trash talk that cut through the crap and spared no feelings—friends, foes, or otherwise. Or maybe it was the moral doppelgangers that peppered the first episode; they haunted me like Lilly Kane long after the credits rolled. Sure, Veronica was threatened by the PCHers in the middle of the night, but it was a gang of 09ers who vandalized her car in broad daylight—a gang that was driven off by the menacing PCHers. In another moral double take, the same surveillance tape that almost sealed the PCHers' fate in court and Wallace's fate on the flagpole also ended up sealing Wallace's position of power over the PCHers. Symbolically, just as PCHers held him over classmates' heads by tape, Wallace held a tape over their heads. Wow.

I began to suspect that what I thought was a depiction of the same old racial stereotypes—literally Black and White—was really gray all over, and my second date with Veronica confirmed my suspicions. In "Credit Where Credit's Due" (1-2), I learned that, in Neptune, what I thought was racism is really in-your-face-ism, that the villains are often victims, and that redemption is often elusive and frequently fleeting. I began to see how they make the gray in Neptune.

Like children mixing black and white crayons to make gray, Blackness is layered over Whiteness to create a narrative gray zone in *Veronica Mars*. Neptune, the town without a middle class, is the place where 09ers and PCHers alike wear Blackness by performing it.

"Credit Where Credit's Due" begins with a delicious visual and symbolic inversion that shows the fluidity of race and language in Neptune, as both are alternately borrowed and performed by Blacks, Whites, and Latinos alike. In a Neptune High hallway, Veronica decoded 09er signs in a party flier for Wallace, the outsider, letting him know that neither was welcome at the party. The very next scene featured Troy, an 09er in economics class but an outsider socially, engaging in an exchange with Duncan in which they performed a self-mocking version of Black vernacular before joining the party where they *were* welcome:

> TROY: Whaddaya say, dawg? You ready to get this party started? You ready to burn this mutha down? Upjump…the boogie?
> DUNCAN: My plan, and I haven't worked this out entirely yet, so bear with me, was to raise da roof.
> TROY: See? That is so you, man, mister old school.

DUNCAN: Me, old school? You're the one who wanted to get jiggy with it.

The vernacular appropriation continued at the party in a Neptune version of "playing the dozens" when the 09ers engaged the PCHers in a beach battle of slurs using rhetorical strategies borrowed from this African-American oral tradition:

LOGAN: . . . She is a good little worker, your grandma . . . yeah, spic and span.
CHARDO: Grandma says you go through a box of tissue a day—your room alone.
LOGAN: What can I say? She's a very sexy lady.

Within the Black community, playing the dozens serves both a performative and a displacement function, as men seek to prove their verbal prowess before an audience while diffusing aggression without resorting to violence. In Neptune, however, when this strategy is performed by Whites and Latinos, they metaphorically cloak themselves in Blackness and contribute further to the visual and narrative gray zone of Neptune.

I also saw one week's villain revealed as the next week's victim, as Weevil Navarro willingly confessed to stealing credit cards from the Echolls family to protect his grandmother, the Echolls' housekeeper, who was accused of the crime. The roots of Weevil's mask of bravado became evident when I saw his grandmother willing to let Weevil serve time for what was, in reality, his cousin Chardo's crime. When Veronica confronted Leticia Navarro about Chardo's guilt, Mrs. Navarro openly admitted to letting Weevil do Chardo's time because, at seventeen, Weevil would only have to serve four months in a juvenile facility; eighteen-year-old Chardo would have had to serve hard time in an adult prison. Leticia's confidence in her decision quickly disappeared, however, when she learned from Veronica that Chardo used the credit cards to impress Caitlin Ford, a "spoiled, rich, *White* girl" (emphasis Veronica's) who was dating Logan Echolls.

Weevil's redemption was a difficult one, but it also affirmed Veronica's location in the gray zone. As Veronica fought to clear Weevil, Wallace reminded her that Weevil had taped him naked to the school's flagpole and that she should have been trying to prove Weevil's guilt. Even Weevil was less than enthusiastic about Veronica's investigation on his behalf, challenging Veronica to question her assumptions about him (the same way she so often forces others to question their assumptions about her) by reminding her of her own fluid position in their world: "You think you're this big outsider, but you're still one of them, you think like one of them" ("Credit Where Credit's Due"). With a family willing to let him serve time for a crime he didn't commit—a sentence he willingly served out of loyalty to a disloyal grandmother—Weevil evolved from a stereotypical villain into a complex man.

Weevil's redemption was short-lived, however. At the episode's end, he hunted down and found Chardo at Caitlin Ford's home. After the relationship between Chardo and Caitlin was finally revealed, Logan and the 09er boys showed up at Caitlin's to attack Chardo when he arrived to carry Caitlin away. The attack, eerily similar to a scene from the film *American History X*, had the 09ers poised to stomp Chardo's head against the curb before his cousin Weevil and the PCHers showed up to rescue him and ride off into the sunset. But Chardo's salvation was also short-lived, as the PCHers took him to the beach to beat him out of the gang. The next day, Caitlin faced her own beat-out, 09er style, when she was frozen out of prime lunchtime real estate by former friends who denied her access to their tables. Neptune, it seemed, was a battleground for a race-class-gender war that had no clear villains or victors and no clear path to redemption.

Come on Now, Sugar, Bring It On, Bring It On...

Villains in Neptune, we frequently learn, usually occupy the gray zone as a result of their past victimization. Logan's insensitivity to others, from his mocking of Veronica's absent mother to his staged fights between homeless men, becomes, if not excusable, then at least rational when considered in reference to the crimes of his abusive and murderous father. Cassidy's reprehensible rape of Veronica and murders of his classmates on the bus are clearly attributable to his sexual abuse by Woody Goodman. Even the not-so-villainous Neptuners straddle the line between black and white. Sweet, virtuous Meg became petty and vindictive toward Veronica after Duncan broke up with her; we learn later that her change stemmed from her unwanted pregnancy and her fear of her abusive father's response to it. And ironically, Meg's pettiness saved Veronica's life when she let the school bus pull off from the gas station without Veronica on board. Jackie Cook's spitefulness masked her insecurity about her illegitimacy and working-class background.

These Neptune villains' "black" deeds, when viewed against their obvious loss of innocence and sense of self, make it impossible to vilify them. It is equally difficult to locate the victors in Neptune. Aaron Echolls appeared to get away with Lilly's murder, only to be killed by Clarence Wiedman on Duncan Kane's orders. Veronica appeared to achieve her dream of reuniting her family, only to lose both Lianne, to alcoholism again, and the check that should have been her college money. Weevil Navarro survived his loss of status among the PCH gang members and managed to pass algebra in order to keep the promise he made to his grandmother to graduate, only to be arrested before receiving his diploma. Like Neptune's villains, its victors' deeds are shaded in gray, making it impossible to thoroughly enjoy their often short-lived victories.

Lasting redemption seems nearly impossible for young people in Neptune, because the real monsters—the people who keep things nice and gray—appear to be their parents. The people who actually created the class and power distinctions that split Neptune's youths along their current class, gender, and race lines are the same people whose abuse and adultery keep Neptune's youths apart; parental influence and authority undermine their children's better impulses. Logan and Weevil in particular seem perpetually on the brink of becoming better people than their parents. They bonded together during detention to pay back the teacher who sentenced them by putting his car on the school's flagpole. When the prank backfired and Weevil got kicked out of school, Logan was taken aback: "I didn't know they expelled people at our school." "Not our people," Duncan responded. Logan went to the vice principal to get Weevil back in school by confessing that he helped Weevil in the prank—while dangling his dad's famous boots, which the vice principal had wanted for the school charity auction, before the vice principal as an unspoken bribe ("The Girl Next Door," 1-7). This alliance, seemingly temporary, remained a tenuous bond between the two of them as they were both alternately accused and exonerated of several murders in Neptune. And it is flexible alliances like this one, alliances which hold the potential for redemption that keep me coming back.

Just Remember Me When...

Nothing is ever clear in Neptune and nothing is ever final; Veronica and friends live in the gray zone, like the rest of us. Sure, I still escape the gray by getting my slay on in Sunnydale, but Neptune is where I go to deal with the real. There are no monsters for me to hide behind; everyone has *inner* demons in Neptune, demons that come from real pain and that lash out in real violence with very real consequences. It certainly isn't a place for the faint of heart and it certainly isn't a place to hide from the real world. It's a place to learn how to confront it. And it's just the place I want to be.

LYNNE EDWARDS, Ph.D., is associate professor of Media and Communication Studies at Ursinus College in Collegeville, PA. She is the author of several essays about popular culture including, "Slaying in Black and White: Kendra as Tragic Mulatta in Buffy the Vampire Slayer" in *Fighting the Forces: What's at Stake in Buffy the Vampire Slayer* (Rowman & Littlefield, 2002), and "Victims, Villains, and Vixens: Teen girls and Internet Crime" in *Girl Wide Web: Girls, the Internet, and the Negotiation of Identity* (Peter Lang, 2005). Lynne currently is writing *The Other Sunnydale: Representations of Blackness in Buffy the Vampire Slayer* (Lexington Books, exp. 2006).

During season one, we did a mall tour in which we had the cast appear in several shopping malls across the country. I attended the first one in Seattle, and we were shocked that, despite our paltry ratings, there was a line stretching the length of the mall. It took people a couple hours to get through the line. I mention this only because it was the backdrop for a conversation I had with a mother who had brought her fourteen-year-old daughter to the signing. She mentioned to me that she loved the show, but that our portrayal of the minority characters in the show made her uncomfortable.

"Why are they the criminals?" she asked.

Now, while the PCHers were mostly (but not exclusively) Latino, and they certainly steal cars, I hadn't thought we had portrayed our minority characters in any negative light.

Well, that's not quite true.

I didn't think I had portrayed them any more negatively than our rich White kids. Certainly, Wallace is the moral core of the show. His ethical backbone is certainly stronger than Veronica's.

And I never considered stealing cars any worse than organizing bum fights, or crossing the border for drugs, or setting fire to the community pool. Noir thrives in a world of moral ambiguity and, outside of Wallace, I don't think anyone is clean. Even Mac takes advantage of her classmates for a profit.

Amanda Ann Klein

The Noir of Neptune

I N THE VERY first episode of *Veronica Mars*, Veronica, our hard-boiled private eye, sits alone in an outdoor high school cafeteria—the kind that only seem to exist in the California-colored worlds of *Beverly Hills, 90210* and *The O.C.*, where it never rains during lunch and where there's never gum stuck under the cafeteria tables. Veronica is eyeing a group of smug, well-coiffed teenagers—her former clique, we soon find out—enjoying their freshly delivered pizzas. As she stabs at her cafeteria-prepared meatloaf with a plastic fork, Veronica explains, in her characteristic monotone, "This is my school. If you go here either your parents are millionaires or your parents work for millionaires. Neptune, California: a town without a middle class" ("Pilot," 1-1).

With these words *Veronica Mars* established the central role that location, with its implicit ties to class and caste, would play in the series. And it is this incessant focus on location, borders, and who lives in what zip code that places the series so firmly within the long, rich tradition of the *film noir*.

Of course, when we think of the principal settings used in the classic *film noir*, images of the city at night, with its low-rent apartments, shadowy alleys, blinking neon signs, and seedy bars, are summoned up. We recall the image of a doomed Frank Bigelow racing through the dusky streets of Los Angeles to inform the police of a murder—his own—in the opening scene of *D.O.A.* (1950) or of Gilda singing "Put the Blame on Mame" on a smoky stage in a Buenos Aires casino in *Gilda* (1946). The words *film noir* call to mind unshaven private dicks like Philip Marlowe, Sam Spade, and Mike Hammer, who are only able to find their key clues after the sun goes down and only in the most unsavory of locales. Even the name—*film noir*—implies that the settings will be "black," both literally and metaphorically.

However, these iconic images allow us to forget that in many *films noir*, it is not the dark, rain-soaked city, but the sunny, California suburb, with its manicured lawns, idyllic homes, and crystal blue swimming pools, that serve as the backdrop for the film's twisted plots. In *Double Indemnity* (1944), for example, Walter Neff and his platinum-blonde *femme fatale*, Phyllis Dietrichson, hatch their murder plans amidst row upon row of identical canned goods in a local supermarket, making a seemingly innocuous location feel as nefarious as any dingy bordello. And one of the first images of *Sunset Boulevard* (1950) reveals a glorious Los Angeles mansion with trimmed hedges and stucco walls; the only thing awry is the presence of our narrator, Joe Gillis, floating facedown in the mansion's swimming pool. From beyond his watery grave Joe describes himself in third person: "The poor dope! He always wanted a pool. Well, in the end, he got himself a pool—only the price turned out to be a little high." What is threatening in these two films is not the back-alley watering hole and the square-jawed thug, but rather the machinelike conformity of the suburban supermarket and the crumbling mansion of the washed-up actress. Crime is found not in the stench of poverty but in the perfume of wealth. Indeed, Walter is intoxicated by the sickly sweet scent of Phyllis's honeysuckle perfume, which he claims smells just like "murder."

In such *films lumiéres* the criminals are not hiding in back rooms, shadowed by fedoras or too much cheap make-up; instead they stand proudly in the public eye, wearing tasteful, tailored suits and pastel-colored sweater sets. This vilification of suburban living and the upper middle class accoutrement makes sense in the context of postwar America, when the concept of the man in the gray flannel suit driving to his nine-to-five job replaced a more romantic vision of America as agrarian, as a country built on the sweat of good, old-fashioned manual labor. Indeed, the seeming homogenization of American society was almost more frightening than the "big city," and the affluent, not the destitute, generated distrust in the popular imagination, making suburban living a subject ripe for exploitation in the 1940s and 1950s.

Today the conceit of the sinister, upper middle class suburb is a familiar one in both film (*Blue Velvet*, 1986) and on television (*Desperate Housewives*), and *Veronica Mars* banks on this familiarity. Although the series does contain its fair share of villains from the "wrong side of the tracks," like the violent Fitzpatrick clan or the treacherous Thumper, it reserves its most stunning transgressions for those characters with the largest bank accounts living within the wealthiest of zip codes. And in this series, there is only one zip code that matters: 90909.

Neptune, 90909

WEEVIL: Hey, let me ask you something. Have I ever asked you if I could come play through at Torrey Pines? Have you ever run into me surfing down at Cape Crescent? Bro? Huh? Have you ever even once come home to find us throwing a kegger in your backyard? No? Then what the hell do you think you are doing on *our* beach? ("Credit Where Credit's Due," 1-2)

A running theme throughout *Veronica Mars* is that location, synonymous with class, is destiny. In "The Girl Next Door" (1-7), Eli "Weevil" Navarro complained to Logan Echolls, "All that matters [in this school] is who your parents are and the zip code your mom shot you out in," after they were both issued detention for very different infractions—Logan publicly humiliated the teacher, while Weevil merely chuckled at the joke. The difference is that students like Logan can bribe teachers by calling upon their parents' wealth and influence, and students like Weevil are usually the first to be suspected of any crime committed on school grounds precisely *because* of who their parents are.

As a result of this seeming distance between characters from different zip codes, "turf" battles frequently ensue, usually pitting the 09ers (led by Logan) against the PCH bike gang (led by Weevil). In season two, for example, Logan and some friends set fire to a community pool at the height of the summer heat wave, knowing full well that such a move would most impact the PCHers and their families, who are too poor to afford pools in their backyards (unlike the 09ers). That such battles have a hint of the cliché to them is not lost on the show's writers (who revel, like all good *noir* scribes, in overwrought narration and melodramatic confrontations). In the pilot episode, Veronica's "boy Friday," Wallace Fennel, described a physical showdown between Logan and Weevil as something out of *The Outsiders*, to which Veronica quipped, "Be cool, Soda Pop" ("Pilot," 1-1).

Location is so important in this series that a major plotline of season two revolves around Mayor Woody Goodman's plans to incorporate the town of Neptune. Though Goodman reasoned that his plan would make for a "cleaner, safer" Neptune, on par with other chic California vacation spots like Carmel, it was more likely motivated by his desire to price the lower classes out of Neptune. When incorporation was later voted down, Keith Mars astutely noted, "What's a yacht without barnacles?" ("Look Who's Stalking," 2-20).

Keith's comment highlights the significant, symbiotic relationship between the classes of Neptune. The "barnacles" on Neptune's perimeters, like south Neptune (where much of the Mexican population resides), the River Stix (the watering hole that caters to the likes of the Fitzpatricks), or the ubiquitous Camelot Motel, are necessary in that they provide 09ers with a place to conduct their unsavory business in order to avoid sullying their own pristine zip code. The very first image of the series, for example, is of the Camelot Motel, where the pillars of the Neptune community, like Jake Kane, go to have their affairs, where presumably disgruntled students who are planning to blow up Neptune High School supposedly rendezvous, and where Woody Goodman (purposefully) created a public scandal by appearing to bed an intoxicated campaign staffer.

Although the 09ers try to distance themselves from their crimes by limiting their criminal acts to Neptune's seamier edges, try as they might, they can't help but track mud into their own homes. In fact, the deviant acts committed on Neptune's outskirts are relatively minor—the threat to blow up the school even turned out to be a hoax—in comparison with the atrocities committed *within* Neptune, making

Neptune itself the site of murder and torture. For instance, the murder of Lilly Kane, the event that forever changed the course of Veronica's existence and the mystery driving season one, was not committed in some back alley or dingy hotel room, but on the "Kane estate," beside the family's designer pool.

It is also significant that this crime was perpetrated by Neptune's own beloved action hero, Aaron Echolls. Aaron, a man who regularly had legions of devoted fans posted by the iron gates of his magnificent home, not only slept with his underage son's underage ex-girlfriend and murdered her when she threatened to expose their relationship, he also attempted to kill Veronica and her father when they finally discovered the truth. Being charged with statutory rape and murder, however, seemed to help, rather than hurt, Aaron's Q-rating, as evidenced by the *Tinseltown Diaries* episode that appeared shortly after his arrest. Not surprisingly, Aaron's celebrity and zip code were impressive enough to get him cleared of all charges, much to Veronica's chagrin. As in any good *film noir*, official society, represented by the courts, due process, and popular opinion, ultimately failed to produce any real justice.

Likewise, in "Nobody Puts Baby in a Corner" (2-7) we discover that the wealthy, God-fearing Manning family kept their youngest daughter Grace locked in a closet and scribbling penances in composition notebooks as punishment for various minor transgressions. Despite the overwhelming evidence against them, the Mannings were never charged with child abuse. And when Veronica reported that she was raped by an 09er during one of Shelly Pomroy's big parties, Sheriff Lamb assumed she was lying, taking the side of Neptune's elite instead: "Is there anyone in particular you'd like me to arrest, or should I just round up the sons of the most important families in town?" ("Pilot," 1-1). In all three cases it appears to be impossible to accuse 09ers of any wrongdoing, no matter how strong the evidence is against them.

This emphasis on zip codes, on location, affects not only the social hierarchy of Neptune students, it also affects their location *in the* school, or at least the classes they take. In "Return of the Kane" (1-6), for example, an episode that cleverly highlighted how the social politics and caste systems of Neptune High School are a carbon copy of those found in Neptune proper, Wanda Varner, a non-09er, faced off against Duncan Kane, 09er par excellence, in the race for student council president. Wanda ran on a simple platform—she planned to abolish the "Pirate points" system that awarded students with certain privileges, such as having their lunches delivered to the school, for participating in extracurricular activities. The system was elitist, however, due to the fact that the only activities that counted towards Pirate points were varsity sports and student council—that is, activities dominated by 09ers.

Since the majority of Neptune High students supported Wanda's bid for the presidency, Madison Sinclair, an 09er and one of Veronica's primary nemeses, took it upon herself to rig the voting. In a nod to the Miami-Dade County election hijinks of 2000 or perhaps to the double-dealings of Tracy Flick in the black comedy *Election* (1999), Madison tampered with the voting directions in the classrooms most likely to carry Wanda supporters—band, auto shop, and art, where the students favor black clothing and tattoos over polo shirts and relaxed-fit khakis. The episode (somewhat problematically) implies that these are the activities (and clothing styles) of the school's underclass, that sports and student council are reserved for only the wealthiest of students. The 09er classes, of course, received the correct voting instructions, ensuring Duncan's victory. Thus, even Neptune High School is zoned by social class, and this zoning is, more often than not, the source of the show's weekly mysteries.

Of course, Veronica, as the *noir* hero, is granted access to all parts of Neptune, but only with the caveat that she will never be fully accepted by either the 09ers or their economically challenged peers. When, for example, she went to Weevil's home to convince him to turn his duplicitous cousin, Chardo, in to the police ("Credit Where Credit's Due," 1-2), Weevil accused her of being an 09er: "You think you're this big outsider, but, push comes to shove, you're still one of them. You still think like one of them," and then promptly dismissed her from his yard. And as we learned from countless voiceovers and flashback sequences, such as her ill-fated decision to attend Shelly Pomroy's big party after her father's public fall from grace, Veronica is not welcome on 09er turf either. Just as Sam Spade and Phillip Marlowe are roughed up by both the thug and the policeman, Veronica has sacrificed the acceptance of her peers, on both sides of the tracks, in order to be a lone wolf pursuing the truth.

Mexico

VERONICA: Did you meet anyone odd or were you followed? Did
  you see any suspicious activity?
TROY: How about all of the above? Have you ever *been* to Tijuana?
  ("You Think You Know Somebody," 1-5)

In the *film noir* there are locations that unambiguously connote comfort and goodness, such as Dave Bannion's idyllic, middle-class home—
shot in high key lighting and soft focus—in *The Big Heat* (1953). And
there are locations that unambiguously connote criminality and im-
pending doom, like the boarding house where the Swede accepts his
untimely demise in *The Killers* (1946). But there are also locations that
cannot be defined in such black-and-white terms. These liminal spaces, which exist on the border between two more defined entities—safety and danger, law and criminality, good and evil—are often a refuge
for *noir* characters. Because there is no law or consequence, these car-
nivalesque spaces are where characters go when they need to start over,
disappear, or just lie low for a while.

For various geographic, political, and economic reasons, including
California's proximity to Mexico, Franklin Roosevelt's "Good Neighbor" policy, and the importance of the Latin American market to the
postwar U.S. economy (Naremore 229–230), 1940s *films noir* posited
Latin American locales as foreign lands filled with exotic primitives
and as safe havens for doomed lovers and the perpetrators of botched
robberies and crimes of passion.

In *Out of the Past* (1947), for example, the protagonist, Jeff, recalls his torrid love affair with a *femme fatale* in Acapulco as a fever-
ish dream, a pastless present in which both were free of obligations
and former ties: "I never saw her in the daytime. We seemed to live
by night. What was left of the day went away like a pack of ciga-
rettes you smoked...don't know what we were waiting for. Maybe
we thought the world would end. Maybe we thought it was a dream
and we'd wake up with a hangover in Niagara Falls." And Mexico
is where a mortally wounded Walter hopes to flee after he murders
Phyllis and confesses his crimes to his boss, Barton Keyes, in *Double
Indemnity*. Except Walter knows this plan is impossible; he is dying
and Mexico is a dream that will never be realized. As James Naremore
points out in his seminal study *More Than Night: Film Noir in Its Con-*

texts, "No matter how the Latin world is represented...it is nearly always associated with a frustrated desire for romance and freedom; again and again, it holds out the elusive, ironic promise of a warmth and color that will countervail the dark mise-en-scéne and the taut, restricted coolness of the average noir protagonist" (230).

By the 1950s, however, the image of Latin America as a utopia for doomed *noir* protagonists, as a place free from America's "unfair" notions of law and order, began to change. With the onset of the Cold War, the postwar notion of "good neighborliness" started disintegrating. Latin America, specifically Mexican border towns like Tijuana and Juarez, became more threatening and ambiguous; Mexico was both too close and too foreign to be trusted. In Orson Welles's baroque *Touch of Evil* (1958), for instance, the border between Mexico and the United States becomes a space where white men can pass as Mexicans (Charlton Heston as Ramon Vargas), women can pass as men (Mercedes McCambridge as a butch gang leader), and concepts like guilt and innocence are meaningless, defined by the whims of an embittered and vengeful detective (a bloated Orson Welles).

The writers of *Veronica Mars* have clearly done their *noir* homework, as Mexico is repeatedly invoked throughout the series as the place of escape from Neptune's (appearance of) law and order as well as a space of criminality and potential danger. As they say in *The O.C.*, another teen drama that uses Tijuana as a carnival space where characters can obtain drugs and alcohol and escape from their white-bread worlds, "What happens in Tijuana, stays in Tijuana" ("The Escape," 1-7).

Tijuana is where Logan was able to purchase the "Liquid X" (or GHB), that was later responsible for Veronica's rape ("A Trip to the Dentist," 1-21). And Tijuana was also the focus of "You Think You Know Somebody" (1-5). As the episode opened, we heard mariachi music playing. Soon we saw Logan, the closest thing the series has to a *femme fatale*, vomiting outside of Troy's BMW. While we assume that these 09er boys had only been drinking and consorting with prostitutes, we find out later that one of them has also nabbed himself a piñata full of steroids, which was later stolen. By the end of the episode it is revealed that Veronica's seemingly upstanding new beau, Troy, had in fact stolen the drugs and hidden them in the bathroom of the Border Diner, where the boys had stopped for a quick nosh after crossing over into the U.S.

It is significant that the border between the United States and Mexico—signified by the liminal space of the Border Diner—becomes a site of subterfuge and potential escape from Neptune. After retrieving his stash, Troy had planned to ditch high school, his family, and poor Veronica, to rendezvous with his partner in crime, the unseen Shauna. But as in all *films noir*, such heists, no matter how perfectly planned, are almost always foiled. The thief or murderer always makes some fatal mistake, a mistake he or she never saw coming. In Troy's case, this mistake was to date and, even worse, to *underestimate* the sleuthing prowess of Veronica, who, before Troy could make his pickup, had already replaced his hidden stash of stolen steroids with candy and a snarky note: "In case you're wondering, the former contents of the package are somewhere between my toilet and the Pacific Ocean. Say hi to Shauna for me. She sounds like a keeper." Even when her heart is breaking, Veronica knows how to craft a good zinger.

The most inventive use of Mexico appeared in the convoluted but rewarding episode "Donut Run" (2-11), in which the baby-napping Duncan found solace and safety with his newborn daughter by crossing the border.[1] In the episode's climactic final minutes, Sheriff Lamb, who was pursuing Duncan, entered a Mexican restaurant with a sign reading, "American also spoken" (thus echoing Lamb's claim earlier in the episode to the FBI that he knew a little "Mexican": "Enough to get by. Tell 'em to turn their music down."). But when he produced a photograph of Duncan and asked the proprietor if he had seen anyone resembling him, the latter replied with a grin, "No, but you all look alike to me."

Here, Mexico becomes the space where the gringo, because of his ethnic difference, can, paradoxically, blend in. A few moments later it is revealed that Duncan, donning a blonde wig and fake beard, was able to pass by Lamb, undetected, with a group of American backpackers. Unlike the classic *noir*, in "Donut Run" the star-crossed lovers *do* achieve their too-crazy-to-possibly-work plan. Veronica and Duncan outwitted the police, their enemies, and even their closest family and friends, allowing Duncan to ride off into the sunset, lit-

---

[1] This was not Duncan's first attempt to disappear from Neptune. In "Weapons of Class Destruction," (1-18), Duncan stole $10,000 and fled to Havana, Cuba, when Veronica accused him of committing Lilly Kane's murder.

erally, with his love-child, the appropriately named Lilly. Success, of course, is a relative concept in the *film noir*. Like the classic *noir* hero, Veronica invariably unearths the truth and foils her enemies at the close of each episode, but always at the cost of her personal (often romantic) happiness. The end of "Donut Run" finds Veronica paying for her success with loneliness; we see her standing on the edge of Neptune staring out at the sea, caught between the haves and the have-nots, the suburb and the ghetto.

Veronica Mars, with its obsessive focus on zip codes, border crossings, and class conflicts, is not unlike *Beverly Hills, 90210, The O.C.*, or even the "reality" series *Laguna Beach: The Real Orange County*. On the surface they appear to be light adolescent dramas about wealthy, photogenic kids, sunny California locales, and angsty love triangles, all set to killer soundtracks (available for downloading on iTunes).

The only difference is that in *Beverly Hills, 90210*, living in 90210 usually means a character is most likely to win homecoming queen or student council president; in *Veronica Mars*, living in 90909 usually means a character is most likely to commit mass murder, steal drugs, or, perhaps, be the ringleader of a few illegal bum fights.

AMANDA ANN KLEIN is an assistant professor of film studies in the English department at East Carolina University. Her publications include essays in the journal *The Quarterly Review of Film and Video* and in the anthologies *Deadwood: A Western to Swear By* and *Media(ted) Deviance and Social Otherness: Interrogating Influential Representations*. She has also published online essays and reviews in *Critical Quarterly Debates, Reality Blurred: Exposed,* and PopMatters.

References

Beverly Hills, 90210. Darren Star (creator). Fox, 1990–2000.

The Big Heat. dir. Fritz Lang. Perf. Glenn Ford, Gloria Grahame. Columbia Pictures, 1953.

Blue Velvet. dir. David Lynch. Perf. Kyle MacLachlan, Isabella Rossellini, Dennis Hopper. De Laurentiis Entertainment Group, 1986.

Desperate Housewives. Marc Cherry (creator). ABC, 2004–.

D.O.A. dir. Rudolph Maté. Perf. Edmond O'Brien, Pamela Britton. United Artists, 1950.

Double Indemnity. dir. Billy Wilder. Perf. Fred MacMurray, Barbara Stanwyck, Edward G. Robinson. Paramount Pictures, 1944.

Election. dir. Alexander Payne. Perf. Matthew Broderick, Reese Witherspoon. Paramount Pictures, 1999.

"The Escape." *The O.C.* Episode 7, Dir. Sanford Bookstaver. Fox, 16 September 2003.

Gilda. dir. Charles Vidor. Perf. Rita Hayworth, Glenn Ford. Columbia Pictures, 1946.

The Killers. dir. Robert Siodmak. Perf. Burt Lancaster, Ava Gardner, Edmond O'Brien. Universal Pictures, 1946.

Laguna Beach: The Real Orange County. Dir. George Plamondon, Jason Sands. MTV, 2004–2006.

Naremore, James. *More than Night: Film Noir in its Contexts.* Berkeley: University of California Press, 1998.

Out of the Past. dir. Jacques Tourneur. Perf. Robert Mitchum, Jane Greer, Kirk Douglas. RKO Radio Pictures, 1947.

The Outsiders. dir. Francis Ford Coppola. Perf. Matt Dillon, Ralph Macchio, C. Thomas Howell. Zoetrope Studios, 1983.

Sunset Boulevard. dir. Billy Wilder. Perf. William Holden, Gloria Swanson. Paramount Pictures, 1950.

Touch of Evil. dir. Orson Welles. Perf. Charlton Heston, Janet Leigh, Orson Welles. Universal Pictures, 1958.

I've said it before, and I'll say it again, if I could get away with doing a completely grounded teen series like Freaks and Geeks, I'd be doing it. Veronica Mars is...hmm...what's the euphemism I'm looking for? Let's go with heightened.

Discussion question: At the end of one of our big mysteries would fans of the show prefer we have Veronica call the sheriff's department to arrest the bad guy, or put Veronica in harm's way? One choice is the "reality" choice; the other is the "heightened" choice. I submit that most people would choose the latter.

I wonder sometimes if our audience thinks we're getting away with TV constructs. I'll give an example. Our dorm rooms are two to three times larger than any dorm room I had in college. We need the space. Great big cameras are rolling around in there with operators and sound people. When I read the comment, "No one has a dorm room that size," I wonder if the poster thinks we don't know that. I also wonder if the audience would prefer a tiny dorm room if they knew that—while it would be truer-to-life—every time we shot in the dorm room, we'd be forced into the same camera angles. There would be little to no possibility of original blocking of a scene.

We certainly strive for reality in terms of asking our audience to believe the motivations, reactions, and behavior of our characters, but do I know when Veronica has time to do her homework? Not really. We attempt to be consistent with our version of reality—what we'll believe in Veronica's world. I don't want to imply that reality isn't important to me. It is. It's just that I'm only trying to achieve a swallowable TV reality. I'm not trying to make it as real as my own (relatively) uneventful life.

I'm pleased to see that, for Jesse, we do land in that nexus of escapist entertainment and emotional truth.

Jesse Hassenger

Reality on *Mars* and Neptune

TELEVISION ISN'T REALISTIC. That much we know. New York City apartments are not cavernous; friends, rivals, and in-laws do not trade quips on a daily basis; doctors are not uniformly attractive; vampires do not exist. Even the genre called "reality" isn't particularly believable, unless you're frequently afforded the opportunity to eat yak testicles for money.

Once in awhile a show will come along and display a modicum of realism; usually, swift punishment is in order. Television professionals look on in horror as shows like *Freaks and Geeks* or *I'll Fly Away* begin a death march almost as soon as they premiere; the terrified result is that even many of the best shows traffic in some degree of implausibility—from storytelling conveniences to the physical attractiveness of the characters—if you snap yourself out of the sexy fun spell they cast over you. In a way, these leaps of faith are even more audacious than the well-documented feats of ridiculousness performed by Hollywood movies, because television can demand a recurring suspension of disbelief of up to six, twenty, or 200 hours, depending on how long your program of choice manages to survive. That survival, in turn, may depend on how well a show can entertain the largest amount of people for the longest amount of time without going too far over the top—which leaves some shows scrambling desperately to float in some kind of mid-air compromise between entertainment and restraint.

It should come as no surprise that this recurring suspension can leave viewers in a fog, unable to discern how realistic a show actually is. I had long suspected, for example, that much of *Veronica Mars* is patently absurd. I'm not even talking about Veronica's impossibly frequent snappy comebacks, or her ability to, as a teenager, find weekly stand-alone mysteries and solve them with prompt professionalism (augmented by frequent snappy comebacks). These are familiar television conceits: the wittier-than-life dialogue, the sexier-than-yours mysteries of life (Veronica never spends an hour looking for anyone's car keys; we're supposed to find her adventures entertaining, after all). It's the world of the show that spins my head—the made-up town of Neptune, California.

The central conceit of Neptune is that it's a "town without a middle class"—an area where a bunch of millionaires and their kids clash with the lower-class citizens who often work in servitude to said millionaires and children thereof. The less privileged citizens of Neptune are not content with random street crime, though. Not only does this California town boast an Irish mafia of sorts (the Fitzpatricks, natch), but that crime family has a tempestuous relationship with Neptune's very own biker gang, nicknamed the "PCHers" after the Pacific Coast Highway. Yes, these teenage PCHers wear leather jackets. I don't even know why you asked.

Neptune's rich kids are no slouches when it comes to outlandish behavior, either; spend one school year in the vaunted 90909 zip code and you'll witness kidnapping, drug deals, pet murders, breaking and entering, and long cons that outwit the FBI. And these are just the B-stories. (The PCHers seem almost too distracted by their sweet rides and camaraderie to compete with this level of mayhem.)

All of these wealthy shenanigans at least sort of explain Neptune's thriving private-investigation subculture—this small town sustains at least two—though I'm still not clear on the database subscriptions that give said private eyes access to all manner of informational shortcuts—just enough to keep the crime-solving well under an hour.

I'm not being flip; I really have no idea, during a typical episode of *Veronica Mars*, whether it's remotely possible for Veronica to track a license plate or a credit-card bill online through a private-eye Web site, or whether the Irish mafia has really been able to gain a significant foothold in coastal California. It's just a sneaking suspicion that the show is snowing me—followed by guilt, like I'm accusing my best friend of exaggerating about his road trip to Tijuana.

So before I can really assess the realism of my beloved *Veronica*, I turn to my own middling detective skills to get the facts of the case straight. This never happened during, say, six years of lazy on-and-off *Dawson's Creek* viewership, possibly because the facts of the show disappeared into the ether shortly after each episode. But the sleuthing of *Veronica Mars* is infectious.

First stop: the most commonly called-out anachronism on the show, that pesky biker gang. A quick scan of news wires for biker news turns up a lot of Hell's Angels stories. This seems logical, though I wonder if a younger, PCH-level biker gang finds this sort of coverage disproportionate and biased towards baby boomers, like how *Rolling Stone* still puts rockers from the sixties and seventies on its covers. I do find one story that mirrors a *Veronica Mars* plotline in which PCHer Felix is murdered and PCH leader Weevil goes on a half-season-long rampage to find the guilty party. In real life, a Hell's Angels member was murdered in California, possibly by another biker gang called the Mongols, and Hell's Angels members "sought revenge in California and Nevada," according to the *Las Vegas Review-Journal*. However, perhaps due to their boomer prosperity, the Hell's Angels apparently utilize more sophisticated equipment than their youthful fictional counterparts: wiretaps reveal that members discussed using "night vision goggles, a firearm, and scope" to exact their revenge, far outclassing the PCH-preferred camera-phone and fists. Suddenly even the largest-scale PCH ideas, like getting a betraying gang member chained to the radiator of a stadium earmarked for demolition ("Plan B," 2-17), seem downright primitive, rather than anachronistic. Let's split the difference and call them charmingly retro.

At this point—the point at which I'm debating which methods of biker-gang revenge sound more realistic—I wonder if I'll ever feel qualified to evaluate the realism of any television show. Still, I press on. My search for information on Irish gang activity in California is even less fruitful; apparently, this "Irish mafia" business is much more popular in the United Kingdom. If the Irish are harboring a long-simmering conflict with motorcycle-riding teenagers, they have become adept at hiding it. Maybe that stuff about hating the English is just an elaborate cover.[1]

Finally, on the subject of private-eye databases, I find a lot of ads for these types of information-rich databases—not exclusively for private eyes, mind you, but for the run-of-the-mill stalker with a couple hundred bucks to burn (in fact, the kind of guy that Veronica busts mercilessly on the show). I also locate an article from *PC Magazine* evaluating how scared you should be of such sites. The answer: kinda. Some are rip-offs, says the *PC* writer, but others happily provide social security numbers. I conclude that perhaps this aspect of *Mars* is semi-plausible, though the information retrieval process looks far less sketchy on a TV screen.[2]

For the moment, my private-eye career seems stalled, my investigation inconclusive. On the surface, these various implausibilities just seem like more imaginative versions of TV's serial truth-bending. After all, the teen soap—a genre in which *Veronica Mars* could easily fit, what with the twenty-somethings playing high school seniors and its focus on the lifestyles of the rich, attractive, and scandalous—is especially, sometimes gleefully, prone to exaggeration. Teen dramas are celebrated and derided for their ridiculousness in equal measure; if anything, celebration has the edge. When smart-girl Veronica goes on and off with sensitive bad boy Logan, the show is dutifully falling in line with *90210*, *The O.C.*, and *Dawson's Creek*: gorgeous people enacting soapy hookups in the sun, as plot suds swirl around them.

And teen shows have been just as happy to apply a tasteful dash of class-barrier lipstick, even—especially—if it wears off from all the making out. *The O.C.* has a boy of humbler beginnings living among a wealthy-elite not far removed from Neptune's upper class; *Dawson's Creek*'s Joey was allegedly a struggling working-class tom-

---

[1] *Editor's Note from Rob*: As far as the youthful motorcycle gang and the Irish crime family go—I made them up.

[2] *Editor's Note from Rob*: A funny note about the P.I. Web sites: These are extraordinarily real and spooky. Our private detective consultant has shown these off to us, and he can find out information on people that you simply wouldn't believe. The reality is that real private detectives do almost all of their work on the phone and on the computer. But what fun would that be for us? It's fun to have Veronica trick people for information. It's fun to have her sneak into places she's not supposed to be. It's fun to have her interview people face-to-face. The truth is that Veronica could find *much* more information on the computer than we allow her to.

boy—the kind whose family owns a bed-and-breakfast in a picturesque small town.

Similar charges could be leveled against Veronica—that she's a hot genius detective who's somehow supposed to be disadvantaged. But the class tensions of Neptune simmer around her, backing up her occasional claims of hardship and easing up any potential narcissism. If the familiar circumstances of Neptune, California—sexy teenagers, warm weather, and the combustion of the two—render *Veronica Mars* far from documentary-like realism, they also keep the show equidistant from its less distinguished peers.

One of the most distinctive aspects of Neptune, setting it apart from Capeside or any Orange Counties real or imagined, is its disappearing middle class—it's explained early in the series as a town where everyone's parents are either millionaires or work for millionaires. The literal lack of middle-income families in Neptune turns out to be less exaggerated than you'd hope. A 2003 Census Bureau report found that in the latter half of the nineties, more members of the middle class left the state than arrived, with demographers pointing to the state's record-high housing costs. Statistics on what percentage of these middle-class citizens were single private-detective fathers were not available, but real life nevertheless confirms (albeit more dramatically) Veronica's place in the middle, inhabiting a middle-class no man's land. If, after the events of the first season, it seemed to stretch plausibility that Veronica remained ostracized from the popular crowd, the series found a reasonable explanation for the show's status quo: no amount of dramatic catharsis, nor reunions with Duncan or Logan or any 09er, could extricate Veronica or her father from the middle-class squeeze.

If class warfare alone doesn't provide enough nagging reality tugging on the show's fantasy, *Veronica Mars* has also found a clever way around the inevitable Hollywood glamour of a television show about sexy teens: by incorporating Hollywood into the world of the show, with at least one eye on the seedy underbelly at all times. While a show like *The O.C.* may rely on wish-fulfillment guest turns from George Lucas, the character on *Veronica* with the strongest Hollywood ties turns out to be one of the most unequivocally corrupt: raging, conniving, underage-girl-sexing, son-abusing, wife-alienating, Lilly Kane-murdering Aaron Echolls, also a movie star who, even after a fiery season-one unmasking, had no trouble beating said murder rap in court. The idea of glamour and sleaze as a sort of peanut butter and jelly of the rich is certainly a familiar one; look no further than the now-almost-yearly celebrity trial *du jour*. The lines between grit, sleaze, and glamour are in a constant, blurring flux; my biker-gang research even turned up an article about those badass Hell's Angels suing Disney for alleged use of its trademark to market an upcoming film.

Before the Echolls verdict was delivered late in the second season, the episode "The Quick and the Wed" (2-15) introduced *Tinseltown Diaries*, an E! True Hollywood Story-style program that covered the Aaron Echolls saga in lurid detail; it popped up repeatedly throughout the season to trouble his son Logan. Other citizens of Neptune may have lousy lives, but Logan Echolls is always in the running for lousiest family, with a presumed-suicide mom, the aforementioned abusive and murderous dad, and a has-been actress half-sister, Trina, played with sloshy spite by Alyson Hannigan. Trina, like almost anyone on the show with a Hollywood life, is rich, semi-famous, and kinda pathetic; the show's parodies of entertainment-industry side culture and castoffs, embodied by Trina and *Tinseltown Diaries*, lack the inside-joke affection of countless other self-referential Hollywood productions. The seaminess underneath the well-kept appearances of Neptune also deepens Veronica's oft-voiced desire to leave her birthplace behind—another potential cliché sidestepped by the show. Veronica doesn't want to get out because Neptune is a dead-end small town (though it is), but rather because it's an actively unwelcoming environment, a depository for faded movie stars and smug software kingpins. It's a land of opportunity exclusive to those who don't need, or deserve, any additional breaks.

Neptune is also, then, a land of opportunity for the show's writers: the town is structured to hold both the outlandish stories required for weekly episodes and the class-conscious realism required for those episodes to be worth watching on a weekly basis. There is a crucial distinction when considering *Veronica Mars*: It may not always be realistic, but it rarely, if ever, goes over the top. A season finale can end with Veronica trapped in a refrigerator which an about-to-be-disgraced movie star prepares to set aflame, rescued at the last minute by her fist-swinging father, and yet a faithful viewer will not be thinking, *Echolls would've just stabbed her in real life*, or even, *There's no way my dad could win in a fight with Harrison Ford*. No, lucky fans of the show are free to simply enjoy the fisticuffs, perhaps with the side thought of, *Well, that's what happens when you systematically remove the middle-class and offer tax breaks to the rich*. After a year or two of immersion in Neptune, the coexistence of class war and juicy scandal doesn't seem ridiculous so much as, well, inevitable.

Veronica and Keith strike a similar balance within Neptune itself. As private detectives, they are involved with the hot messes created by Neptune's wealthy elite, and as citizens they deal with the practical problems that their wealthy neighbors do not share. Their compact family unit comprises the heart of the show's middle-class struggle. Keith's presence in particular works as an antidote to the show's sudsier leanings. Many teen-centric programs marginalize parents as conflict devices (my parent doesn't understand my desire to fit in/stand out/attend college/not attend college) or sentimentalized supporting parts (my parents are splitting up/dying/teaching me more than I ever could have imagined), but Keith Mars is a constant in Veronica's life, much more so than her romantic relationships, the most successful of which would charitably be categorized as on-again, off-again. There doesn't seem to be room for much more; the prevalence of Neptune's soul-sick upper class infects even those who attempt to find their place in the disappearing middle. Look no further than Lianne Mars, if you can find her. Veronica's mother, former prom queen of Neptune High who married upstanding Keith, was missing throughout most of season one; she returned only to reveal her alcoholism and then, finally, treachery, stealing $50,000 from Veronica and Keith before disappearing again. Veronica and Keith may have an idyllic father-daughter bond, but the extent of their isolation is nonetheless clear. Neptune's merciless class system doesn't even have room for a family of three in the middle.

The refusal to bring Lianne back into the fold is another example of canny realism used to maintain a TV-style status quo. It is more dramatic, of course, to have Veronica and Keith on their own (not to mention both single); it is also unrealistic to expect an alcoholic to recover quickly and happily. *Veronica Mars* finds realism in the corners of TV plotting; as if paying back its audience for these semi-leaps, it also finds drama outside of its flashiest plots.

In fact, despite the barrage of twists, one of the show's most dramatic moments so far came with a small gesture; in the second-season episode "Donut Run" (2-11), when Veronica was questioned by police about a kidnapping plot and responded with her customary flip remark, Keith cracked down, banging on a table and ordering her to keep it serious. Their relationship is so believably affectionate and functional that Keith's outburst is startling even upon re-viewing, as is his stern loss of trust in Veronica by the episode's end, after he figures out her elaborate hoax, which not only fooled him, but also local and government authorities. In one of the show's boldest uses of misdirection, we're fretting over Keith's reaction even though we should be asking questions about the competence of these duped federal agents.

The emotional gambit works. Veronica's near-fantastical detecting skills are directly attributed to her even more crack investigator of a father, so for Keith (and us) to see that craftiness turned against him creates a sensation not unlike the best superhero comics, where the super-powered deal in recognizable human emotions rather than grand, super-impossible feats of strength.

Some fans of the show consider the lack of ramifications of the "Donut Run" rift throughout the remainder of the season to be a cop-out, but really, could anyone expect Veronica and Keith to stay apart? They're almost too human for interpersonal drama, their keen detecting brains having long figured out that no one else in Neptune truly understands them (almost literally, since so many middle-class families have apparently left town. In fact, come to think of it, the seemingly middle-class hacker girl Mac is also crafty to a degree that makes us question the skills of our own supposedly computer-savvy friends; this is either a scheme to subtly flatter a middle-class audience, or an even more insidious plot by the rich to make us all feel kinda lousy by comparison).

Of course, the idea that Veronica and Keith's shared specialness makes them more believable might seem paradoxical; since when is extraordinary intelligence considered realistic and human, especially on television? But the Marses' alienation is genuine, even if their professional abilities are sometimes beyond belief. It doesn't really matter, either, if the Neptune biker gang accurately reflects California biker gangs throughout history, or if it's possible for a public high school to not have any unattractive students. It all goes toward creating a made-up environment utterly believable in its hostilities—hostilities with unreasonably high entertainment value. By planting its feet in the imaginary Neptune, *Veronica Mars* finds dual paths, to both escapist entertainment and emotionally true art. I'd like to think that even the Hell's Angels would approve.

> JESSE HASSENGER was born in Saratoga Springs, New York, a small town without an Irish mafia or a biker gang. He graduated from Wesleyan University in 2002 with a major in English, and currently lives in Brooklyn, New York. His reviews have appeared in PopMatters, *The L Magazine*, and on filmcritic.com; his fiction has appeared in *Me Three* and *Dirt*, and he is a member of the Blackout Writing Collective. He enjoys many types of pie and rarely writes in the third person.

References

"Market Whispers: Hell's Angels." *The Independent on Sunday*. 12 March 2006. 11.

"Wiretaps Hear Revenge Plot in Biker's Slaying." *Las Vegas Review-Journal*. 14 July 2003. 1B.

"Priced-out Californians High-Tailin' It For Cheaper Digs." *Daily News*. 10 August 2003. B1.

The writing staff *doesn't bat an eye when Veronica lies in an attempt to gain information from anyone she doesn't have a personal relationship with. When Veronica lies to Keith or Wallace or a boyfriend, we do have lengthy discussions about it in the writer's room. Whether an audience member forgives her or not, on those occasions we (and so, in turn, Veronica) are not being flippant about it.*

John also mentions Keith telling Veronica he wouldn't be able to trust her again. William Goldman relates an interesting anecdote in Adventures in the Screen Trade *about how Susan Sarandon ruined* The Great Waldo Pepper *by being too good. When she died, the audience wouldn't or couldn't forgive Robert Redford. Everyone was too bummed to enjoy the rest of the movie. We suffered from a similar problem. Most audience members probably know that our episodes are written weeks ahead of when they're shot and months ahead of when they're aired. It's difficult to "fix" something midstream.*

I actually wrote that scene between Keith and Veronica, but it wasn't until I was directing it, and I saw Enrico and Kristen perform it that I had a moment of clarity about the consequences. Frankly, it was so much more powerful when I heard it performed than when I heard it in my head that I thought to myself, "Oh shit. That's gonna really resonate, and other than some lip service to it in the next episode, we aren't playing the ramifications of that moment."

The resulting grumbling was deserved. As I said in the commentary about the previous essay on reality—I'm not trying to make our show about a teen girl detective absolutely "real," but I do want to hit the emotional truths, and not playing fallout from that discussion was a mistake.

John Ramos

"I Cannot Tell a Lie.
And If You Believe That..."

DO YOU VALUE honesty in people?

Does it bother you when people, including yourself, tell lies?

Do you think the world would be a better place if people were more honest with each other?

It would take a very, for lack of a better word, *honest* person to answer "no" to those questions. Yet if you were asked to describe the eponymous lead character of the television show *Veronica Mars*, while several complimentary words would no doubt spring to mind—strong, resourceful, witty—you'd probably admit that the less flattering description of "liar" fits her as well...or at least that she bends the truth very frequently. Not that she's alone in that regard—in her noir world, almost every character we're familiar with has told a whopper at one time or another. But the point is, from what I know of viewers' opinions, including my own, we like Veronica. She's a sympathetic character. So how can we reconcile our positive view of her (and other rather less-than-honest characters) with the realization that lying comes as easily to her as her impossibly sharp and acerbic comebacks?

On the brilliant and all-too-short-lived television show *Arrested Development*, one of the character Maeby's most memorable lines came when she noted to herself, "Okay, now I'm just lying for no reason." What makes that line real comedy is that very few people in truth or fiction actually do that. In *Story*, one of the definitive works on screenwriting, author Robert McKee tells us that true character is revealed in the choices we make under pressure. He explains, "If a character chooses to tell the truth in a situation where telling a lie would gain him nothing, the choice is trivial; the moment expresses nothing. If a character insists on telling the truth when a lie would save his life, then we sense that honesty is at the core of his nature."

Veronica's core is clearly not as impossibly pure as that of McKee's example character, but what do the lies she utters and the deceptions in which she engages tell us about her true character? Let's start with the untruths that are most numerous—those she tells in pursuit of solving her one-off cases, or "Mysteries of the Week," as they're commonly known. It's tempting just to dismiss these lies as part of Veronica's job—if she told no lies as a private investigator, not only would she not get anywhere, we would have one boring show on our hands. And often, these lies are harmless—for example, in "Lord of the Bling" (1-13), Veronica amusingly posed as a hospitality clerk at a hotel in order to get some information from an unsavory rap star and his entourage. Only the most inveterate pearl-clutcher would castigate Veronica for lying in that situation. Similarly entertaining excursions into untruth occurred in "Betty and Veronica" (1-16), when Veronica posed as a student at the Bizarro Neptune Pan High, and "Green-Eyed Monster" (2-4), when she unsuccessfully set up a "temptation scenario" for a guy who turned out to be too good for his insanely jealous girlfriend. While these lies are often told in the service of justice, it's important to remember that they're just as often told in the service of Veronica's financial gain. Yet, despite the fact that many of us would agree that telling the truth should be more important than profit, these lies are typically forgotten as easily as the cases that prompted them.

Sometimes, however, Veronica's deceptions can give us a little more pause. One such example came in "Mars vs. Mars" (1-14), when Veronica committed a serious invasion of privacy by telling an unaware-as-always Duncan that her doctor was retiring, setting into motion a chain of events that led to her discovery of Duncan's secret medical condition. More unsettling was when she told the attendant at the bank that her mother had died, and produced a fake death certificate to boot, all for the purpose of gaining access to her mom's safety-deposit box in "You Think You Know Somebody" (1-5). Nothing evokes stronger emotions in people than death, particularly when said death is being related by an impossibly cute and distraught blonde teenager, and playing on a stranger's sympathies in that manner (reprised, to some degree, when she told a mechanic that she was the deceased Curly Moran's niece in "Cheatty Cheatty Bang Bang," 2-3, and when she told a wig-shop attendant that she was looking for her runaway sister in "The Rapes Of Graff," 2-16) for the sake of an errand that's ethically questionable to begin with isn't so easy to laugh off. Nor is it a laughing matter when Veronica's deceptions have unintended consequences—for example, when she used Deputy Leo's genuine and uncomplicated attraction to her to further her own ends. When her carelessness in leaving the evidence room unlocked led to Leo being suspended from his job for a week in "Silence of the Lamb" (1-11), the collateral damage Veronica's lies caused crossed the line from theoretical to disturbingly tangible. Of course, in this particular instance, the writers made it easy for us to forgive Veronica in light of the fact that she and Leo started dating very soon after this incident. Because if he can forgive her, we unconsciously think, why shouldn't we?

And this is not to say that, as silver-tongued as Veronica may be, she doesn't feel the occasional pang of remorse when she twists the truth into a pretzel. She told us as much in one of her patented voiceovers—VMVOs, as my typing fingers love me to call them—when she said she felt awful about playing on Leo's feelings. But no matter how big the lie told, no matter how much the lie makes it a little harder for her to look at herself in the mirror, she convinces herself that her greater mission—finding her best friend Lilly Kane's killer, in the first season—is worth the ethical price. And indeed, that seems to reflect her more general feeling about the falsehoods she tells in service of her cases: lies told in pursuit of the truth are acceptable. Moreover, the greater the stakes of the case, the greater and more damaging the lies it's acceptable to tell. It's an ethical matrix that's certainly logical enough, if somewhat unsettling to find in a teenaged girl. But it's not the logic that makes lies told in pursuit of the truth acceptable to us as the audience—it's the belief in Veronica's ultimate goal. Who among us didn't want to see Veronica solve her rape? Reveal Lilly's killer? Find her mom? (Okay, in retrospect, two out of three ain't bad.) The point is, somewhere deep down, we understand that some degree of sacrifice is necessary to solve such tangled mysteries, and the truth is not going to escape unscathed. We mentally give Veronica license to lie, as long as she doesn't abuse our generosity. And when she does abuse it, we notice. For example, when Wallace asked about Logan's use of an untraceable tardy slip in "A Trip To The Dentist" (1-21), Veronica lied that she gave it to him so they could go over some details of his mother's case, when in fact, unless said details were to be found on the roof of Logan's mouth, she simply wanted to fool around with her clandestine boyfriend. And while said fooling around may have caused a significant percentage of the viewing audience to swoon with delight, even the most diehard Logan/Veronica fan had to be disturbed by Veronica's bald-faced lie to her best friend, which was told in the service not of truth but of shame. (She apparently made up for it with a tearful confession later that episode, but since it happened off-screen, it was somewhat lacking in emotional resonance.) The point is, that lie was worse than any lie told in service of her cases, for two reasons: One, it was motivated by less-than-honorable intentions. And two, could you lie to Wallace while looking him in the eye?

Well, then again, maybe you could, if the situation were right. After all, Wallace's upstanding mother Alicia looked Wallace in the eye and told him that his father was dead. Obi-Wan Kenobi might say that what she told him was true, from a certain point of view, but even he would have to admit that it wasn't the whole story—the man who died was Wallace's adopted father; Alicia had fled from his natural one before Wallace was born. Said story culminated in Wallace skipping town with his biological dad for several episodes, leaving Alicia to regret not telling her son the truth. But we understand why she lied—she was trying to protect him. And some of Veronica's best lies, so to speak, occur when she's trying to protect other people. Sometimes the protection is physical, such as when she lied to the rather scary archery aficionado Harry that she was unable to find his dog's killer in "Nevermind the Buttocks" (2-19). She did so because she knew that Harry would most likely put a bolt between the eyes of her mortal enemy Liam Fitzpatrick, and while a VMVO admitted that she "wouldn't miss [Liam]" (most likely because he was within inches of decorating her face like an Irish cereal box in "Ahoy, Mateys," 2-8, and because he tried to shoot her father earlier that episode), she couldn't live with the thought of Harry going to jail for the rest of his life. Sometimes the protection is more emotional, as when Veronica told Abel Koontz that his daughter Amelia was happy. While the glib might point out that Veronica's statement is only true in that Amelia at that point is in, euphemistically, a happier place, Veronica chose to lie in order to give her onetime enemy a consoling thought with which to die. We not only understand Veronica's motive for telling these lies, but can't really even imagine *not* telling them were we ourselves in her situation. These lies reveal pieces of Veronica's true character, and in turn, our identification with Veronica reveals pieces of our own.

And said pieces of Veronica's character, like those of so many good characters both real and fictional, often conflict. Nowhere is that more evident than in "Donut Run" (2-11), the episode in which Veronica lied so big that for the first forty minutes even the audience had no idea what was really going on. Veronica, sure that her then-boyfriend Duncan's child was unjustly going to be taken away from him, conspired with him and her private-investigator pseudo-nemesis Vinnie Van Lowe to get Duncan and his baby girl to Mexico one step ahead of the law. In doing so, she and Duncan faked a public breakup, led the FBI on a number of wild-goose chases, and even got the often-hapless Sheriff Lamb to unwittingly carry Duncan over the border in his trunk. Veronica gave up her boyfriend, risked taking on the FBI, and lied to everyone, including the viewers, because she simply couldn't accept how unfair the world can be, a trait of hers that resurfaces time and time again. (The term "vigilante" is often used to describe Veronica, but that's a whole other essay.) In service of her single-handed mission to right the wrongs that unfairness creates, she lied. She even lied to her dad, leading to an emotional scene wherein he told her he could never trust her again. Many viewers rather grumpily noted that he seemed to forget about this declaration immediately afterward, which is certainly a fair point—while we expected that "never" would turn out to be an exaggeration, we didn't expect the argument to seem as if it had been forgotten *by the next episode.*

But before we castigate the writers too quickly for forgetting how they portray Keith from week to week, it's worth wondering whether he (if he really existed, I'm not delusional) might have let go of his resentment and mistrust because he thought twice about that little speech, more specifically to ponder this question: Does Keith bear some of the responsibility for his daughter's untruths? Because regardless of whether you believe in nature or nurture, you'll admit that when it comes to lying easily, the phrase "Like father, like daughter" has rarely been more aptly applied. In the second episode of the show, "Credit Where Credit's Due," Veronica and Keith (highly entertainingly, it must be said) teamed up and posed as a pregnant teen and her irate father to convince a hotel receptionist to give up some vital information. But since this lie ultimately resulted in Paris Hilton's comeuppance, no one's likely to remember it in any way other than fondly. Similarly, when Keith posed as a DEA inspector to aid Veronica in bringing down a pair of criminal techno-geeks in "The Wrath of Con" (1-4), one couldn't help but feel that these lies were told in the service both of heartwarming father/daughter teamwork and of justice.

However, lying is a slippery slope, and when Keith and Veronica bring their lies to bear on each other, we stop cheering and start feeling uncomfortable. Keith was portrayed as a liar in Veronica's eyes in the very first episode of the series, when he told Veronica that a license plate she photographed belonged to someone involved in corporate espionage when in fact it belonged to her mother, whom Keith knew Veronica was desperate to find. Veronica also learned in the pilot that Keith was still investigating Lilly's murder, when he had both officially and to the best of Veronica's knowledge dropped the case months earlier. Veronica, via VMVO, speculated that perhaps Keith was lying in an effort to protect her, but these bombshells make us feel that the importance of honesty is not a value that father is clearly imparting to daughter. Indeed, that Keith and Veronica keep their own counsel even when it comes to each other has been an ongoing theme throughout the series, although Veronica deserves credit in "Return of the Kane" (1-6) for telling Keith that she didn't want their relationship to be, as she put it, "[their] own game of *Spy vs. Spy*." You might point out that some of said credit has to be repossessed for offenses like infiltrating a cult against Keith's express orders in

"Drinking the Kool-Aid" (1-9) and sending him a misleading picture to convince him she was in an art gallery instead of investigating Amelia DeLongpre's disappearance in "Rat Saw God" (2-6). But would she be Keith's daughter if she did otherwise?

And the question of Veronica's parentage brings me to the last famous example of lies told in the relationship between Veronica and Keith. In "Drinking The Kool-Aid," Veronica lied that she needed a sample of Keith's blood for a health assignment, when in fact she planned to use said sample for a biological test to determine once and for all if Keith is her father. Frankly, it's a shocking violation of trust, even for this show. Of course, Veronica decided not to read the results at the eleventh hour, leaving it to Keith to pull a similar invasion of privacy on Veronica later in the season. And as we all know, in "Leave It to Beaver" (1-22) when Keith produced the paternity results that proved he is in fact Veronica's biological father, the resultant outpouring of emotion yielded one of the most touching moments of the series. Looking at the happy ending, it's tempting to wonder what the problem was—why didn't they just go get tested together, rather than resort to these underhanded shenanigans? The answer is obvious when you think of what would have happened if the test had come back the other way. Despite Veronica's assertion that she was ready to make Jake Kane cough up enough money to send her to Stanford for the next 100 years, I think Veronica was planning to keep that knowledge to herself—to bear a heavy burden to protect Keith from a heartbreaking realization. She couldn't go through with it, leaving it to her stronger father to face doing the same for her. In their own way, these lies are an expression of love, and, viewed in this light, make Keith and Veronica appear almost admirable for telling them.

Ultimately, it behooves us to remember that Neptune is a noir universe, and even a mostly beloved character like Logan can reprehensibly twist the truth, such as when he told Hannah he liked her when really he was only using her to influence her father to drop his testimony against him ("Ain't No Magic Mountain High Enough," 2-13). (Yes, his feelings eventually changed. Duly noted.) But we still don't generally think of Logan as dishonest, because he only lies when something big is at stake for him. In contrast, a lie that on the surface was far more innocuous was nonetheless seized upon by many viewers: Duncan told Veronica he was studying for a Latin quiz when in fact he was watching television ("Green-Eyed Monster," 2-4). Viewers use this incident to label Duncan as shifty and dishonest, despite the writers' assertions in the press that Duncan is supposed to be a nice, upstanding guy. The branding of Duncan with the "L" word as a result of that incident may seem like an extreme overreaction, but it all goes back to McKee's rule—by extension, if a person lies when he has nothing to lose by telling the truth, he's a liar by nature. Veronica, in contrast, never lies for no reason. She lies for good reasons and bad reasons, but usually, she lies because she thinks that lying is the right thing to do in the given situation. And the fact that we find her sympathetic, and even cheer her on, suggests that we understand and condone this behavior. So have we learned anything from this walk down the road of good intentions? If we look within ourselves, I think we'll find that despite the fact that we all profess to value honesty, lying is not only part of human nature, but a fundamental and necessary part of the human condition. And if anyone tells you otherwise? Don't believe a word he says.

JOHN RAMOS graduated from Princeton University in Princeton, New Jersey. Following college, he was a journalist at the business magazine *Across The Board*, a publication of the business research and membership organization The Conference Board (http://www.conference-board.org/). He then moved into the financial markets, wherein he worked as an options trader for ten years before becoming a film producer and aspiring screenwriter who resides in New York City. He also recaps *Veronica Mars* for the well-known Web site, Television Without Pity (www.televisionwithoutpity.com) under the handle "Couch Baron."

References

McKee, Robert. *Story: Substance, Structure, Style, and the Principles of Screenwriting.* USA: Regan Books, 1997.

Contrary to what *might be demonstrated in* Veronica Mars, *I actually have an average, possibly even above-average, faith in law enforcement and the criminal justice system. As I believe I admitted earlier, I didn't have any great insight into noir. It was a genre I neither gravitated toward nor avoided. When I began to develop the show, I purchased a couple of books about noir and boned up. I learned that a corrupt legal/law enforcement system was an almost universal element of noir.*

I was lucky to have read that because, as Alafair also points out, had I written Sheriff Lamb as a hard-working honest man, Veronica Mars *could not exist. There would be little need for her.*

A sidenote: I've always believed that Lamb actually leaked information to the press during the original Lilly Kane investigation. The one thing Lamb has ever done successfully he did as deputy, and that was stab Keith in the back.

Alafair Burke

Lawless Neptune

OWE THE READER of this essay an initial disclosure. I am a compulsive, insatiable, and wholly devoted fan of *Veronica Mars*. I TiVo. I pause and rewind. I pre-order the DVDs on Amazon. I yearn to be BFFs with Kristen Bell and writing partners with Rob Thomas. Yet despite my passion, an occasional guilty pang of disloyalty prevents me from calling myself a proud, unapologetic devotee. Why? Because, whenever I tout my fondness for all things *Veronica*, I find myself serving up an explanatory defense on the side.

The conversation usually goes something like this:

FRIEND: I'm addicted to [insert well-known water cooler TV show here: *Lost*, *CSI*, *24*—whatever].

ME: Yeah, that's all right, but the best show on television is *Veronica Mars*.

FRIEND: Isn't that about that teenage detective?

ME: [long pause] Um, it's hard to explain. She's in high school. And her dad used to be the sheriff, but now he's a detective. And she solves all these mysteries, but it's not like Nancy Drew. It's darker. And also funny. But really dark. It's like *Buffy* without the vampires. And, hey, they actually give you answers every season, not like that other show.

By the end of the conversation, my friend is seriously questioning my judgment in show selection, and I find myself frustrated. I'm a criminal law professor. I'm a former prosecutor. I write mystery novels with sex, violence, and cuss words. And I am convinced that loving *Veronica Mars* in no way undermines my gritty crime-story cred.

And yet that awkward moment at the proverbial water cooler remains. Explaining Veronica to the uninitiated is awkward because the very premise of *Veronica Mars* sounds dubious. A high school student solving crime? At best, it might be light entertainment: a female Encyclopedia Brown solving cute little mysteries at her quaint little high school, a young Jessica Fletcher for the *O.C.* crowd. But a teenager solving rapes, murders, and bus explosions? The notion sounds like off-the-deep-end farce, yet it never is—not in the Neptune that Rob Thomas has created. And there must be a way to explain that to others, besides saying, "But Steve King loves it, too." There must be a way of explaining to *Veronica* virgins how a show about a teenage girl detective manages to be more suspenseful, powerful, and poignant than any series about terrorist investigators, mafiosi, or the best looking set of castaways this side of Gilligan's Island.

So, there you have my disclosure in black and white: I have an agenda. So that I never again have to apologize for worshiping the best show on TV, I am out to explain how Rob Thomas manages to make a sass-talking teenage crime-solver believable.

In the real world, when girls get raped, boys get molested, and bodies get blown up, people look to the law. They look to the police, prosecutors, jurors, and judges to dole out some justice. They don't call the high school-aged daughter of the disgraced former sheriff. The key to understanding why we believe that the people of Neptune need Veronica Mars lies in Rob Thomas's depiction of the alternative. In Neptune, the criminal justice system is consistently either indifferent or incapacitated. Neptune, in short, is lawless.

Take a look at what we learn about Neptune in the pilot episode. Veronica first met perennial sidekick Wallace Fennel when he was duct taped naked to a pole outside the high school—his punishment for diming out members of Weevil Navarro's gang for shoplifting beers from the Sac-n-Pac. How did the gangbangers know who dropped the dime? Sheriff Lamb brought Wallace before the glaring, bike-revving gang to question him. Wallace claimed he'd hit the silent alarm button accidentally, but to no avail. Sheriff Lamb arrested the shoplifters anyway based on a videotape from the store's security camera, and then mocked Wallace's cowardice for good measure. "Go see the wizard," he advised. "Ask him for some guts." Message: Don't trust the cops. Like Lucy with Charlie Brown's football, they'll screw you every time.

We also learn from the pilot that Sheriff Lamb's insensitivity to the citizens of Neptune extends well beyond beer-run investigations and is particularly acute when it comes to Veronica Mars. Again in flashback mode, we watch a long-haired, visibly distressed Veronica inform Sheriff Lamb that she has been raped by an unknown assailant at a party. In the privacy of his office, Lamb revealed the depth of the animosity he holds for both Veronica and her father, the man who previously held Lamb's office with competence and dignity. Using her father's public disgrace as a backdrop, Lamb taunted Veronica with the lack of evidence, bringing her to tears. Just in case we doubted Lamb's mean-spiritedness (or lack of originality in the insult department), he advised her to see the wizard as well: "Ask for a little backbone." Lamb is a small man who, at least in his own eyes, lives in the shadow of his predecessor. As a consequence, he's big on belittling Veronica at every opportunity, even if it's on the heels of a sexual assault.

With Sheriff Lamb set up as our antagonist, it was our heroine who wore the proverbial—and no doubt fashionable—white hat. She negotiated a deal with Weevil: Lay off my man Wallace and I'll make sure your boys get their shoplifting charges dropped. Manipulating her knowledge of when so-called "random" locker searches took place, she whipped up a little Veronica magic and pulled off a switch-a-roo in the sheriff department's evidence room. Abracadabra. At the gangbangers' trial, instead of the Sac-n-Pac video tape, the judge was treated to the sight of one of Lamb's deputies enjoying a little afternoon delight in a squad car. Hey, as the song says, when it's right, it's right.

Only because of Veronica's black-market intervention was the judge able to see an important truth—one that had nothing to do with shoplifting and everything to do with Neptune's inept and boorish law enforcement. Message: While the cops are getting their shields polished, Veronica's dusting off a little old-fashioned justice. And sometimes, in this lawless world of Neptune, justice is something negotiated between Veronica and a gang leader, beyond the callous eye of law enforcement.

But the concept underlying *Veronica Mars* relies on more than just its depiction of cops as either bumbling or cruel. Its portrayal of the criminal justice system is not just an indictment of the individual personalities entrusted to execute the law. Rather, it is a challenge to the power of law itself. At each possible turn, Thomas subtly reinforces our doubts about the ability of formal legal systems to remedy the very real problems we witness on the screen.

When Wallace's mother, Alicia, was stuck with a tenant that made *Pacific Heights*'s Michael Keaton look like friendly Fonzie in the Cunningham garage apartment, a sheriff's deputy told her the best he could do was oust the creep in sixty days. Veronica's father, former sheriff Keith Mars, did the job himself—illegally and by force—telling Alicia (and us), "I know how the law works—slowly" ("Like a Virgin," 1-8).

Thomas depicts the law as working not only slowly, but rigidly. True justice, in contrast, is flexible and discretionary. If punishment must be doled out, we want the dealer to have good judgment and character, and to dole only after fully considering the surrounding context and mitigating circumstances. But when the father of a working-class Neptune High student harassed a pampered 09er to level the competition for the prestigious and plentiful Kane Scholarship, his son learned that in Neptune there is no room for mercy: his father would be arrested and prosecuted unless the spoiled 09er dropped charges ("Kanes and Abel's," 1-17). We viewers might debate the level of wrong in the father's conduct, but Thomas's point is that the automated response of the law leaves no room for debate. Because the law's response is inflexible, the son paid for the sins of the father and was forced to withdraw from consideration, and Veronica ultimately wondered if perhaps the truth would have been better left undiscovered. "Life," as Veronica reminded us in her narration, "is fundamentally unfair," at least when life's clumsy approach to justice goes unshaped by Veronica.

Time and again, Thomas uses the juxtaposition of the law's ineptitude against Veronica's savvy to convince us of our heroine's power. When Veronica served as a juror, at first only one Latina juror was willing to believe the word of a Mexican alleged prostitute against two white 09ers. But even after that sole hold-out made her point, she relented, offering to cave if the rest of the jury disagreed. It took our little pain-in-the-butt Veronica to cast the determinative vote to continue deliberations and to come up with the winning arguments that the police and prosecutor had overlooked ("One Angry Veronica," 2-10). When another 09er framed Veronica for knocking out fake IDs, Lamb responded on auto-pilot, searching her locker, finding the IDs, and charging her with a felony. It fell to Veronica to prove who did it, sending Lamb to fetch himself a new fake ID in a controlled buy while she alibi'd herself in his office, "chillin' like a villain" ("Clash of the Tritons," 1-12). Indeed, even attorney Cliff McCormack regularly comes to Veronica to help him get what he wants for tawdry clients like exotic dancer Loretta Cancun. McCormack is no Barry Zuckercorn. He may have flunked criminal law, but he knows how the system in Neptune works.

But wait a second. If formal law is so corrupt, slow, incompetent, and inflexible, why doesn't my friend at the water cooler instantly believe that Veronica and Keith could be the ones to save the day? After all, if this is really our perception of the law, then we in the real world should also look to extra-legal actors to bring us our justice. The answer is that in the real world, we continue to trust the legal system. We trust it because in *most* cases, the legal system—despite some occasional doubts about its promptness, precision, and proficiency—is good enough.

Rob Thomas, in contrast, nimbly convinces us that in Neptune, our suspicions about law's occasional inadequacy are in fact the prevailing, everyday norm. How does he manage to pull that off? Part of the trick is Thomas's decision to exaggerate the occasional shortcomings and to flesh them out in full in every episode. But that move wouldn't work on its own. A smart viewer would say, *But in the real world, law works better than that.* We know that in real life, when rich, attractive white girls get murdered, and when busloads of kids are blown to bits, the cases don't get short shrift. In real life, the law enforcement A-team steps in.

The key to understanding why we believe in a lawless Neptune is to look at the *kinds* of crimes Thomas uses to define the context in which these other high-profile, season-defining crimes take place. The big mysteries tackled by Veronica (Who killed Lilly? Who blew up the bus?) may be headline stealers, but the smaller ones wrestled with on an episodic basis are not. In his choice of crimes for the episodic mysteries, Thomas reinforces our perception of a lawless Neptune by focusing on crimes that *are* routinely ignored, not just in Neptune but everywhere. Specifically, he uses the old classics of race, gender, and class to remind us in each episode how much we distrust the criminal justice system.

In credibility contests between 09ers and the regular folk, guess who comes out on top? When it's the word of a white guy against a group of Weevil's PCHers, again, guess who wins the pissing match? And speaking of the PCHers, they cause an awful lot of trouble for both themselves and others, and yet the police never seem to touch them. It's no coincidence that this echoes the real-life gang violence that is infamously difficult to prevent and prosecute. One exception to the PCHers' invulnerability was Weevil's heartbreaking arrest, just prior to the moment his devoted grandmother was set to see him graduate from high school ("Not Pictured," 2-22). But even this exception demonstrates the rule. Weevil is of course the most sympathetic of the PCHers, helping Veronica out repeatedly with a devilish smile and penetrating double entendre. And when Weevil did go down in season two's finale, it was for opening up a long-delayed, well-earned six-pack of whoop ass on the traitorous Thumper—who'd managed until then to literally get away with murder, thanks to the bumbling Sheriff Lamb.[1]

Thomas is particularly artful in his use of realistic depictions of crimes against women and children to persuade us that Veronica lives in a lawless Neptune. From the disclosure of Veronica's own rape in the pilot episode, we know that Sheriff Lamb couldn't care less if a passed-out party girl loses her virginity to an unknown assailant— especially when the girl is Veronica. And we believe it, because we know in the real world that date rapes are routinely ignored and unprosecuted. But Veronica is no typical victim. She may be the ultimate outsider—provoking the sheriff to taunt even a rape victim—but she has the ultimate insider's knowledge. Combining modern high-tech high jinks with the old-fashioned know-how she picked up from her father, cagey Veronica scouted, spied, queried, and hoodwinked until she discovered the truth about that traumatic night on her own.

---

[1] As of this writing, we all wait to see what will become of Eli "Weevil" Navarro in season three.

When we were temporarily convinced that Veronica was not in fact raped, but instead had succumbed to a roofie-induced but consensual moment with Duncan ("A Trip to the Dentist," 1-21), Thomas again reminded us of the commonplace role of date rape in young lives, law enforcement's flawed response to it, and Veronica's wily ways by having ex-beau Troy face false accusations of raping a co-ed while visiting the Hearst College campus ("The Rapes of Graff," 2-16). Lamb treated the case as open and shut, relying on Troy's presence with the victim before she passed out and then awoke with a shaved head. Despite Veronica's own doubts about Troy, she wasn't satisfied. After some nimble legwork involving a sob story to a wig shop and a little breaking and entering, Veronica managed to clear Troy's name and lay the blame at the door of Hearst's bawdiest frat house. Importantly, though, even with Veronica's intervention, the real rapist eluded detection. Sometimes even a demi-goddess can only do so much.

Thomas reminds us of law's failures not only in cases of sexual violence against women, but also physical violence and psychological terrorism. When Veronica suspected that the pregnant woman upstairs was being battered ("The Girl Next Door," 1-7), neither she nor her father even thought to call the police. Of course they didn't. That's because everyone knows the police can't do anything. It's precisely because we accept this powerlessness as a given that we actually rooted for the loathsome Aaron Echolls when he erupted in a violent explosion against daughter Trina's battering boyfriend, beating him with a belt, patio furniture, garbage, a tiki torch, and just about anything else he could lay his vengeful hands on, all to the soothing accompaniment of "That's Amore" ("Hot Dogs," 1-19). As Logan said in the immediate aftermath, "Father knows best." This was arguably Aaron Echolls's single decent moment, as he stepped in to fill a gap we all know exists in the formal justice system.

Veronica did the same for Carmen when her future ex-boyfriend Tad went all Sizemore on her and couldn't accept their break-up ("M.A.D.," 1-20). When it was clear that his pleas for reuniting had failed, Tad dropped all airs of Peaches and Herb sweetness and threatened Carmen with the release of a video of her getting nasty with a popsicle in a hot tub. The ploy worked, forcing poor, manipulated Carmen back to Tad the Cad and his wife-beater tank top and gay jokes. Her only alternative, as she so eloquently explained to Veronica, was to "end up a downloadable national joke...right up there with Paris Hilton or that *Star Wars* kid....Just google 'popsicle girl' and there I'll be for the rest of human history." Most importantly, Carmen recognized, "*And I can't stop him.*" If the law does little for women who are beaten by their boyfriends, it does even less for the Carmens of the world.

Veronica, however, didn't miss a beat; she knew immediately that the solution to Carmen's problem would be found not with formal legal actors, but in a partnership with Veronica. She told Carmen her only choice was to get something "that would ruin Tad back. You know, get your own A-bomb and it prevents him from launching a first strike. Mutually assured destruction." When Carmen worried that boring Tad had no dirt to uncover, Veronica assured her, "Leave that to me." With some creative role-playing, photoshopping, and audio dubbing, Veronica armed Carmen with a Web site entitled "Our Precious Secret," convincingly dedicated to Tad's (non-existent) gay romance. And so Veronica's plot for justice was hatched: If homophobic Tad was going to release Carmen's Cold Throat video, he could do it under threat of his own greatest fear.

Perhaps Thomas's darkest forays into the law's limitations are found in his depictions of violence against children. When we watched Aaron Echolls force Logan to select the leather belt that would deliver his barebacked beating while mother Lynn sipped her drink in what appeared to be blissful ignorance, we wished for—but knew we could not have—some semblance of justice other than Logan's public charitable pledge of half a million bucks on a surprised Aaron's behalf ("Return of the Kane," 1-6). We believed that Logan had no other recourse because we know from our own experience that the word of a celebrated celebrity like Aaron Echolls—think Tom Cruise before the sofa-jumping—would outweigh the word of a trouble-making teenager who webcasts bum fights. (Hello? Michael Jackson anyone? And Harry Hamlin's work is far less creepy than MJ's, and Logan has way more baggage than that Neverland kid.) The costs of law's tendency to undervalue children's reports of abuse is perhaps most transparent in Cassidy Casablancas. Beaver would not have developed into the criminal mastermind that he became if he thought anyone would possibly believe that Woody Goodman was a serial child molester. His name might've been Woody, but come on, who'd buy a guy as smiley as Steve Guttenberg as Chester the Molester?

Thomas reminded us again about the law's inability to protect children after Veronica and Duncan learned that the pious Manning family was locking cute, helpless Grace in the closet ("Nobody Puts Baby in a Corner," 2-7). Unfortunately, they had to break into the Manning home to make their discovery, and Mr. Manning turned the tables on them by calling Sheriff Lamb. Lamb's decision to release Veronica and Duncan—and the suggestion that Lamb's own father was abusive—is Lamb's most sympathetic portrayal in the series. Note, though, that his beneficence results not from a decision to enforce the law against Mr. Manning, but rather from his decision *not* to enforce the law against Veronica and Duncan. Only by neglecting the expectations of his office is he able to do the right thing. The law, Thomas is telling us, is an impediment—not a vehicle—to justice.

In episode after episode, law and the people who enforce it prove unhelpful—until, of course, Veronica gives the system a little shove. Ultimately, Thomas's masterful and believable depiction of formal legal systems as inadequate is the grounding that makes the rest of the show work. Without this context, Veronica's many witticisms, the multi-layered plots, and the best father-daughter relationship on television wouldn't fly. It's precisely because cops, prosecutors, lawyers, and judges are credibly depicted as lazy, reactionary, and/or powerless that we satisfied viewers can swallow a series based on a high school student solving not just little mysteries about fake IDs and missing dogs, but also weighty ones, like murder, molestation, and mass violence. We would never buy the notion of Veronica's importance if she existed in a world with meaningful governmental response. We believe in her importance because she lives in lawless Neptune.

ALAFAIR BURKE is an author and law professor. After graduating with distinction from Stanford Law School and serving as a deputy district attorney in Portland, Oregon, she is now an associate professor at Hofstra Law School and frequently serves as a legal and trial commentator for radio and television programs. She lives in New York City and is the author of the Samantha Kincaid series of mystery novels (*Judgment Calls*, *Missing Justice*, and *Close Case*). Her first stand-alone thriller, *Dead Connection*, will be published in July 2007. Alafair welcomes contact from readers at www.alafairburke.com.

Veronica is certainly a vigilante, and here at VM headquarters, we love her for it. We love her for it in the same way we love Bruce Wayne throwing on a cape and becoming Batman. There's something twisted in both of their psyches that makes "seeking justice" or "wreaking vengeance" a compulsion. When an occasional character (Meg, Carmen) suggests that it might be healthier for Veronica to rid herself of this compulsion, well, yeah... they're probably right. That said, Meg or Carmen would be equally correct in pointing this out to Bruce Wayne. I hope people don't think we're holding Veronica to a different standard because she's a young woman.

Kristen Kidder

The New Normal

Breaking the Boundaries of Vigilantism in Veronica Mars

URING THE FIRST two seasons of *Veronica Mars* we watched our dynamic heroine's social status vacillate between sharing limos with the popular 09er crowd to lunch room isolation and back again. She couldn't seem to make up her mind about Duncan and Logan. In fact, she shape-shifted so often that one of the only things we can say with any degree of certainty is this: she *really* wanted a pony. In fact, she had probably wanted one since she was a little girl; it's the kind of thing that gets tacked onto the end of birthday or Christmas lists, the kind of thing that—after years of wanting and never getting—comes to represent something else entirely.

Veronica references her pony frequently; it's part of the Mars family vernacular. It was the first thing she squealed for when her father handed her an envelope at her high school graduation, and it was her request when he suggested that they spend an evening doing something regular fathers and daughters do. (Tough break there—in lieu of the pony, Keith thought Veronica might instead like to rub his feet.) Although it's entertaining, the metaphor is hardly worthy of Mensa: what the detectives Mars are really longing for is normalcy;

the pony is just part of their shtick. And who can blame them? Two seasons on the air and they've already weathered their fair share of trauma: divorce, alcoholism, rape, murder, ostracism. Their mutual desire to blend into the woodwork makes perfect sense.

The search for normalcy is at the very center of *Veronica Mars* and, in many ways, has become synonymous with the show's struggle for truth. "Normal" is presumably what will be left once Neptune, California, has been stripped of all its dysfunctionality and deceit; it's the goal assumed to be shared by its residents, regardless of their race, gender, and socio-economic status. As our local do-good detectives, Keith and Veronica aren't exactly superheroes, but they are the champions of normalcy, the characters charged with restoring moral order to their undeniably corrupt environment. And, like many social crusaders, their actions and behaviors quickly become lightening rods for criticism—an analysis of which reveals a firmly entrenched cultural bias relating to gender and power.

Keith and Veronica each bring their own personal code of ethics and unique set of values to their detective work. As the former sheriff of Neptune, the elder Mars has a clear respect for established authority and conventions; his daughter, to put it mildly, does not. In fact, her style leans strongly towards a reliance on vigilante justice, the kind of work where the hero famously takes the law into his or her own hands against the perceived insufficiencies of established authority. Popular culture is filled with these kinds of figures—most recently personified by 24's Jack Bauer—but classically depicted by the likes of Rambo, Dirty Harry, Shaft, and virtually every comic book character. It is thanks in part to this fictional boys club that vigilantism has become synonymous with masculinity, which creates an interesting paradox: because Veronica attempts to bring justice (and therefore status quo) to Neptune via a highly gendered and controversial method, her actions provoke a strong response from those around her, thus ensuring that her life will never be normal—the very thing she seems to long for.

Yet that is not to say that there is not pop cultural precedent for female detectives. On the contrary, Veronica is a clear descendent of Nancy Drew—in fact, finding a review of the series that does not reference the twentieth century's favorite girl detective is a formidable challenge. And a propensity for sleuthing is not the only thing these characters have in common: significantly, both young women are only children being raised by a single father, and both are described as being highly intelligent with an upbeat, sassy personality. These rhetorical devices are likely present to explain both teens' "unladylike" behaviors and the relative ease with which they are able to solve cases that baffle adults. There is, however, one very important difference in their character- izations: while Nancy relies heavily on consultations with her father, teachers, law enforcement, or other experts to solve a case (thereby implicitly urging her readers to do the same), Veronica defies all such conventions. It's a subtle, but important, change. Veronica's willingness to go her own way, to take the law into her own hands, could be viewed as a booster shot of feminism right into the heart of a genre that is not generally hospitable to woman—or it could serve as a cautionary tale to girls of a similar mindset.

Unlike most heroic conventions (like flying, super-strength, or the ability to turn into some sort of arachnid), vigilantism has definite real world applications. The most cursory look at a local newspaper reveals that there are vigilantes all around us, citizens who take action when they feel the law is standing silent. Significantly, as long as the vigilante's notions of justice remain in line with those of mainstream America, the term is not likely to be used as a pejorative. Defying all popular stereotypes of women in general and female detectives in particular, Veronica's vengeance is swift, exacting, and almost com- pletely outside the established legal and judicial order—particularly when she's called upon to crack a case in which a man has harmed a woman through some form of violence or sexual coercion. In season one, this scenario plays out with alarming frequency.

The motivation behind Veronica's thirst for vengeance was estab- lished early in the series: aside from the unsolved murder of her best friend and her father's unseating as sheriff, a flashback revealed that the new sheriff literally laughed in her face as she arrived at the police station, torn and tattered, to report that she was raped at an end-of- the-year party. Her attitude towards the resolution of that crime—"I'm going to find out who did this to me and I'm going to make them pay"—later became her goal for every young woman at Neptune High who approached her for help. And while *Veronica Mars* is hardly a cata- lyst for teenage would-be delinquents, community response to her ac- tions serves as an interesting barometer of cultural zeitgeist—even if the community in question is the fictional Neptune, California.

Veronica soon discovered that the consequences of working outside the established moral order were particularly pronounced and gendered—a dichotomy that was painstakingly revealed when father and daughter worked side-by-side on a case. In "The Girl Next Door" (1-7), Veronica alerted her father to the fact that their upstairs neighbor, a young pregnant woman named Sarah, had apparently gone missing after a night of fighting. Suspecting foul play, Veronica asked her father to look into the case, a request that he ultimately denied, citing the standard twenty-four hours that must pass before an adult is declared missing. Veronica would not accept this explanation, and immediately began her own search for the young woman.

Because Sarah was not officially missing—a designation even her boyfriend was unwilling to make because he said she "tends to disappear sometimes"—Veronica was left to her own devices. She broke into the upstairs apartment when no one was around to look for clues, made fraudulent phone calls to her doctor to uncover the results of recent medical tests, and made several reconnaissance trips to the high-end retail store where Sarah worked. Keith Mars, in the meantime, did little to assist with the investigation of the case besides offering his official detective services to Sarah's parents when they arrived from Ohio to look for her. In fact, Keith did everything he could to discourage his daughter's efforts, primarily because cases where attractive young girls go missing "often end badly." Undeterred, Veronica continued to follow her intuition while investigating the disappearance, going so far as to enlist the local biker gang to disrupt Sarah's place of employment in an attempt to get her manager to return the young woman's diary. He did.

Veronica's unconventional sleuthing was ultimately more effective than her father's traditional methods, and she soon found Sarah, unharmed, hiding out along the seashore. The young woman returned home to her apartment, where her boyfriend had been entertaining her mother and stepfather. This seemingly idyllic family reunion was shattered, however, when Keith and Veronica heard shouting coming from the upstairs apartment. In this, the moment of truth, Keith ordered his daughter to stay put while he went up to investigate—and Veronica uncharacteristically obeyed his request. Keith interrupted the argument just in time to defend Sarah by shooting her stepfather, who we learned was the baby's father.

What made "The Girl Next Door" significant was that the episode was bookended by the aftermath of Keith Mars's shoot-out—in fact, the action opened on the entryway of the apartment complex, its darkness punctuated only by the flashing lights of emergency response vehicles. Before plunging into flashback, Veronica reflected in a tone heavy with regret:

> I look over the past week and wonder if things could have turned out differently. If I hadn't met the girl, if I hadn't initiated the case, if I hadn't interfered, would tonight be just another dull, quiet night in our apartment complex?

It was an interesting reaction, considering that Veronica's meddling returned a young pregnant woman to her otherwise supportive and loving family. And while it was true that Sarah's stepfather was shot as a result of the conflict that followed, he wasn't mortally wounded—and even that is a consequence that is likely to be viewed by many as being relatively lenient in comparison to his crime. Veronica acknowledged this paradox at the very end of the episode when she rationalized, "Sure, the real tragedy happened long before I came along—I just brought it to the surface." Still, it's clear that her faith in vigilante justice is at best inconsistent, as she left the audience with a loaded question: "Are some things better left buried?" While the "things" Veronica alluded to are necessarily vague—depending on which angle you approach season one, they could refer to the identity of her rapist, Lilly's killer, or questions of her own paternity—her hesitation hinted at one of the series's central questions: Is Veronica willing to trade her reliance on vigilantism (and all of the positive, albeit masculine, traits it demands) for a chance at a "normal" life?

The following episode, "Like a Virgin" (1-8), would suggest not. In that installment, an online purity test wreaked havoc on Neptune High, as students paid ten dollars each to discover their classmates' sexual pasts. The results of some of the surveys were, of course, fraudulent, with less popular students appearing to have scores so low that they ranked well within the realm of deviant sex fiend. (Veronica herself rated a fourteen, with the test indicating that she had "pleasured the swim team while jacked up on goofballs.") But when purity mania ruined the reputation of Meg Manning, one of the few 09ers who still called Veronica a friend, Veronica promised her usual brand of vengeance, declaring, "We'll clear your name and make someone pay."

In an unrelated plotline in the same episode, Veronica's father took it upon himself to evict an unwanted tenant from Alicia Fennel's apartment. Presented side-by-side in the episode, these stories illustrated the contrast between father and daughter—or rather the contrast in the reactions they garner from those they try to help. When Keith Mars initially approached the single mother, he offered his assistance because he knew how "the law works—slowly." Mrs. Fennel categorically refused. "If I have a problem I'll go to the police," was her stern response. Similarly, when Veronica explained her sleuthing philosophy to Meg—"You get tough. You get even. Works for me"—the popular girl's reaction, much like Alicia Fennel's, was steeped with concern for the status quo: "Does it bother you, the things they say?" she asked Veronica, betraying her obvious concern for social standing.

Predictably, both members of the Mars family remained undaunted in the face of criticism. Keith took matters into his own hands by stealing Wallace's house keys. He then spent the night in the apartment, terrorizing the freeloading tenant, who moved out at the first light of dawn. Similarly, it didn't take long for Veronica to uncover the identity of the purity test falsifier and orchestrate a videotaped confession, which was promptly aired to the entire school. Mission(s) accomplished.

While the outcomes of the Mars' investigations might have been uniformly positive, the reactions from their clients were not. Alicia was uncharacteristically contrite: "The fact that you helped me, even though I was awful to you. You're a very decent man." That encounter sparked a renewed friendship, and eventual romantic relationship, between the two. Meg's initial reaction was similar, insinuating that Veronica was her knight in shining armor as she quipped, "I was looking for a white horse." However, her gratitude quickly shifted gears as she offered Veronica the following words of wisdom: "Getting tough? Yeah, that was good advice, and I needed that. The getting even part—you might want to rethink that one." In those scenarios, both Keith and Veronica assumed the traditional male role of savior to a distressed, helpless woman, and both were forced outside the socially accepted boundaries of law and order in the process. And, while their assistance was eventually accepted with gratitude, only Veronica was condemned for her transgression.

A similar scenario played out in "M.A.D." (1-20), an episode in which Veronica attempted to stop her classmate Carmen's vengeful ex-boyfriend Tad from releasing an embarrassing, sexually charged cell phone video. Because it was impossible for Veronica to recover every copy of the digital file with any degree of certainty, she switched strategies, deciding instead to produce her own incriminating piece of media. The finished product: a homosexuality-themed Web site, designed to send the homophobic, Naval Academy-bound Tad running for cover. In a move lifted straight out of the Cold War, Veronica gave Carmen control of its dissemination, convinced that when faced with the prospect of his own reputation's demise, Tad would have no choice but to discontinue his threats.

She was wrong.

However, Carmen's thirst for revenge inexplicably waned once the video was released, despite the fact that she had instantaneously become Neptune High's latest cautionary tale. Veronica did not hesitate, and presented her with a laptop, email written and ready to send. With just one click, Carmen had the power to send the inflammatory Web site to each member of the Naval Academy freshman class, all but guaranteeing the end of Tad's military career. Carmen instead chose to erase the message, over Veronica's futile cries.

Carmen's reasons for deleting the e-mail are similar to Meg's in that they privileged the traditionally feminine traits of forgiveness and understanding over the masculine dominance associated with vengeance. Carmen's tone was masked with an air of superiority as she informed Veronica that "tearing Tad down is not going to make me feel any better." She cut off any further protests with a curt, "I'm sorry, Veronica, I guess revenge just isn't my thing." The audience was clearly left with the impression that Carmen's character was taking the high road.

It's a theme that's not unproblematic, considering that *Veronica Mars* is founded on the premise that the title character is a tough-talking, empowered role model for teenage girls. The pervasive nature of the criticism throughout suggests that this ideology is not accidental or even included for diversity; the condemnation Veronica received from her female peers continued even into the end of season one. During those climatic sequences, Veronica's quest for vengeance built to an almost literal crescendo as she systematically approached every man who may have had knowledge of her rape, despite Meg's advice that she "let it go, you'll just make yourself crazy." Of course, Veronica did not let it go, ultimately (appearing to) solve that mystery in addition to uncovering Lilly Kane's murderer. Score one point for vengeance.

Yet the obvious success of her vigilante methods did not preclude Veronica from continuing to seek her ever-elusive pony. In fact, the title of the season two opener, "Normal Is the Watchword," suggested that she was willing to trade her signature style for a healthy dose of the mundane. And while Veronica Mars's life was never exactly quiet, there appeared to be a marked difference in her attitude towards justice and the law during her senior year of high school—in other words, she seemed to have developed a renewed deference for authority. (Or at the very least she was taking a page out of her father's book and working within the established boundaries.) From there on out Veronica's trials were literal: not only did the specter of Aaron Echolls's court case hang over Neptune during the entire season, but she was called for jury duty during Christmas break.

In that episode, titled "One Angry Veronica" (2-10), she ostensibly did the work of twelve men, re-imagining a crime scene involving a prostitute, her pimp, and a couple of 09er classmates. As jury foreman, she was the Veronica we love—smart, self-assured, creative—we just weren't used to seeing her be all these things in such a formal environment, working to preserve the integrity of a system that had failed her so blatantly in the past. This inversion of style grew more pronounced in "The Rapes of Graff" (2-16), when Veronica fought to clear the name of a purported rapist—ex-boyfriend and sleazy steroid dealer Troy Vandegraff—accused of drugging and violating a young woman at a college party. Although the case was practically a carbon copy of the situation that fueled her vigilante revenge throughout the previous year, Veronica had surprisingly little empathy for the victim, choosing instead to align herself with Troy. While she succeeded in exonerating him, she never identified or apprehended the rapist. Worse yet, she appeared to never have intended to.[1]

Perhaps the first half of the second season of *Veronica Mars* was crafted to send the message that the judicial process is like AA: it works if you work it. But that theory was (quite literally) blown away

---

[1] In retrospect, this quirky characterization was clearly setting us up for season three, which lends even more credence to the theory that Veronica's abandonment of vigilantism was a temporary–even understandable–reaction to being locked in a refrigerator and set on fire.

in the season finale with Aaron Echolls's acquittal and his vigilante-style execution at the hands of Clarence Wiedman. Clearly, the show's attitudes towards justice, gender, and vigilantism were at a crossroads: Veronica's apparent embrace of normality could largely have been reactionary, a not unrealistic and temporary response to the events of the previous year. Or Aaron Echolls's violent (and completely justifiable) murder could have indicated that this vigilante stuff was best left to the boys.

The penultimate scenes of season two were as close to a Norman Rockwell painting as we're likely to ever see in Neptune: our heroine was happy and in love, ready for summer adventures, and looking forward to tackling the rigors of college. Things appeared—dare we say it—almost *normal*. But normal, as a concept, is entirely subjective, culturally specific, and generally (although somewhat ironically in this case) propagated by the mass media. *Veronica Mars* functions as a kind of meta-text: as the characters search for the mundane in their own lives, their actions—and their peers' reactions to them—establish the context of the same for their audience. To Veronica, "normal" may mean living in a world where young women can live without fear of verbal or physical abuse, where they are free to grow into competent, capable adults. To the residents of Neptune (and to some extent the rest of society) that same designation may represent a world where women are tethered, happily, to the constraints of their gender.

And while I would love nothing more than to see Veronica riding off happily into the sunset, here's hoping that she never gets her pony.

KRISTEN KIDDER is a writer, cultural scholar, and recovering academic who lives in Brooklyn, New York. Although her earliest work focused almost exclusively on female music fans—in 2004 she was sent to Germany to lecture on the subject with 1960s super-groupie Cynthia Plaster-Caster—nowadays she spends most of her time mining little nuggets of feminism from the weekly television line-up. A long-time contributor to *Bitch* magazine, Kristen's work has also appeared on PopMatters, *Alternet*, and *Clamor*. She recently bought a TiVo specifically so she could record *Veronica Mars*.

For Christmas last *year, my wife framed the first six Mallard Fillmore cartoons that included the* Veronica Mars *mentions. She was able to talk Bruce Tinsley out of the originals. Afterwards, I exchanged a few e-mails with Bruce, and we actually discussed why* Veronica Mars *might be perceived as conservative-friendly. As part of the Hollywood Liberal Media Elite myself, I was confused by the phenomenon. Our ratings are undeniably better in red states. Strangely, we have a bigger market share in Lincoln than Seattle. I told Bruce my theory—a theory Chris also mentions in his essay:* Veronica *metes out a particularly uncomplicated Old West brand of justice. Criminals get what's coming to them. Bruce had a different theory. He suggested that liberals wouldn't be able to fathom a teen show as worthy; they'd write it off as uncool without even sampling it. Conservatives, he suggested, wouldn't be dissuaded by the teen girl detective logline.*

A footnote that I found interesting. . . .

Bruce's wife is a lefty human rights lawyer. She sent her own e-mail to me saying that Veronica Mars *provided a weekly date night. It was one piece of pop culture they could agree on.*

Chris McCubbin

The Duck
and the Detective

CELESTE KANE: Jake, honey, when did we become Republicans?

—"Leave It to Beaver" (1-22)

I T ALL STARTED with a little black duck in a fedora....

The specific waterfowl in question was Mallard Fillmore, the star of the comic strip of the same name by Bruce Tinsley.

In case you haven't seen it, *Mallard Fillmore* is the graphical musings of a duck who works as co-anchor of a network news show, despite holding an avowedly conservative political viewpoint. Mallard's mission in life is to skewer the liberal establishment (in Mallard's world "liberal" and "establishment" are practically redundant) at every available opportunity.

In the early months of 2006, Mallard started to talk about his great admiration for *Veronica Mars*—no bones were made about the fact that the duck considered the show to be not only the best-written thing on TV right now, but in fact one of a meager handful of shows even worth watching.

Take, for example, the cartoon from January 27, 2006. As in many *Mallard Fillmore* cartoons, Mallard himself doesn't appear—but we still know that the viewpoint expressed is Mallard's (which, Tinsley is on record as saying, is pretty much the same as saying that the viewpoint expressed is Tinsley's[1]). The cartoon shows a pudgy, smirking Hollywood mogul type. Under the header, "TV Producers' New Year's Resolution," we are given a little poem:

> *We resolve to stop feeding you drivel . . .*
> *Relying on our big-name stars . . .*
> *Now that we see what good writing can do . . .*
> *On shows like "Veronica Mars" . . .*

Again, this was only one of several cartoons praising *Veronica Mars*'s superiority to pretty much everything else on TV.

Of course, it must be admitted that there's nothing particularly amazing about a newspaper cartoonist geeking out over a favorite TV program or movie. *Foxtrot*, for example, was practically guaranteed to do a week or so's worth of strips about the excitement of the nerdish youngest son Jason every time a major fantasy blockbuster is released (the *Fellowship of the Ring* vs. *Harry Potter* strips a few years ago were particularly memorable).

So, for example, if Gary Trudeau did a series of *Doonesbury* strips praising, say, *Snakes on a Plane*, you probably wouldn't want to assume that it was because *Snakes* had a particularly liberal political context. But there's a difference. Trudeau is a liberal cartoonist, doing a strip that often speaks to his liberal viewpoints. But *Doonesbury* is also about personal relationships, the absurdity of modern life, popular culture, and a whole slew of other topics. Bruce Tinsley, however, is a conservative doing a strip about conservatism. It's a subtle but important difference. Pretty much every *Mallard* strip speaks directly to conservative thought or a conservative slant on current events. Characters, from Mallard himself on down, exist only as mediums for the political message. Popular culture usually enters *Mallard Fillmore* only as an object of scorn.

So I got to wondering: what is it about *Veronica Mars* that would appeal so strongly to a conservative as dedicated to his viewpoints as Tinsley, that he'd take time out from a strip as focused as *Mallard Fillmore* to single the show out for praise?

---

[1] "Mallard really is about as close to me as you can get," Tinsley has said.

I'm sure there are tons of conservatives out there who love *Veronica Mars*...but the question the *Mallard Fillmore* strips made me ask was, "Is there something about *Veronica Mars* that appeals to political conservatives *because* they're political conservatives?"

"A Working Class Hero Is Something to Be...."

KEITH: Wow, that's some cake.

VERONICA: Isn't it, though?

KEITH: I love it. Ever notice how everything you make just tends to lean a little to the left?

VERONICA: [examining the cake] I do that on purpose.

("You Think You Know Somebody," 1-5)

Because, on the face of it, Neptune is hardly the kind of Norman Rockwell, traditional-values place we associate with the Republican Party platform. In fact, with its teenage sex, crime and drug use, its general political corruption, its high proportion of rich and bossy Hollywood media elite types, and the pretty much complete absence of religion from the social fabric...if anything, Neptune is a conservative's vision of hell. (Not that there's anything wrong with setting a TV show in a vision of hell; it worked for *Buffy the Vampire Slayer* for seven seasons.) The Mars family itself, with its absentee, substance-abusing mom, messy end, and questions of paternity, is hardly an exemplar of traditional family values.

Perhaps more importantly, Veronica herself seems to have few obvious conservative viewpoints. She's gay positive, sex positive (always assuming the sex is consensual), and possessed of a highly mutable respect for both rules and the law.

KYLIE: Sorry to blow your mind, but I'm a lesbian, Veronica.

VERONICA: Oh. Well...that's cool.

KYLIE: Only when you're in college.

("Versatile Toppings," 2-14)

Obviously, then, if there's something in *Veronica Mars* that calls out to conservatives, it's not directed at the "traditional values" religious right wing of the movement, who have the habit of sitting through prime-time TV with clickers in their hands, ticking off every violent act, sexy scene, and dirty word to determine numerically which programs are the most decadent.

> MR. DANIELS: You know, the glow of your father's wealth and celebrity may be enough to sustain you through high school, Mr. Echolls, but do you know what it will get you in the real world?
>
> LOGAN: [sarcastically] Please say "high school English teacher." Please say "high school English teacher."
>
> [Weevil snickers]
>
> MR. DANIELS: Mr. Navarro, I wonder if you'll find Mr. Echolls so amusing ten years from now—when you're pumping his gas.
>
> ("The Girl Next Door," 1-7)

Then there's the most fundamental political level, the economic. The predominant conservative view—the viewpoint of those who like to label themselves as "Reagan Conservatives"—is that it's okay to be rich. Under the theories of so-called "trickle down" economics, the very prosperous spread their wealth around to the community at large, creating increased prosperity for all. And if you want to be one of the rich, thanks to our capitalist system all you have to do is work hard and invest wisely, and in due course you'll move up. The poor are that way because they're too lazy to prosper.

Veronica Mars, in contrast, seems to present a world that sometimes seems almost Marxist in its perspective, where the rich are corrupt, entrenched, and oppressive. They use their wealth to control and humiliate the poor, and to evade the law and their civic responsibilities. This is true both of the adolescent 09ers and of their parents. Veronica herself is often cast in the role of Robin Hood, metaphorically hijacking the ill-gotten gains of those who should already consider themselves rich enough, and channeling it to the more morally deserving underclass. This is hardly a conservative model of capital redistribution.

> VERONICA: I'd be the best rich person, seriously. I'd be the perfect combination of frivolous and sensible. Money is so wasted on the wealthy.
>
> ("An Echolls Family Christmas," 1-10)

To the Right of What?

Obviously, contemporary American conservatism is not a monolithic, easily defined movement. Even when you identify the different threads and themes in modern American conservatism, it's impossible to apply them exclusively to individual conservatives—it's more like a buffet, where people take a little bit from one theory and a little bit from another. We've already mentioned the traditional values conservatives and their close cousins, the religious right. We've also touched on economic conservatism. Neither one of these movements seems particularly appealing to the *Veronica Mars* fan.

There's the national security conservative, whose main concerns are strong national defense abroad and strong law enforcement at home. This seems a bit closer to the mark—*Veronica Mars* is definitely pro-justice. On the other hand, the show is less-than-friendly to public institutions (namely the Neptune police), and pretty much unconcerned with foreign affairs.

Political pundits have recently identified a bloc of potential voters that they've dubbed "*South Park* Republicans," or "*South Park* conservatives." The name is, of course, drawn from the notoriously transgressive Comedy Central cartoon show, which often focuses its satirical sights on liberal ideas—particularly the Hollywood liberal elite. The term was coined by commentator Andrew Sullivan, and has been popularized by author Brian C. Anderson through his book, *South Park Conservatives: The Revolt Against American Media Bias*. Of course, the right wing is not immune to *South Park*'s satirical broadsides either, but that's sort of the point. The *South Park* conservative viewpoint is most neatly summed up by the show's co-creator Matt Stone, who's on record as saying, "I hate conservatives, but I really fucking hate liberals" (Stone). This kind of "pox on both your houses" cynicism seems to go well with the hard-boiled detective side of *Veronica Mars*, and I bet that lots of *South Park* conservatives—jaded and pop-culturally aware—are big *Veronica Mars* fans, so we're close. . . . But this *South Park* conservatism is definitely not the kind of true-believer conservatism espoused by *Mallard Fillmore*.

Mostly, I think the show's appeal speaks to the libertarian wing of the movement—the kind of conservative who wants to keep government small, taxes low, citizens armed, and the common man in charge of his own destiny.

Libertarian conservatism is embodied in the libertarian political party, but it also pervades (albeit usually in more moderated or diluted forms) the Republican Party. It must be said, for the record, that Mallard Fillmore has never identified himself as a Republican (and Republican national figures are often the target of the strip's satire—usually for not being conservative enough). He has claimed—once—to be a libertarian, but it wasn't clear whether he was talking about the political party or just the school of thought.

So now that we've identified the kind of conservative who might be drawn to *Veronica Mars* by something a bit deeper than the beauty and charm of Kristen Bell, what are the specific elements of the show that would appeal to a *Mallard Fillmore* conservative?

It seems pretty obvious to me that the creators of *Veronica Mars* never set out to create a political metaphor. Rather, the deep fissures in the social fabric of Neptune arise from the contradictory influences the show so brilliantly combines. *Veronica Mars* blends hard-boiled detective fiction and film noir, where everything is corrupt and fundamentally hopeless, with the family drama/coming-of-age story, which is wholesome and intrinsically hopeful. Both Mickey Spillane and Louisa May Alcott feature prominently in *Veronica Mars's* family tree.

Allow me to suggest that it's this synthesis of two seemingly contradictory genres that holds the key to *Veronica Mars's* appeal. The conservative loves the potential of the free human spirit, the essential nobility of the properly channeled human will. This is the coming-of-age story, where the young hero (of whatever gender) breaks away from the nurturing family and is tested by the outside world—not always passing each test perfectly, but growing stronger and wiser along the way. This is Veronica's story.

At the same time, the conservative deeply distrusts the dominant social order, which can all too easily turn predatory and corruptive without constant vigilance. This is the hard-boiled-detective story, where the hero can never trust anybody but himself, and any individual, no matter how beautiful, and any institution, no matter how august, can at any time turn out to be rotten, evil, and plotting against the hero's life. This is Neptune's story.

Let's look at some of the ways this plays out in the show.

The System Is Broken

Ms. Dent: Good morning, Veronica. I was thinking maybe you'd be interested in covering the election for the student newspaper.

Veronica: Sure, I'll write it up this afternoon.

Ms. Dent: The election's tomorrow.

Veronica: And I can already see the headline: "Brown-Nosing Résumé Packer Wins in a Landslide."

("Return of the Kane," 1-6)

Outwardly, Neptune is pretty, prosperous, wholesome—the American dream. The core, however, is rotten. The leading citizens are selfish, hypocritical, and corrupt. The poor are lawless and desperate. The police are ineffectual and self-serving, and even the city government (as we learn in season two) is pretty much a wholly owned subsidiary of white-collar organized criminals like Mr. Casablancas, Dick and Beaver's dad, manipulating the public good to get the most profit out of his shady real estate scams.

A libertarian conservative (let's just go ahead and call him a *Mallard Fillmore* conservative) might grudgingly admit that government is necessary for functions like defense, law enforcement, and public transportation, but he definitely believes that government works best when it does the least. When government has too much power, libertarian thought states, it begins to strain and buckle under its own weight. Efficiency is lost. More importantly, supporting a massive and bloated government requires that the government confiscate an undue portion of its people's money in the form of taxes (and then it has to charge more taxes to pay for collecting the taxes). Finally, an overly powerful government creates a culture of entitlement among the populace, where people expect the nanny-state to take care of every need and wish as a "right." This leads to a decadent, corrupt, and immoral culture of weaklings. Neptune is a pretty powerful metaphor for the arrogance of power.

This overall social breakdown can be seen in several different recurring themes in the show. To name three....

Public Schools

KEITH: How was school?
VERONICA: You know—mean kids, indifferent teachers, crumbling
infrastructure.

("M.A.D.," 1-20)

So let's look at Neptune High. The 09ers spend their time doing
drugs, hooking up, running scams, and throwing wild parties while
their grades get automatically inflated to the point where they can get
into any school their parents can afford. Meanwhile the PCH greas-
ers are selling them the drugs while bullying the weak. The teachers
are burnt-out and uninspired, and the few intelligent, motivated students, like Veronica, are pretty much left to fend for themselves. The
only kids with any hope of any kind of upward mobility are the jocks,
like Wallace. Buffy's Sunnydale High had an excuse—it was built over
a Hellmouth. But Neptune High is just corrupt.

To a certain subset of the modern conservative movement, this
portrait of U.S. secondary education isn't a dramatic exaggeration—
it's pretty much a documentary. There's a strong current among conservatives that the government has no business collecting taxes for a
mandatory, secular public education system that many feel is a joke
to the rest of the world. It's not much of a stretch to guess that this is
one theme that works particularly well for Tinsley and *Mallard Fillmore*. Tinsley considers the U.S. public education system completely
broken, and his alter-ego has often said so in the strip.

Defense Lawyers

CLIFF: I failed criminal law.

("Like a Virgin," 1-8)

Ladies and gentlemen, I give you Cliff McCormack, the Mars family's lawyer friend—always available to provide justice at a reasonable
cost. Though Cliff is often actually on the side of the angels (usually
despite himself), defending those who really are innocent (or at least
pure of heart), the fact remains that basically Cliff is presented to us
as cowardly and opportunistic. This jibes well with the prevailing
wisdom of the conservative movement. Prosecutors put criminals in

jail, defense lawyers get criminals out of jail. Conservatives—at least those not currently under indictment—tend to prefer the former to the later.

Hollywood Types

> AARON: Have you heard from your sister?
> LOGAN: Yeah. She sent a telegram. Heartbroken. Stop. Can't make it back from Sydney. Stop. Underwater scene shoot tomorrow. Stop. Entire crew said prayer for Mom. Stop. Love you. Stop.
>
> ("Lord of the Bling," 1-13)

Conservatives believe that the American culture of the moment is dominated by a "liberal media elite" that distorts the values of the average American and screens out information the elite considers "politically incorrect." The poster children for this media elite are Hollywood stars, with their trendy, liberal social causes, their immoral and immodest lifestyle, and their often uninformed outspokenness.

The Echolls family doesn't completely conform to this stereotype. Aaron—by far the worst of the lot—seems to be a square-jawed, action-movie type in the Arnold Schwarzenegger/Clint Eastwood/Charlton Heston mold, and conservatives don't tend to have much trouble with that particular sort of star. On the other hand, George Clooney makes action movies, too, and plenty of conservatives would love to see him share Aaron Echolls's fate. Plus there's Trina, Aaron's ditzy actress daughter, who fully embodies the image of Hollywood irresponsibility. Trina's signature is social conscience as a career move—she pretends to have principles, because she thinks principles are something celebrities are supposed to wear in public, like Manolo Blahniks. This sort of ideological opportunism is exactly what conservatives (especially the *South Park* conservatives mentioned earlier) really despise about "Hollywood liberals." It's a fundamental clash of cultures—rich conservatives quietly (sometimes covertly) give piles of money to candidates who believe the same things they do, while famous liberals (so conservatives believe, and often the evidence seems to be on their side) endorse candidates when it means they'll have a chance to share in a photo-op and get their picture in a part of the paper other than the Lifestyle section.

Right Is Right

VERONICA: [voiceover] So this is how it is. The innocent suffer, the guilty go free, and truth and fiction are pretty much interchangeable.... There is neither a Santa Claus, nor an Easter Bunny, and there are no angels watching over us. Things just happen for no reason, and nothing makes any sense.

("Not Pictured," 2-22)

Poor Veronica has every right to feel disillusioned from time to time. After all, in her world, things are all too often not at all what they seem. Friends turn away, authority figures fall.

However, for us, the viewers, things always eventually come into sharper focus. Once all the mysteries are solved, we know who the bad guy is, and who the good guy is—and the mystery always gets solved in the end, even if it takes all season.

And pretty much everybody does turn out to be either a good guy or a bad guy. The good guys aren't perfect (Wallace has made a misstep or two along the way, and even Veronica occasionally pushes the limits of acceptable behavior), and a few of the victims have a sympathetic side (Terrence Cook, the fallen baseball star, has made a mess of his life, but he'd really like to be a better dad). Some of the characters are very complicated (Weevil, Logan, Lilly), but in the end even they shake out to one side or the other—Weevil and Logan, despite their faults and bad choices, are basically good kids, while Lilly Kane, despite her charm, was probably always doomed.

Liberals are notoriously comfortable with nuance and shades of gray, but conservatives like a world that's more black and white. For proof, just look at the military policy of the current administration. The people we're fighting, or that we think we might have to fight some day, are not rivals or adversaries—they're evil: "Evildoers," an "Axis of Evil." Our whole foreign policy under the Bush administration is based on the idea that, first, we can tell the good guys from the bad guys, and second, that we have a moral right to take down the bad guys because they're evil.

In *Veronica Mars* the good guys come from the family story side of the fence, while the bad guys creep in from the hard-boiled surroundings. Having both, and being able to tell the difference, gives the show much of its appeal.

Veronica Gets Even

KEITH: Have you been playing nice with the other children?
VERONICA: You know, Dad, I'm old school, an eye for an eye.
KEITH: I think that's actually Old Testament.

("Meet John Smith," 1-3)

Veronica likes to get payback. Most sixteen-year-old girls who suspect they've been drugged and raped at a party would want to think about it as little as possible, but Veronica is driven to find the responsible party. When Jackie embarrasses her on Madame Sophie's public access show, Veronica is determined to find a way to make her regret it. Veronica jeopardizes her own scholarship to see Aaron Echolls pronounced guilty and sentenced for Lilly's murder. Of course, it must be noted that this drive for vengeance doesn't always serve Veronica well—her anger at Jackie caused a split between her and Wallace, and Aaron was found not guilty, so she lost her chance at the scholarship for nothing. But even though she doesn't always get her personal paybacks, Veronica is still very effective at bringing the guilty to justice.

Veronica Mars is a very vengeance-friendly show, and conservatism is a very vengeance-friendly philosophy. Though in general, conservatives may consider themselves to be solidly behind Jesus and his teachings, they do tend to have a bit of a problem with all that "turn the other cheek" stuff. By nature, they favor the Old Testament methods mentioned by Keith, above.

Look at our criminal justice system. Liberals say that they'd rather see 100 guilty men go free than one innocent man face punishment but conservatives are more concerned with the possibility that innocent blood might go unavenged. This is most obvious on the question of capital punishment: liberals worry about the possibility of error, the economic practicalities of the institution, and whether the ultimate penalty is being applied fairly across boundaries of race and class, but law-and-order conservatives tend to think that such sweeping questions are meaningless—the only thing that matters is that in each specific case the condemned was guilty of the crime and is suffering the just consequences of that guilt.

Veronica's not the only avenging angel in the show. At this writing, the season two finale made it appear as though Aaron Echolls had successfully manipulated the criminal justice system to regain his freedom, only to discover that there's more than one kind of justice. By the time you read this, we'll have a more detailed picture of Aaron's fate, but it's pretty clear he got what he had coming.

Self Defense

There's not a lot of gunplay in *Veronica Mars*. In particular Veronica and even Keith are seldom seen with firearms. It makes the Mars family more heroic to have them think their way out of confrontations with armed enemies. Plus a teenaged girl with a gun is a rather disturbing image—and Veronica's routine skirting of the law would seem less spunky and mischievous and a lot more felonious if she were packing heat. However, the show makes no bones about the fact that it's okay for honest citizens to defend themselves with whatever means are at hand. Backup the pit bull serves as a fine lethal weapon when Veronica is imperiled. Like conservatives, *Veronica Mars* has no problem with the First Amendment's right to self defense.

> VERONICA: [voiceover] Tragedy blows through your life like a tornado, uprooting everything, creating chaos. You wait for the dust to settle, and then you choose. You can live in the wreckage and pretend it's still the mansion you remember. Or you can crawl from the rubble and slowly rebuild. Because after disaster strikes, the important thing is that you move on. But if you're like me, you just keep chasing the storm.
>
> ("Meet John Smith," 1-3)

So, in the end, we're left with this: *Veronica Mars* is a show about a young woman who knows what's right and courageously acts on that knowledge. She doesn't let fear of personal danger, or social disapproval, or even arbitrary rules and laws stand in her way. It's a story everyone can relate to—and if it's a particularly powerful scenario to a conservative aquatic waterfowl, that's by no means the only group to which it speaks.

CHRIS McCUBBIN has written more than twenty books, mostly about games (computer and otherwise). He's a co-founder of and writer/editor with Incan Monkey God Studios. Chris lives in Austin, Texas, with his wife, Lynette Alcorn, and his dogs, Penny and Sammy.

References

Tinsley, Bruce. *Mallard Fillmore* daily comic strip, 27 Jan. 2006. King Features Syndicate.

Tinsley, Bruce, Interview with Bill Steigerwald. "Meet Mallard's Daddy," *Pittsburgh Tribune Review*, 22 Oct. 2005.

Stone, Matt. Verbal remarks given at a People for the American Way awards dinner, 2001.

Anderson, Brian C. *South Park Conservatives: The Revolt Against Left-Wind Media Bias*. Washington, D.C.: Regnery Publishing, Inc. 2005. Anderson credits blogger Andrew Sullivan with originally coining the term "South Park Republican."

I'm not entirely sure that Veronica's need to dole out retribution is entirely behind her. In writing an ongoing fictional creature I'm tugged in a couple different directions. There's the part of me that thinks Veronica should grow and evolve. She should get past her pettiness. She should learn how to forgive. (We just finished a script in the past couple of days for season three in which she unexpectedly heeds the advice of a televangelist speaking on the subject of forgiveness.) The other part of me wants to keep her complicated. Difficult. Testy. I don't want her to soften into angelic heroine who consistently does the "right thing."

Like America, Veronica and I are at a crossroads.

Deanna Carlyle

The United States
of Veronica
Teen Noir as America's New Zeitgeist

HAVE SOMETHING IN common with Veronica Mars.
Last year I was sexually molested, and the cops laughed it
off. The incident left me in danger of becoming a cynic. But it
also taught me a hard truth, a truth that teen detective and TV
sensation Veronica Mars learned an even harder way after her rape,
when, with unnecessary cruelty, Sheriff Lamb let the case drop.

The truth is, sometimes even the "good guys" aren't looking out
for us. Ultimately, we're thrown back on ourselves and our own self-
preservation instinct. What then? Who can we turn to? The new
task, maybe even *the* task for our times—the one *Veronica Mars* gives
us the tools to tackle—is figuring out how to protect ourselves without putting too much faith in an external authority or blocking out
feelings that make us vulnerable, feelings like trust, empathy, and
love. The temptation is to join our violators' ranks by walking away
from responsibility or acting out in some eye-for-eye campaign for revenge, a temptation Veronica struggles with mightily. But as Veronica
learned after she was repeatedly condemned for her reliance on vengeance, that way lies misery, hate, and solitude.

That way lies our current zeitgeist. That way lies teen noir.

"Tensions in Neptune Are the Highest They've Ever Been."

That *Veronica Mars* falls squarely within the *film noir* tradition has been shown by sharper pens than mine. What I'd like to explore here is *why* teen noir is surfacing now and what it can teach us. Why does it hit a nerve that hurts so good? Why do adults and teens alike respond so deeply and enthusiastically to the show? Because it's a direct expression of America's current zeitgeist, that's why.

The guarded, snarky noir voice and personality of Veronica's world are symptomatic of the modern American struggle to protect our vulnerability and recover our lost innocence in these cynical times. In a very real, if fictional sense, we *are* the United States of Veronica.

Wartime, loss of innocence and stability, distrust of authority figures at local, national, and international levels—this is our current American climate, and it creates a pattern of response that is not unlike the way Wallace described Veronica in the show's pilot episode: "Underneath that angry young woman shell, there's a slightly less angry young woman... You're a marshmallow, Veronica Mars, a Twinkie" ("Pilot," 1-1).

I'll go further. I'll say Americans have become like a smoking, burnt-out s'more at some sadistic teen's marshmallow roast, charred and crusty on the outside, oozing fear and repressed sadness on the inside. Oh, we'd like to think we're tough and invincible. We used to be in some illusory golden age. But the hidden truth is we're frightened and vulnerable. We're mourning the loss of our collective innocence and our shattered illusions—illusions about ourselves, our leaders, and our democratic way of life—just as we did in the postwar forties and the war-torn seventies, and now again in the wartime naughts.

It's a tough time, and we're hurting. And our poster child is Veronica Mars.

"There Is No Santa Claus, Veronica."

When creating a character, screenwriters often talk about a character's need, or "ghost." By this they mean the character's past trauma and resulting emotional wound, which create a deep, unfilled need that in a sense haunts the character throughout the story. If all goes well, story events will both irritate the wound and help it to heal, and ultimately the character will come out having met a subconscious need. This is what happy endings are all about, and it's what *Veronica Mars*'s main plot is all about, when it provides Veronica the upbeat closure she craves each season, a faint glimmer of hope in an otherwise dark and pessimistic world.

At the same time the show's subplots tend to end each season on a down note, especially Logan and Duncan's, reminding us that not all of us get our happy ending, not if our parents have abandoned or violated us. This is the character wound that may or may not heal, and this is what creates the real suspense in *Veronica Mars*, at least for me. Will Duncan, Logan, and Veronica be able to heal their wounds, or will they repeat the cycle of violation and neglect their parents taught them?

In Veronica's case, her "ghost" during the first season is threefold: her best friend Lilly was murdered, her boyfriend Duncan inexplicably dumped her, and her mother abandoned her without explanation. Veronica's wound and theme are thus abandonment, with a sub-theme of violation at the hands of her peers and community elders.

Her two character wounds—abandonment and violation—are reflected, doubly or singly, in nearly every character in *Veronica Mars*, lending the series a marvellous thematic unity—no mean feat for such a complex storyline, especially one in the mystery and thriller genres, a form that traditionally has been more about surprise and suspense than character growth.

All this is to say, just as our American zeitgeist can be seen as the "United States" of Veronica, so too can the other characters on the show. Each reflects a different aspect of Veronica's character, whether it's her destructive and vengeful side, reflected in Duncan and Beaver, or her protective and generous side, reflected in Wallace and Keith.

Thus Veronica—and we—can use their good (and bad) examples to learn how to deal with our own sense of abandonment and isolation. But let's back up a moment to look at the big picture: exactly where did America's sense of abandonment and isolation come from?

"You Know, No One Seems to Care. I'm Practically an Orphan."

Just as 9/11 was the defining event for America's current sense of violation, the New Orleans flood was the defining event for America's current sense of abandonment. When Hurricane Katrina destroyed much of the Louisiana and Mississippi coastline and endangered thousands of American lives, national resources were *not* mobilized as efficiently as they were, say, to invade Afghanistan and Iraq to hunt down a comparatively small band of dangerous terrorists who turned out to have nothing to do with Iraq (surprise, surprise).

The New Orleans debacle and *Veronica Mars* have this in common: they bring to the surface an American theme that has been psychologically denied and barely kept in check for much of the present decade—namely, that many of our high-ranking authority figures, our political leaders, the "fathers" and "mothers" of our nation, may not truly care about protecting us, their citizen children, but may in fact be more interested in bending the truth and securing their own power base.

Like Lianne Mars when she abandoned Veronica without explanation and later stole her college funds, and like Woody Goodman after he sexually abused his Little Leaguers, our political leaders have left the scene of the crime. They have treated human beings, at home and abroad, as objects whose needs and subjectivity, whose very lives, are to be ignored, destroyed, or endangered. Is this who we want to be?

And although it's true that Lianne Mars was also trying to protect her daughter, her means did not justify her ends. She owed Veronica more information and better communication. Her weak moral fiber was only confirmed when she bolted again at the end of season one, violating Veronica by stealing her college fund and abandoning her by putting her own agenda first.

Welcome to Veronica's world. And welcome to the picture of our times: a selfish, abusive authority figure and his or her dependent child, a child whose resulting pain, rage, and drive for self-protection, if acted out—the way Beaver did in season two—will only repeat the cycle.

"The Getting Even Part? You Might Want to Rethink That One."

But getting from rage to its healthy release doesn't happen overnight. Witness our current decade. Our era is the scene of an epic inner struggle between the base instinct for revenge and higher moral ground. A few of us—like Veronica—will come out winners on the side of self-mastery and wisdom of choice. More than a few of us, however, will not.

Or am I being pessimistic? What if I'm wrong? What if most of us *will* overcome our drive for revenge? A girl can dream, can't she?

Early in the series, I wasn't sure whether Veronica had what it took to overcome her weakness—a weakness that I define as her drive for revenge and her inability to let down her guard and open her heart. "Here's what you do," Veronica told Meg, whose reputation was being dragged through the mud at Neptune High. "You get tough, you get even." Later in the same episode Meg told her, "Getting tough? Yeah, that was good advice. And I needed that. The getting even part? You might want to rethink that one." ("Like a Virgin," 1-8).

Meg had a good point. In season one, Veronica exacted revenge for offenses committed against her and those she loved, much in the way the U.S. bombed the Taliban out of power in Afghanistan after 9/11, hunting down and killing al-Qaeda members throughout the world. True, Veronica never resorted to murder, but she did get people arrested and publicly humiliated—and she got chastised for it by her peers.

By season two Veronica began learning from her mistakes. When she had the chance to take revenge on Jackie, for instance, by publicly outing the girl's father as a gambling addict, she decided against it. For someone as ensconced in her shell as Veronica, backing down like this takes extra guts because, for her, backing down is akin to admitting defeat, and admitting defeat means showing her throat, and showing her throat makes her vulnerable to getting it bitten again, just like when she was an innocent kid, powerless to defend herself against the people around her.

"I'm Asking You to Let It Go."

So now that we've diagnosed the American wound, how do we treat it?

The way I see it, *Veronica Mars* presents us with several coping strategies for dealing with our teen noir times, some of them effective, some of them less so. First the ineffective strategies:

We can (1) *laugh the problem off*, the way Logan did when he pretended he was accepting an Academy Award during his police line-up ("Oh, wow, I'm stunned. You like me! You really like me!" ["Rat Saw God," 2-6]]), which is only a partial solution—and I say this as a comic fiction writer—because laughing at something without also confronting its reality is a form of denial. Or we can (2) *numb out*, like Duncan did when he went catatonic after finding Lilly's body and later took antidepressants to avoid his feelings, another form of denial. Alternatively, we might (3) *grow an impenetrable shell*, the way Veronica did early in the series, a strategy that leads nowhere because toughening up without also opening up is as much of an opiate as Duncan's antidepressants. Or, just as ineffectively, we might (4) *flee responsibility*, as have the many deadbeat parents in *Veronica Mars*, leaving their children behind to fend for themselves. And finally, we might (5) *fight fire with an apocalypse*, the way Beaver did when he bombed the school bus, murdered Curly, and committed suicide (not an effective strategy, as the tragedy that is Iraq clearly shows).

So much for what *not* to do. Let's look at what works. While *Veronica Mars* presents more than a few positive strategies for healing the national psyche, three of them are key:

1) Allowing Pain, Truth, and Vulnerability

The truth can hurt. When Veronica broke down and cried behind the wheel of her LeBaron after visiting Abel Koontz in prison, I believe it was because she had finally opened her heart to the painful truth about her mother, who at some level just didn't care about Veronica (or at least not enough). Veronica learned from Koontz that her mother lied to her and that she herself might be Jake Kane's daughter and Duncan's sister. Just being reminded of her mother's lies and abandonment must have hurt, but instead of blocking the pain the way she had earlier in the series, she allowed herself to feel it.

Allowing vulnerability like this was an important step for Veronica. It let her more easily identify with and accept other characters who were suffering, and forgive them when they repented their crimes. This is harder to do than it sounds. In order to feel another person's pain, we first have to feel our own, a challenge for hardened people like Veronica who are afraid of lowering their guard.

But Veronica braved her fears, allowed the painful truth about her mother, and so by season two was able to sympathize with and even forgive Koontz, who'd perjured himself in court over Lilly's murder, thus helping to tear apart Veronica's family. Veronica's forgiveness of Koontz also allowed her natural generosity to come to the fore; she later helped him locate his daughter Amelia, fulfilling his dying wish, and allowed him to die believing Amelia was happy and healthy.

Veronica was also able to forgive Logan and risk trusting his love, a love which, to her way of thinking, might at any moment turn into an attack or be ripped away, as her mother's love had been.

> LOGAN: I'm the one who's responsible for what happened to you. And I can't take that I hurt you like that. I can't take that I hurt you when all I want to do is protect you....I want you to trust me.
> VERONICA: (softly) I do.
>
> ("Trip to the Dentist," 1-21)

Her love for Logan was only possible once she had allowed herself to identify with the full range of his humanity, including his suffering. And that, for Veronica especially, took guts. It's much easier to hate the person who has harmed you than to understand him.

Without such understanding, without sympathy (or "suffering with" in Greek), the milk of human kindness would sour, with war and vengeance as likely results.

2) Protecting our Innocence

Another positive strategy for treating the current malaise is to acknowledge and protect innocence—in ourselves and in others. Time and again, Veronica has been called on to learn the truth about an abused innocent, and if possible to protect that innocent. First there's her best friend Lilly, who in a sense stands for Veronica's innocence— something Veronica spends all of season one trying to regain by solving Lilly's murder. Then there's baby Lilly, Duncan's infant, who must be protected by Veronica and Duncan from ending up the victim of

Meg's parents, who locked their daughter Grace in a closet for extended periods to discipline her.

And yet again, there was the abandoned newborn in the Neptune High School bathrooms, a crime uncovered and exposed by Veronica twenty-five years later.

How does acknowledging our innocence help in the grand scheme of things? It calls forth our generosity and protective instincts—impulses that are life-affirming, not life-denying.

3) Releasing the Need for Revenge

Then there's the third and final strategy, *the* turning point task for healing what ails our times, and that is: releasing the need for revenge.

While revenge can feel protective and empowering in the moment, ultimately it's a dead end, as Veronica began to realize early in season two:

> VERONICA: So you got even? Is that it?
> BUTTERS: It looks that way.
> VERONICA: You're playing a dangerous game. Kelvin will take your head off if I tell him you're the reason he's off football this year.

("Normal Is the Watchword," 2-1)

Ironically, one of the psychological functions of detective fiction like *Veronica Mars* is to allow us to experience revenge vicariously—which we rationalize to ourselves as justice—and therefore to release extreme emotions like rage. It's a sort of steam valve on a pressure cooker, if you will.

This experience is what Aristotle in his *Poetics* calls "catharsis," a term he understood in a medical sense. According to Aristotle, spectators feel fictional dangers and sympathies so strongly that they show reactions like widened pupils and sweating hands. During a story's climactic scenes these reactions are at their most intense, and when the story concludes, resolving all conflicts, spectators experience a healthy physical release.

For Aristotle, catharsis also has a moral dimension. In his view, one of the strongest forms of catharsis is the reinstatement of moral rectitude, or justice. The more injustice an innocent character has experienced during the story, the greater the moral pleasure afforded the spectator when the scales of justice tip back in the victim's favor.

But if crime fiction is to say more about the human condition than just "let's sock it to the bad guys," if it is to reach the level of art, I believe it must also include a moral dimension that shows characters making existential choices for better or worse, the way they do in *Veronica Mars*. To take revenge, or not to take revenge. That is the question. Not just "Who done it?" and "Did they get away with it?"

And this is the crowning achievement of *Veronica Mars* as art and craft. The series seamlessly combines a character-driven storyline with a plot-driven one in such a way that we experience fear and hope for the victims as well as surprise and suspense during the story's many plot twists. In the end, the inner and outer stories come together in a grand finale each season, when inevitably, spectacularly, and (thank goodness) wisely, justice is done.

"Justice," Vincent "Butters" Clemmons told Veronica at the beginning of season two, "it can be a bitch" ("Normal Is the Watchword," 2-1). Yes, I agree. The bully's brand of justice can do more harm than good. But there's a difference between that kind of justice, which is closer to vengeance, and the tempered justice that occurs when a suspect receives a fair trial and a convicted killer is put behind bars. There's a difference, too, between the bully's brand of justice and karmic justice, described so well by Keith at the end of season two:

> KEITH: However wrong it turned out, it's done. We're people with lives, and we will not obsess. We move on. Aaron Echolls will get his justice in his own way.
> VERONICA: You really believe that?
> KEITH: Yes.
>
> ("Not Pictured," 2-22)

Maybe Keith was right. Maybe justice doesn't need us. Maybe it will take care of itself. Meanwhile, back on earth, mere humans like me and Veronica have to battle the instinctive drive to strike back against both real and perceived attacks. I don't know what I would have done out on that rooftop of the Grand Neptune Hotel at the end of season two (probably run back downstairs screaming), but I'm glad that by then Veronica's moral fiber had grown strong enough to pass this ultimate test:

> LOGAN: Veronica, don't.
> VERONICA: (crying) He killed my father!
> LOGAN: Now give me the gun, Veronica.
> VERONICA: He killed everyone on the bus! He raped me!
> LOGAN: Look, you are not a killer, Veronica. Give me the gun.
>
> ("Not Pictured," 2-22)

Veronica had the chance to kill Beaver then, but didn't. She overcame her true weakness—not her vulnerability, but her need for revenge—and she let Logan take the gun from her hand. In other words, she won the real battle against the real enemy—not against the killer, but against the killer in herself.

"Can You Feel the Love?"

At the risk of over-romanticizing American culture, the way German patriots did in the thirties when they spiritualized concepts like *Zeitgeist* and *Volkgeist*, I'd like to posit that Veronica is a hero for our times, and that when she and all of us who emulate her fulfill our inner need, when we give up our anger at having been abandoned and violated and release our need for revenge, we will be able to experience more love and hope, and our teen noir era will come to an end. A new American era will then emerge, with new lessons to be learned and new heroes to live them out for us, leading the way.

> Author and screenwriter **DEANNA CARLYLE** writes comedy, mysteries, and thrillers. She is the winner of the James D. Phelan Literary Award and co-founder of the International Women's Fiction Festival held each year in Matera, Italy. Visit her online at http://www.deannacarlyle.com.

References

Hiltunen, Ari. *Aristotle in Hollywood.* Exeter, England: Intellect Books, 2002.

Parker, Philip. *The Art and Science of Screenwriting.* Exeter, England: Intellect Books, 1999.

Scaruffi, Piero. "A time-line of the USA." *Piero Scaruffi's Home page* 2006. <http://www.scaruffi.com/politics/american.html>.

Full disclosure: *I'm not a car guy. I don't know much about cars. My assistant Alex and writer Phil Klemmer generally make decisions about the cars we use in the show. I've made a few of the calls. The LeBaron was modeled after the car my then-girlfriend (now wife) drove, and it was motivated primarily by the need for a convertible Veronica could afford with a back seat large enough to allow Backup to jump and attack a PCHer in the pilot episode.*

As for Mr. Daniels's car, I was inspired by the movie Election. *I wanted to see a teacher who walks out into the parking lot and sees 90 percent of his students driving nicer cars than he can afford.*

Lawrence Watt-Evans

I'm in Love with My Car
Automotive Symbolism
on Veronica Mars

NEPTUNE, CALIFORNIA—A COASTAL town somewhere not too far from San Diego. It's fairly typical of southern California in many ways, deliberately so. It's got its share of the very wealthy—movie stars, software millionaires—but most of the town isn't so fortunate. If you work your way down to the bottom of the social ladder, you'll find the Hispanic families who supply the wealthy with maids and gardeners.

In Veronica's voiceover introduction in the pilot episode of *Veronica Mars*, she told us Neptune has no middle class—just the wealthy and the people who clean their homes and tend their gardens. This isn't literally true, by any means, as we see plenty of schoolteachers, mechanics, and the like, but it's uncomfortably close.

Perhaps as a result, the people of Neptune, including the students at Neptune High, take social status very seriously. They're always alert to the markers that indicate who's better than whom—the clothes they wear, the accents in their speech, their manners, the cars they drive....

Oh, yeah. Definitely the cars they drive. In Neptune, what you drive tells the world who you are. And someone at the show clearly put a lot of thought into who drives what.

Once upon a time, if they showed cars at all, TV shows would typically give every character a fairly generic vehicle; often, every car on a given show would come from a single manufacturer, who provided them free as part of an advertising deal. The closing credits would include a line like, "Vehicles courtesy of Ford Motor Company," and every character would drive a different model of new Ford.

This is far less common than it used to be; I'm not sure any scripted shows still do it, though reality shows do. I'm very glad that the producers of *Veronica Mars* didn't try it, though, because the vehicles here add significant flavor to the show and tell the viewer something about the characters.

Everyone on *Veronica Mars* drives—which is hardly surprising in modern America, but if you think about it, it's far from universal on TV shows. Does anyone on, say, *How I Met Your Mother* own a car? Can you identify the make of a single character's vehicle (excluding Dr. House's motorcycle) on *House*, even though it's set well out in the New Jersey suburbs? Buffy Summers didn't have a car; the sisters on *Charmed* teleported everywhere; the doctors on *Grey's Anatomy* apparently drive but we almost never see the vehicles. Cars are far less visible in TV Land than in the real world.

And when cars do appear, especially if they're important story elements, they tend to be so eccentric as to almost be characters in their own right—Batman's Batmobile, the General Lee on *The Dukes of Hazzard*, or even Giles's battered 1963 Citroën on *Buffy the Vampire Slayer*. You can find fan Web sites devoted to these vehicles, just as if they were characters. In the most extreme cases, the cars *are* characters, like KITT on *Knight Rider* or the 1928 Porter on *My Mother the Car*.

But on *Veronica Mars* that's not the case. The cars are cars, all recognizable as real world vehicles, neither ignored nor elevated to iconic status. They're not exaggerated, but they're important. There are as many scenes in the high school parking lot as there are in class, as many scenes in cars as in homes. Everyone owns a car, and everyone *cares* about his or her car. Each one fits the character's personality and circumstances.

For example, Veronica herself drives a Chrysler LeBaron convertible, an American classic "fun" car, a car that represents the stereotypical laid-back California lifestyle—wind in the hair, sun on the face. It's not a sports car; she's not into speed and power for its own sake.

It's not an import; she's an all-American girl. Nothing too expensive; she's not an 09er, not one of the rich kids. It's black and white, not anything too flashy. A good car, representing the good life—but it's a 1998 model, not anything recent, because not only was her family never really rich, but that good life all went away when Lilly Kane was murdered. Veronica's car is a leftover, a relic, a reminder of what she *used* to have.

It's also convenient for the writers to have her driving a convertible, of course; she can hop in and out as the script demands, or keep the top up when needed. She even has a blue cover she can pull over it when she needs privacy.

What she doesn't have is a cute name for her car, or any special gadgets or modifications. It's not a character. It's a LeBaron. She calls it "my car," or, at least once, "the LeBaron."

Name another TV show where the protagonist refers to his or her car by model. I can't think of one. But plenty of people in the real world do exactly that.

The other major characters are also all appropriately wheeled. Duncan Kane, being the rich but quiet sort that he is, drives a new gray Mercedes M-Class SUV, redolent of power, quality, and class.

Logan Echolls drives an SUV as well, but it's much flashier—a bright yellow Nissan Xterra, advertised as a fun car. Hardly in the same price range as Duncan's Mercedes, but newer and more costly than Veronica's LeBaron and able to hold all his buddies.

Why SUVs? The traditional expensive toy for rich Californians is a sports car, of course, not an SUV—the sort of sports car that Aaron Echolls, that walking collection of unfortunate Hollywood clichés, drives. Aaron *of course* drives a high-end sports car, specifically an Aston-Martin; the only surprise is that it's cream-colored, rather than cherry red, and that we never see him with a blonde in the passenger seat, showing off her cleavage. Aaron plays the part of the movie star to the hilt, and loves it.

But Duncan and Logan don't drive sports cars. Duncan isn't into any sort of unnecessary display; he likes his privacy, and doesn't want to show off. The quiet gray SUV suits him. But he still wants quality, and isn't trying to hide his money any more than he wants to flaunt it, so his SUV is a Mercedes.

It might be theorized, actually, that Duncan didn't pick the car out himself, that his parents bought it for him; apparently he shared it with Lilly, which would seem unlikely if he'd bought it on his own. (It's a safe bet *Lilly* didn't buy it—there's no way she'd have chosen something so tame.) Probably Jake and Celeste Kane chose a "safe" car for the son they were determined to protect. Still, whoever chose it, it fits Duncan's personality.

Logan, meanwhile, is determined not to be like his father—or anyone else, for that matter. That yellow Xterra stands out anywhere, and proclaims Logan's refusal to conform to *anyone's* expectations.

Another point about an SUV—there's plenty of room to get cozy with a girlfriend without bumping heads or worrying about impaling yourself on the gearshift, which is not generally the case with a sports car. Aaron Echolls, of course, doesn't worry about such details, since he's got his mansion where he can take his girlfriends—including a pool house wired for video....

Moving on to the parents of other Neptune High students, Keith Mars drives a drab Ford sedan—but then, as a private eye, he needs something unobtrusive. I've never managed to make out just what sort of Ford it is, only that it's dark and nondescript.

The last time we saw her, Lianne Mars drove a beat-up 1971 Plymouth Satellite Sebring because she'd been beaten down by life—it's a cheap old car, and indicated that she didn't much care about anything anymore.

Jake Kane drives a spiffy new Land Rover—expensive, tough, slightly exotic, but not showy or frivolous.

Celeste Kane's car is actually the first parent's car we see—a red Jaguar. She *does* fit the red sports-car stereotype, showy and expensive, complete with a vanity plate reading KANE2 that lets Veronica identify it immediately and beyond question when she sees it parked outside the Mars Investigations office. This car may be why Aaron Echolls's car isn't red—they wouldn't want to confuse anyone. Though anyone who can't tell a Jaguar from an Aston-Martin....

But then, Lynn Echolls drives a red sports car, too—a red Dodge Viper, license ECHOLLS2. Nowhere near as nice a car as Celeste's Jag, though; it's sort of a cheap imitation, right down to the license plate. It's nowhere near as nice a car as Aaron's Aston-Martin, either; Aaron clearly keeps the best for himself, and Lynn has to make do with what he allows her.

And then there's Eli "Weevil" Navarro, the outsider, the trouble-maker, who doesn't have a car at all for most of the first two seasons; instead, he rides a motorcycle.

Someone obviously worked these vehicular choices out carefully, and didn't just grab whatever was on the studio lot, but even so, there's no deliberate emphasis on the choices. No one ever says, "Nice car!" or the like; cars are recognized, certainly, but no one makes a point of commenting on them.

Furthermore, throughout the series cars act as their owners' stand-ins, as well as reflecting their personalities. In the pilot, when Veronica planted a bong in Logan's locker, Logan's father punished him by taking away the Xterra (though apparently only briefly, as it was back by the next episode). We found out later in the series that Aaron is perfectly capable of taking a belt to his son, and probably of far worse, but in this case he chose a less direct punishment, one that seemed to get to Logan just as effectively as a beating.

When Logan wanted to retaliate against Veronica for that stunt, he didn't touch *her*; he smashed out the headlights of her LeBaron with a tire iron. Then, when Weevil came to her defense, he did hit Logan, but he also took that same tire iron to the hood of the Chevy SUV Logan and his friends came in, even though he was told it wasn't Logan's. He seemed to feel that if someone hit Veronica's car, then a car must be hit in retaliation, even if it was not the car he'd have preferred.

A few episodes later, in "The Girl Next Door" (1-7), when the temporarily allied Logan and Weevil wanted to retaliate against Mr. Daniels, the teacher who had been giving them a hard time, they did so by impaling his car on the school's flagpole—and the phallic symbolism, the obvious implied "fuck you," is hard to miss.

Incidentally, the car in question is an ugly little blue econobox, probably a Geo Metro, which nicely suits Daniels's rather self-righteous and fun-squelching attitude.

This car-as-proxy business lets the show's creators depict violence without showing blood, or without getting into the typical Hollywood fantasy of two guys trading punches and then walking away unhurt—whacking someone's car shows the capability for serious violence without making one character an irredeemable bastard and without putting anyone in the hospital. That's a useful tool for the writers!

It's hardly the only use they have for cars. Cars are all over the series. They not only reflect and stand in for their owners—they represent wealth and freedom to their owners, as well.

In "You Think You Know Somebody" (1-5), Troy faked the theft of his father's BMW 740i in order to (a) steal the car, and (b) use it to retrieve the $8,000 worth of illegal steroids he'd stolen from his friend Luke and stashed outside of town, in a scheme to get away from parents he saw as stifling him.

Mac's motive for sending out the purity test in "Like A Virgin" (1-8) was to raise money to buy herself a new car—which she did, replacing her ancient and barely functional 1963 Ford Ranchero, which didn't suit her at all, with a spiffy new VW Beetle that nicely reflects who she is.

Terrence Cook collects fancy cars, which reflect his wealth and success more than his own identity—but then, he identifies himself pretty strongly as wealthy and successful. He rents a hangar to store them, which is where incriminating evidence was planted—his display of wealth made him a target. The man who tended to the vehicles testified that the evidence wasn't there all along, however, proving that someone was setting Cook up. The fact that Cook takes care of his cars, that they aren't purely window dressing, saved him.

There's another thing that cars do—they identify people literally as well as symbolically. Right at the start of the pilot Veronica knew Celeste Kane was in the Mars Investigation offices, because the red Jaguar was at the curb.

And of course, the first evidence that Lynn Echolls had killed herself at the end of "Clash of the Tritons" (1-12) was when her red Dodge was found abandoned on the Coronado Bridge, the door standing open. Her body was never found, but the car was there.

Although Lynn was gone without a trace, in the course of the series any number of people *are* located by tracking down their cars— Veronica found Lianne Mars (or at least where she'd been) in Arizona by running her plates, Liam Fitzpatrick was linked to his crimes through his grandmother's green Barracuda, and so on.

People are identified with their cars. In "Kanes and Abel's" (1-17), when Sabrina Fuller asked Veronica whether she knew Caz Truman, Veronica responded, "Basketball player? Drives a Yukon?"

Cars are potent symbols throughout of things other than their owners as well. I've already mentioned the symbolism of impaling Mr. Daniels's car on a flagpole, but that's just the start.

When Weevil left the PCH biker gang behind, he bought himself a car—he was trying to fit into normal society, no longer the angry outsider. He was out to leave all that outcast stuff behind, ready to walk across the stage at graduation and get his diploma.

It didn't work, of course, but still, the car was a symbol of his desire to fit in.

In "A Trip to the Dentist" (1-21), Duncan's reaction to seeing Veronica and Logan together, and being told that anyone who has a problem with them being a couple should leave, was to go back out to his Mercedes—and when he found he'd locked himself out he smashed his car's windows in a berserk fury, a symbolic act of self-destruction.

Cars as extensions of self, cars as symbols of power, freedom, and wealth—it's all amazingly well thought-out and consistent. In fact, the cars are treated far more realistically and consistently than other elements, such as the Mars dog, Backup. Backup only appears when his presence is necessary to the plot—when Veronica needs a way to defend herself she takes Backup with her, when she needs a reason to leave the house she walks him, and so on, but we never see him climb on her lap when she's sitting at home, he never barks when someone comes to the apartment door, and there's never a scene of Veronica or Keith feeding the dog while they talk. The LeBaron gets more screen time and better treatment than the dog, and is more consistent; two different dogs played the role of Backup, while the LeBaron has never changed.[1]

In a way, that's no surprise. Southern California is famous for its love of cars, and *Veronica Mars* is very, very Californian. Many TV series seem a little vague about where they're set, but *Veronica Mars* never is—the beaches, the outdoor school cafeteria, the movie stars, the Hispanic housekeepers, all of it is redolent of southern California. Getting every detail of the cars right is a part of that, and someone did a first-rate job of it. It's impressive, and a general sign of the care and thoughtfulness that went into making the series. Everything fits together into a coherent whole.

---

[1] *Editor's Note from Rob:* Regarding Backup.... We switched dogs because we weren't happy with the level of training on the first dog. We generally only use Backup when we need a stunt, because it costs a ton of money to have a dog trainer and dog on set. It adds hours of shooting time that we don't have. It's not a failure of intent; it's a financial reality.

That's part of what makes *Veronica Mars* so special as a series—*everything* fits together. Characters glimpsed in one scene may turn out to be important several episodes later; throwaway jokes turn out to be vital clues—*anything* may have an unexpected significance.

On other shows, cars serve a few basic functions—as settings for private conversations, as plot devices (like the General Lee), as bits of characterization (like Alison Dubois's Volvo wagon), as cheap gags (like Giles's Citroën). On *Veronica Mars* they do *all* these things, constantly, and others besides. No other TV show has ever come close to making such extensive use of vehicles as a way to communicate important information to the audience. Where most shows treat cars as props, in some ways, *Veronica Mars* treats them more like costumes.

It's one of the things that makes the show such a rich and involving experience. When someone has taken the time and effort to make sure even something as commonplace as the cars the minor characters drive is absolutely right, it adds a depth and realism most shows never approach. That level of detail, that complexity, is what makes *Veronica Mars* so fascinating. It's so *satisfying* to see every car be just what it should be.

The only thing I could never quite figure out is why Dick Casablancas drives an Audi.

> NOTE: Scott Fisher provided invaluable aid in precisely identifying some of the cars.

> LAWRENCE WATT-EVANS is the author of some three dozen novels and more than 100 short stories, mostly in the fields of fantasy, science fiction, and horror. He won the Hugo Award for Short Story in 1988 for "Why I Left Harry's All-Night Hamburgers," served as president of the Horror Writers Association from 1994 to 1996, treasurer of SFWA from 2003 to 2004, and lives in Maryland. He has one kid in college, one teaching English in China, and shares his home with Chanel, the obligatory writer's cat.

It's been repeated many times. Logan was never supposed to be a Veronica love interest. I created him to be the antagonist—the "psychotic jackass" who would foster confrontation and keep Veronica in her place (which, certainly, was not at the 09er table).

When Jason Dohring came in to audition for the first time, it was one of the most powerful auditions I've ever witnessed. Because we didn't have that much dialogue for him in the pilot, I wrote an additional audition scene in which Aaron picks Logan up from school after Veronica gets him expelled for the bong in his locker. In the scene, Aaron has Logan push in the cigarette lighter, and the audience realizes as Logan loses his composure what Aaron plans to do with the lighter. Jason was spellbinding. (He always wanted to perform that scene in the show. It was replaced by the scene of choosing a belt with which to be whipped. I believe the cigarette lighter scene would've led people to believe Aaron was the murderer too early in the series.)

Still, even knowing how good Jason was, I didn't foresee a Veronica/Logan romance until we started seeing them onscreen together. There was a shared pain and a shared disdain for everything they saw around them that was—to quote Catcher in the Rye—"phony."

I wasn't actually pleased with the first Veronica/Logan kiss. Now, I may have been wrong on this front, but it wasn't what I imagined, or really what I think was described in the script. The line of description called for Logan to "devour" Veronica. I wanted it to be—I don't know if sexual is the right word, but—hungry, or a release, or mixed with some self-loathing and confusion. Instead, it came off as singularly romantic. Now the post-kiss moment of the two of them regarding each other—that was everything I hoped for.

It's funny to watch Kristen and Jason "act" together, because they approach their craft so differently. They're both incredibly dedicated, but Kristen can turn it on and off. Jason is very method-y. He works himself up before a scene. You can kind of see Jason disappear and Logan replace him before we shoot a scene. There's the famous anecdote of Laurence Olivier saying to a young Dustin Hoffman, "Have you ever tried just 'acting'?" You could replace Olivier with Kristen and Hoffman with Jason, and you'd have the dynamic between our two stars.

Jason has told me that he hates saying, "I love you" onscreen. The good news is that I hate writing it, so we're a good pair. That said, he delivers it beautifully in "Lord of the Pi's" (3–8). Of course, at the time, he's angry at Veronica.

That's just how they roll.

Misty Hook

Boom Goes the Dynamite
Why I Love Veronica and Logan

I FIRST STARTED WATCHING *Veronica Mars* during the summer reruns following the first season. My sister, who is intimately familiar with my championship of female empowerment, could not believe I wasn't watching a show that prominently featured a strong, intelligent, sassy woman. She also kept mentioning that it was the best show on TV. So, to humor her, I agreed to watch. She was right. I liked it. It was smart, funny, poignant, highly entertaining, and extremely well-acted. Kristen Bell in particular was a joy to watch. I looked forward to it every week but I wasn't obsessed. I sometimes only just remembered that it was on. That wee bit of sanity about the show, however, remained only until The Kiss, which is what diehard shippers (as in those who favor specific relationships) call the first time Veronica and Logan Echolls locked lips. After that, I was a goner. I bought the first season DVDs, joined fan forums, attended a fan event in Austin, read fanfiction about the couple, and eagerly scoured the Internet for all things *Veronica Mars*. The night UPN ran the show became *Veronica Mars* Night and no one was allowed to talk to me until I'd finished watching the episode. I had never done these types of things before and am not usually a gung-ho kind of person, so I was puzzled as to why I was so mesmerized.

Veronica Mars has a lot of fascinating aspects: humor, great plots and dialogue, a solid father-daughter bond, gender reversals, physical and emotional abuse, class issues, scrappy underdogs, cross-racial relationships, and of course, the obligatory romance and mystery. However, it is the relationship between Veronica and Logan that truly captivates me and, let's face it, they are the real reason I watch. Perhaps I am crazy to be so enamored by a fictional romantic relationship, but I am not alone in my insanity. Logan and Veronica's relationship has spawned several Web sites, generated hundreds of fanfiction stories, and even had critics raving about the chemistry between the two. Fans of the show are so passionate about the pairing that even the show's producers reacted by deciding to feature Logan more prominently as a love interest for Veronica. The CW, their new network, responded by including both Kristen Bell and Jason Dohring in their promos for the show. So what is it about this particular relationship that makes it so compelling? Why does it seem that, in many ways, it is the Veronica and Logan twosome that drives the show itself?

Chemistry

One of the obvious draws for the relationship is the incredible chemistry that Veronica and Logan have with each other. Television critics never fail to mention it and even fans who are not crazy about the pairing admit that it is there. Chemistry is one of those things that is hard to describe in words but, just like pornography (as one Supreme Court justice famously said), you know it when you see it. It's kind of like the feeling in the air during a lightning storm: there is a sense of anticipation, an inability to look away, and an intense excitement about what is going to happen next. The writers for *Veronica Mars* were quick to capitalize on this chemistry. The original plan was for Duncan to be Veronica's love interest; Logan was not supposed to be a prominent player. However, after watching the dailies of Veronica and Logan, the writers realized they had hit the chemistry jackpot. The fact that the screen just explodes whenever Veronica and Logan interact was evident even in the pilot, when the two were enemies. The audience was supposed to hate Logan for all the horrible things he had done and was doing to Veronica but you couldn't help but want to see more of the two of them together; there was the sense that their mutual animosity wasn't telling the whole story. By "The Wrath of Con" (1-4), the Homecoming flashbacks of the "Fab Four" made it clear that Veronica and Logan's relationship was complex, and that even when they were both romantically involved with other people, they couldn't hide the chemistry they share. It doesn't seem to matter how they are relating to each other, whether through sarcasm and biting wit or physical contact—their scenes together just ooze sexual tension. Indeed, some of the more powerful scenes of the two of them together are nonverbal: the look they gave each other after Lilly's memorial video was shown, the stares they exchanged after they kissed for the first time, and their silent dance together in "Plan B" (2-17).

Part of what makes their chemistry so potent is the heightened awareness Logan and Veronica have of each other. This attentiveness is something you expect to see between people who are in love or even just in lust. Our interactions with potential lovers are just different than those we share with our friends, parents, or acquaintances. For whatever reason—be it a magnetic pull, pheromones, or something else—attraction affords us the ability to be strongly connected to a person, so much so that we often know where he or she is without even being aware of it. Logan in particular has honed this ability. He always seems to know where Veronica is, whether she is staring at the 09er table in the quad, talking to a possible boyfriend by her locker, on the beach walking Backup, being held down and threatened on a pool table, or mingling at a crowded dance. As the less emotionally aware partner, Veronica is not as practiced at this ability as Logan, but she still has it. When she was looking for Logan at their graduation party, just recall the way that, despite having to plough through a crowd of people in a room full of music and conversation while simultaneously talking on the phone, she walked directly to him ("Not Pictured," 2-22). Sensory overload alone would have dictated a need to search for him among the crush of her classmates, but she knew exactly where he was. She could feel him.

This heightened awareness also includes perceptiveness about your partner's facial expressions, eye contact, verbal inflections, and general body movement. You become tuned into what is going on with the other person and you respond in kind. This is one of the reasons Veronica and Logan were able to be so successfully hurtful toward each other during the first season. Both of them knew almost intuitively what would most wound the other because they could read the damage in each other's eyes and face. Other people could be deceived into thinking that neither Logan nor Veronica were injured by the verbal putdowns or mean-spirited pranks (since both have mastered tough external personas) but the two of them were never fooled. Thus, in the pilot episode, Logan knew exactly how much he was hurting Veronica when he mocked her mother's alcoholism, while Veronica was very aware that Logan would rather take a beating from Weevil than apologize to her.

When their relationship morphed into something more positive, this perceptiveness increased and it became like the steps of an intricate dance. When dancing with a partner, you must anticipate his or her actions: when he pushes you pull, when she goes forward you step back, and sometimes you must simply follow the other person's lead. Veronica and Logan seem to do this dance effortlessly. For example, when Veronica was telling Logan at the end of season one in "A Trip to the Dentist" (1-21) about what had happened to her the night of Shelly Pomroy's party, their dance was in full swing. Veronica began with a push ("I'm so sorry . . .") while Logan responded with a pull ("It's fine. You OK?"). Logan then went forward ("You find something out?") while Veronica stepped back ("I was drugged but I wasn't...."). Later, stunned by Aaron's surprise party and their being outed as a couple, Veronica followed Logan's lead. He held out his hand and she took it. In both scenes, their dance did their talking for them and conversation was so unnecessary that any words were solely for the benefit of the audience.

The very ease with which they are capable of interacting makes those scenes where their interaction is *not* easy incredibly painful. When Veronica suspected Logan of murdering Lilly in "Leave It to Beaver" (1-22), their dance by his locker became stilted. He moved forward ("If you need to do whatever, just let me know.") but she dodged left ("I need to do whatever."). Logan pushed ("Knowing what we do about Duncan, I don't want to believe that it could have been him but it's the only thing that makes sense, right?"), but instead of pulling, Veronica refused to go along ("I don't know."). Finally, he kissed her, but instead of following his lead, Veronica simply looked down. In that scene, Veronica's intentional missteps, and the change they caused in the pair's normally smooth interaction, hurt to watch. In season two, their dance stumbled in the beginning but, as Logan and Veronica worked their way back to each other, their dance again became evident. Conversations were held in close proximity and their bodies started to mirror each other's until, at last, they were twirling together once again.

Body Language

While their awareness of each other makes their onscreen interactions feel both natural and inevitable, it is the ways in which they respond to each other unconsciously, physically, that really make the pairing sizzle. Although there are other couples who possess good sexual chemistry, I can think of no other couple who responds so completely to one another other at such a basic physical level. Kristen Bell and Jason Dohring deserve the credit here, as we can almost see Veronica and Logan's relationship unfold through only their body language.

Although she spends much of the first two seasons fighting against their attraction, Veronica is clearly affected by Logan, and her body gives her away. Her breathing changes, her face freezes, and her body tenses, at least until she gets herself under control. This is especially true when Logan catches her off guard. When Weevil asked Veronica to bug a confessional in "Rashard and Wallace Go to White Castle" (2-12), Veronica certainly didn't expect Logan to be with him. As she became aware of Logan, she took a deep breath, straightened her body, and kept her facial expression blank until she was able to begin snarking at him. Similarly, when Logan put the "Out of Order" sign on the restroom door in "Nobody Puts Baby in a Corner" (2-7), Veronica's version of the Bat Signal, her face was almost completely blank as she spoke with him. It was only after he'd shown his hurt and started to leave that she showed any facial or vocal animation.

In fact, her responses to Logan are often as bland as she can make them; unlike with Weevil or Dick Casablancas, or any number of other students who have challenged or insulted her over the course of the show, she usually responds to Logan's taunts with silence rather than the patented Mars verbal put-down. In the pilot episode, she remained quiet while he was taunting her in the quad and again when he was mocking her mother's alcoholism. Even when he was breaking her car's headlights, she was silent until he forced her to speak. In season two, Veronica didn't say one word to Logan until the third episode. She endured his obvious hurt when he saw her by the school bus with Duncan ("I'm gonna miss you!" ["Normal Is the Watchword," 2-1]) and Logan's ridicule of Duncan's sexual prowess ("FYI, if the cuddling was the best part, he didn't do it right." ["Driver Ed," 2-2]) without comment. It was almost as if she didn't trust herself to speak because, if she did, her response might reveal her to be more affected than the taunts would warrant from anyone else. It is in these silences that Veronica gives herself away most clearly. Perhaps the best example came during Logan's drunken declaration of love during Alterna-Prom ("Look Who's Stalking," 2-20). As Logan reached up to touch her face, Veronica half turned away and gave a shaky sigh that spoke volumes about both her uncertainty and her longing to believe his words were true.

While Logan is more honest with himself than Veronica, he too has engaged in self-deception about his true feelings, and like Veronica, his body continually gives him away. In early season one, despite their status as enemies, Logan's body acknowledged what he in his conscious mind would not: he was attracted to Veronica. Whenever they interacted, Logan always looked at Veronica just a beat too long and this intense stare always made it seem as if he was hungry for contact, even if the only contact he could elicit from her was negative. His facial expressions, wild hand gestures, and sarcastic tone also are dead giveaways that he is conflicted internally. When Logan does not want anyone to know how hurt he is, the dramatics enter in full force. Thus, when Veronica found him in the pool house in order to question him about the poker game in "An Echolls' Family Christmas" (1-10), Logan threw his hands about, asked snidely about her super sleuth kit, and ended with his now famous "Annoy like the wind!" and accompanying gesture. Similarly, when Veronica tried to question Logan about the phone call about the bus crash that came from his house, he broke out the evil mustache twirling and sarcasm, then pretended to look at a non-existent watch as he exited the conversation ("Green Eyed Monster," 2-4). Suffice it to say, when Logan is upset and wants to hide, his acting roots go into full bloom.

However, while Logan's theatrics are his coping method of choice, they aren't his body's only way of revealing his feelings. Whenever Logan is uncertain or hurt, he hangs his head like small children do when they are scolded. Recall his response when Veronica asked him to leave her alone with the federal agent who had just basically kidnapped her (and who Logan had just punched out in an attempt to save her): Logan's head dropped and, with hesitation, he obeyed. When Veronica boarded the bus with Duncan to go on the field trip in "Normal Is the Watchword" (2-1), Logan hung his head before waving goodbye to them. In moments like these, Logan's impulses are battling his mind for dominance, and his posture reflects this internal struggle. With him and with Veronica, part of the fun of watching is waiting to see how and when those impulses will win out.

Psychological Complexity

This kind of physical believability, however, is not enough; characters can push and pull and alter their breathing all they want, but if there's no psychological depth to their relationship, it's just not worth watching. As a psychologist, I always watch to see whether television characters truly reflect the complexity of real people. If, as is usually the case, the characters are two-dimensional (whether good or bad), I become bored and quickly stop watching. Veronica and Logan are not like this and it is a big part of the reason they are so mesmerizing. Through the course of the first season, we got the rare opportunity to observe their family dynamics and truly understand why they each act the way that they do. At first it was puzzling to see their transformation from the seemingly light-hearted people they were before Lilly's death to the morally ambiguous and angry people they became after. People usually don't change that drastically, no matter how traumatic the event; thus the darkness that emerged in them after Lilly died had to have already been part of their personalities. So where did that darkness come from? Once both Logan and Veronica were revealed to be the children of alcoholic mothers, that darkness made sense, and I became excited that, unlike in other shows in which addiction is used to service the plot, in *Veronica Mars* we were going to see the true psychological aftermath of a dysfunctional family.

That both Veronica and Logan are living out that aftermath, not just one or the other, is just perfect. People who have alcoholism in their families tend to be attracted to those who come from the same background, and this is definitely true of these two. Both of them are children of alcoholics and display certain characteristics associated with this, but interestingly, they do so in ways that are complementary rather than similar. Veronica has difficulty expressing emotion, but Logan does not. Veronica finds it hard to relax while Logan relaxes too much. Veronica is overly responsible, and Logan is not responsible enough. Logan exhibits sensation seeking (hello, bum fights!); Veronica radiates calm and, unless openly challenged, remains largely unobtrusive. Logan demonstrates excessive loyalty to his friends while Veronica's ties are often too easily broken by her suspicion and distrust (just think of her willingness to think the worst of Logan, *twice*, at the end of season one). Veronica and Logan both fear loss of control and want people to need them but, again, this is displayed in complementary ways. Veronica wants people to need her in a professional capacity while Logan prefers people to need him emotionally. It is this complexity in response to similar dysfunctional dynamics that is one of the magnetic links that connects Logan and Veronica. They recognize the darkness in one another and are irresistibly drawn to and comforted by it. It is familiar to them and, as such, they actively seek it out.

The darkness also contributes to one of my favorite aspects (and one of the most unusual for TV) of the Veronica and Logan relationship: they're not sweet. They are sarcastic, cynical, and vengeful, and often do not hesitate to use other people to further their own agendas. While they each have their own brand of ethics, their own moral compasses, their threshold for "wrong" is quite lower than is comfortable for most people. That moral complexity makes them fascinating. It's also is what makes them perfect for each other. They are both so powerful, so larger-than-life, that no one else we've seen has succeeded in being what either of them needs. Veronica needs a man who can match her in strength of character, someone she can trust who is not afraid to have her take the lead at times and who can accept her for who she is, warts and all. None of the other romantic pairings Veronica has had throughout the series could meet these criteria. Troy was not trustworthy and Leo was too passive. Duncan never seemed to fully accept her for who she had become. He was either surprised by her skills (as when he didn't believe that she was truly investigating the theft of the poker money in "An Echolls Family Christmas," [1-10] or intimidated by her strength as demonstrated by his dream about Meg and Veronica in "Ahoy Mateys," [2-8]). Only Logan has proven himself to be strong, proactive, trustworthy (when it counts), and capable of loving the Veronica we know now.

At the same time, Veronica is the only woman who can handle Logan. None of Logan's other romantic partners understood the full range of his personality. Lilly didn't appreciate his sweetness, Hannah didn't get his cruelty, and neither Caitlin Ford nor Kendall Casablancas cared about anything other than his money and sexual prowess. Veronica can keep up with his multifaceted personality and match him quip for quip, and she demands things from him that others let slide. She looks beyond his "psychotic jackass" facade to see the wounded and empathic boy underneath, but is not impressed by his wealth or social status and insists that he act decently. Most of all, Veronica gives him the one thing most people withhold from Logan: trust. Of course, this trust was not given overnight (in fact, for all of season one, she actively *distrusted* him) but when push came to shove at the end of season two, Veronica trusted him with her life and, soon after, with her heart.

Thanks to all of this, Veronica and Logan are something rare in the land of television: a three-dimensional couple. While they can be funny and gentle, they're not all sweetness and light. While they can be morally questionable and thoughtless, they're not all darkness. Like the rest of us, they live in the gray areas.

Growth

Complexity, however, is not only about character traits. It's also about character *growth*. *Veronica Mars* allows us to see that growth. Characters who begin the season one way do not end it in the same way; there is movement. Nowhere is this more evident than with Logan and Veronica because their relationship serves as a catalyst for their development.

At the show's start, Logan was set up as emblematic of the kind of treatment that made Veronica who she is today. However, while the rest of the 09ers' behavior toward Veronica was appalling, the fact that it was *Logan* who was leading the charge against her hurt the most because he, unlike the others, mattered to Veronica. In the pre-show flashbacks, we see Veronica mainly interacting with Lilly, Duncan, and Logan. The other 09ers were peripheral at best. Then Lilly died, Duncan became a zombie, and only Logan was left. Since those we love are the ones who can hurt us the most, it was Logan who had the most power to damage Veronica. Thus, while Veronica could have endured the antipathy of those she cared little for, it was Logan's treatment of her that caused Veronica to, as she put it to Meg in "Like a Virgin" (1-8), "get tough." Logan also helped keep Lilly's murder fresh in her mind. Duncan's behavior toward her had changed before Lilly's death, so it was Logan's transformation from goofball to jackass that reminded Veronica how, as the theme song says, they used to be friends.

Veronica shaped Logan just as much as he did her. Veronica started off as his friend but then he believed she betrayed him first by telling Lilly about Logan's extracurricular kiss with Yolanda ("Lord of the Bling," 1-13) and again when she stood by her father in his suspicion of the Kanes. This double betrayal caused Logan to focus his grief and anger into active cruelty; Veronica was a constant reminder of his loss and an easy target for his pain. Later, Veronica's willingness to help him look for his mother, despite the last year of hurt between them, seemed to cause him to soften. Similarly, it was Veronica's suspicion of Logan for murder that triggered Logan's self-destructive behavior at the beginning of season two—and Veronica's rejection of him for it that began to convince him of the need to regain control.

In season two, their involvement and subsequent breakup kept them changing, but largely in negative ways. Without Logan to challenge her, Veronica became less thoughtful and less reflective. Without Veronica to keep him grounded, Logan spiraled out of control and ended up hurting other people as well as himself. Without the other to balance their flaws, they became characters in *The Wizard of Oz*: Veronica is the Tin Man, living in her head without much idea of what to do with her heart, while Logan is the Scarecrow, filled with emotions but without the wisdom to know how to manage them appropriately.

But as each continued to grow into their own skin, they made their way back to each other. Veronica let go of her past when she let go of Duncan, and acknowledged that perhaps she preferred the person she had become. And based on her experience of losing Duncan and Meg, almost losing Wallace, and the looming prospect of losing Logan to time and distance, Veronica also realized that she needed to let down her guard and let other people in. Thus, when Logan finally opened his heart to her during his epic speech at Alterna-Prom ("Look Who's Stalking," 2-20), she was ready to hear it. The Veronica who was learning to let down her walls was able to say what the Veronica who distrusted everyone never would have, telling Logan, "I don't want to lose you from my life either."

Logan learned that his acting out had severe consequences and was not getting him what he wanted. His fight with the PCHers led to a charge of murder, and his efforts to seek revenge cost him his relationship with Veronica. However, in repairing his relationship with Duncan and being honest with Hannah, he learned that people do appreciate the good things he has to offer, and that he is worthy of forgiveness. Consequently, he decided that it was time to let go of the physical risks (the excessive drinking, the constant antagonism of people who could hurt him) and take some emotional ones instead. This allowed him to be upfront with Veronica about what happened with Hannah ("The Quick and the Wed," 2-15) and, later, about his feelings towards her. As a result of what he learned, a sober Logan was physically and emotionally available to help Veronica on the Neptune Grand's roof when she needed him the most.

The TV landscape is littered with thousands of pairings but it is the rare couple who truly strike a chord with viewers. One reason for this is that many TV couples get together with only token resistance to the pairing. They may overcome traumatic events together but they are rarely forced to deal with what is dysfunctional in their dynamic or weather the changes that result from doing so. We like to see Logan and Veronica suffer from heartache as long as it eventually leads to interpersonal rewards; it was much more satisfying to watch Veronica finally admit to Logan that she wanted him in her life because we knew that the admission came at great risk. Most TV couples don't work for their relationships and, as such, don't deserve the rewards of being together. Logan and Veronica do.

Much has been made of the fact that Logan and Veronica are seriously bad for each other. Logan can be cruel, has a propensity for violence, and is destructively impulsive. He used a drugged Veronica as a saltlick during a party, smashed her headlights, and picked fights with gang members. He's also emotionally needy, desperate to experience the love he didn't receive from his parents. Veronica, on the other hand, is actively distrustful and emotionally unavailable. She suspected Logan of many misdeeds and turned him into the police for murder, she lied to his face instead of talking it out with him, and has extreme difficulty with trust and intimacy. Being with Logan will take endless understanding; being with Veronica will require infinite patience.

As such, their relationship is so wrong, it's right. It is like a high-wire act in that the potential for disaster is great, but it's an amazing feat if it works. Whenever Veronica and Logan are onscreen together in any capacity, we're usually treated to the best these two characters have to offer—passion, intelligence, humor, resilience—but when they're with each other romantically, even greater qualities emerge: Veronica demonstrates an amazing capacity for forgiveness while Logan displays gentleness, affection, and even, sometimes, hope.

Because They're Epic

While the chemistry, body language, psychological complexity, and growth are all extremely important in shaping the Veronica and Logan pairing, at the end of the day, it is their epic nature that brings it all together. At the core of it all, Veronica and Logan just *get* each other. They have a long history together, and no one else knows them better than they know each other. Logan and Veronica are also both larger than life; their lives will never be simple. As Logan told Veronica at Alterna-Prom, "I thought our story was epic, you know? You and me...Spanning years and continents. Lives ruined, bloodshed. Epic" ("Look Who's Stalking," 2-20). Although they are still young, their story has indeed spanned years (a long time ago, they used to be friends . . .) and while they have yet to traverse continents (give them time), their relationship has already been marked by ruined lives (the Kanes, the Casablancases) and bloodshed (Lilly, Aaron, Cassidy). Logan and Veronica will never be able to sit on the sidelines, so it is only together that they can emerge damaged but unbroken from whatever else may await them.

However, being epic isn't easy. Veronica and Logan will never experience the happily-ever-after; they will constantly have to struggle to be with each other. Yet it is this battle that makes the show so compelling. Already we have seen the two of them kept apart by murder, other people, violence, fear, and mistrust—yet they always return to each other. Season one began with them as archenemies and ended with them seeking one another's comfort after a night of trauma. Season two began with Logan in Veronica's arms and ended with Veronica in Logan's; the overarching story in between was their struggle to understand and forgive each other. While I don't know what season three will bring, I feel certain that it will involve my favorite couple arguing and separating yet eventually finding their way back to each other because, no matter what happens, they cannot stay apart for long.

So yes, it is their epic nature and the dynamite therein that makes them such a fascinating and wonderful couple. Everyone adores a good love story and Veronica and Logan give us that; they are star-crossed lovers, soul-mates who belong together no matter what the cost. They are each other's destiny and the idea of that is incredibly romantic. Who among us has not wanted a partner who not only sees into our soul but also accepts it? Who among us has not wanted a love that would keep us coming back, no matter what, because we are so right for each other? Who among us has not desired a relationship that is so sexual and loving, exciting and tender? Veronica and Logan give us all of these things, and we can't help wanting more. Consequently, while the mysteries are intriguing and the dialogue is fun, it is the exciting, angst-ridden, and explosive relationship of Veronica and Logan that keeps me coming back week after week. I watch in anticipation of Logan's latest romantic gesture and Veronica's next step on her journey toward emotional intimacy. I eagerly wait for the time when Veronica will fight for their relationship the way Logan always has. In short, they are so dynamite together that I want—no, I *need*—to see more of them together. In a show filled with great entertainment, it is this couple that keeps me on the edge of my seat, and it is their pairing that truly drives the show.

> **MISTY HOOK** received her Ph.D. from Ball State, the place where "Boom Goes the Dynamite" originated, and views that as the show's personal shout-out to her. After getting her degree, Dr. Hook spent five years as an assistant professor of psychology and it was there that she learned how to analyze pop culture. She is now a licensed psychologist in private practice where she sees couples who unfortunately do not bear any resemblance to Veronica and Logan. In her spare time, she enjoys spending time with her husband and son even though they are annoyed by her *Veronica Mars* obsession.

Veronica and Buffy may have a few things in common, but until I read Samantha's essay, I didn't know Buffy received an award and ovation at her prom. I swear. In my earliest notes to myself about Veronica Mars, I had an idea jotted down that I never executed, though it interested me. Originally, in the pilot scene where we see Veronica eying the 09er table and commenting on their elevated status, I had her vowing that she would be prom queen her senior year. Now, this may seem at odds with, oh, everything the show stands for, but I viewed it as an entirely dark notion. She wasn't going to become prom queen by being sweet and by going out with the popular boy, she was going to become prom queen as a "fuck you" to the establishment. She would become the hero of the underclass at Neptune High. She would be the one candidate who wasn't an 09er, and, within the space of those two years, she would come to represent the "anti-them." Veronica wanted the title only because she knew it would cause Madison Sinclair (and those like her) to commit hari-kari. When I decided that Veronica should receive a healthy share of applause at her graduation, it was an echo of that earlier notion. She had become a hero to the underclass whether she knew it or not.

Samantha Bornemann

Innocence Lost
The Third Wave of Teen Girl Drama

ET'S START WITH a show of hands. Who else spent the *Veronica Mars* pilot waiting for the other, supernatural shoe to drop?

Wow, that many....

Well, buck up, my fellow brainwashees. There's no shame in assuming a high school girl needs some kind of mystical hook or higher power to claim a show all her own. Obviously, you're A-plus students of recent TV history.

As for the rest of you, stifle the smirks, please, and consider that Veronica came along a full decade after *My So-Called Life*. As you all *should* know, that series revolved around Angela Chase, a regular fifteen-year-old attending a humans-only high school. (And no, I am not forgetting that the Halloween and Christmas episodes involved ghosts. Those flights of fancy are immaterial here.) Critics raved about Winnie Holzman's intricate writing and the series's uniformly marvelous performances, but the show suffered for Thursday-night ratings opposite a freshman comedy called—that's right—*Friends*. Angela lasted just nineteen episodes as the red-headed step-child of ABC's 1994–95 schedule.

She's lingered far longer, however, as a cautionary tale. Scared off by her example, the networks made sure subsequent high school heroines were special. Buffy was the Slayer. Joan of Arcadia kept company with a corporeal, very bossy God. And *Dead Like Me*'s eighteen-year-old Georgia—well, the gimmick's in the title.

Veronica Mars breaks this pattern. No monsters. No deities. No afterlife. But if we can't lump Veronica in with those "chosen" protagonists, neither can we label the series a throwback to the earnest, dreamy realism of *My So-Called Life*. Rather, Veronica ushers in a new, third wave of teen girl drama, in which the stakes and the hurts are as heightened as the real world will allow, and the lead must bear the brunt of them.

Which is to say, Veronica gets her name in lights because she suffers. A lot.

But I'm getting ahead of myself. How can we pin down this third wave if we haven't fully examined the first two? Let's go back to the beginning, to Angela Chase.

The First Wave: A So-Called Experiment

Signature series: *My So-Called Life*
Signature character: Angela Chase
What makes her special?: That she's not special. She's Everygirl (albeit within the confines of the white, suburban, middle class).
Emblematic struggles: Getting along with type-A Mom. Trusting Dad though she suspects he's having an affair. Making crush Jordan Catalano notice her. Passing geometry.
Key physical transformation: She dyes her mousy hair a vibrant crimson.
Behind-the-scenes quote: "All we do is try to tell the truth and then discover that it hasn't been done before."
—Executive producer Marshall Herskovitz (Mendoza)
Inciting incident: Angela drops her lifelong best friend to hang out with wild Rayanne Graff.

We all knew girls like Angela. Those fifteen-year-olds armed with evasive eyes, secret dreams, and hazy convictions were nearly everywhere—drifting through the mall, hiding at school, moping at the dinner table, perhaps even peering back from the bathroom mirror. The one place you couldn't find them, prior to August 1994, was on television for an hour each week. Winnie Holzman changed all that with *My So-Called Life*.

Her pilot offered the most concentrated dose of what it means to be fifteen and female in suburban America ever seen on scripted television. Full of tears, confrontations, and a naïve classroom outburst in which Angela described Anne Frank as lucky for having been "trapped in an attic for three years with this guy she really liked," it was not a feel-good hour ("Pilot," 1-1). But it was emotionally honest and startlingly real.

We stumbled on Angela just as she was struggling with issues of identity—chiefly, the burden of others' expectations. "Things were getting to me," she explained, "Just how people are. How they always expect you to be a certain way, even your best friend."

Let me be clear about how Angela dealt with this: She took action. She stopped hanging out with Sharon. She dyed her hair (according to new best friend Rayanne, doing so was crucial to, like, her life). She quit working on the yearbook because the premise felt false. This drifting, introspective, half-formed young adult made choices and acted on them—for good or for ill. No label, no power, no comic book villain reared up to make her story worth telling. Holzman gave us just a girl and her mind, and that was exactly enough.

Which brings me to my other favorite aspect of *My So-Called Life*: Its writers took seriously their mission to show life from the female perspective. A chief example of this was episode five ("The Zit," scripted by Betty Thomas), a nuanced exploration of the myriad ways women can be dissatisfied with their bodies. While Angela obsessed over a pimple and the injustice of Sharon having a boyfriend when she did not, her former and current best friends had opposite reactions to their placement on an anonymous poll of sophomore girls' attributes. "Most Slut Potential" thrilled and amused Rayanne, but Sharon was humiliated by her "Best Hooters." Invisible Angela didn't rate at all.

Home offered no refuge, as Angela clashed with mom Patty over their continued involvement in the annual mother-daughter fashion show. Confused by her daughter's resistance, Patty assumed that Angela thought she was too cool for the event. The truth, finally revealed in a teary outburst, was quite different. Angela believed she didn't measure up to her mom's beauty and didn't want to parade that fact as they marched in matching outfits.

Moments like this—the small revelations and tiny shifts in perspective—made more than 9 million viewers fall in love with *My So-Called Life*. And when ABC gave it the hook in 1995, we felt—well, it was a lot like a stake through the heart.

The Second Wave: A Formula That Works

Signature series: *Buffy the Vampire Slayer*

Signature character: Buffy Summers

What makes her special? Well, she *is* the chosen one, the world's lone Vampire Slayer.

Emblematic struggles: Hiding her status from Mom, as well as kids and teachers at school. Defeating one Big Bad after another. Loving a vampire.

Key physical transformation: Did we mention the Slayer thing? That means she's damn powerful, but also a moving target.

Behind-the-scenes quote: "There's never a time when life is more like a TV show, whether it be a horror show, a drama, or anything else." —Creator Joss Whedon (Gross)

Inciting incident: Mom moves her to Sunnydale for a fresh start.

Everything that sucked about high school—and we all know there's a lot—became bigger, badder, and bolder in the Buffyverse. Where Angela opined, rather melodramatically, that school was "a battlefield for your heart," Sunnydale High sat atop an actual hellmouth. Teachers really were evil, sex really could be fatal—like, immediately—and Buffy's mom seriously didn't understand.

Of course, the most obvious metaphor was the Slayer herself. One day, Buffy was a bubbly, kinda superficial teen; the next she learned she'd been drafted into lifelong service as a demon magnet. On the plus side, she'd been imbued with enough power (though steady training was recommended) to kill most of the vamps and monsters she came across. But they'd never stop gunning for her, and she'd be lucky if she made it to twenty-one.

This was dire, horrifying, infuriating—and Buffy knew it. Though she was told she was the "chosen one," she heard the truth: Slaying was a command, not a calling. She had to do her time until she was used up, and then they'd summon her replacement.

Here's where we get to the "Buffy rocks!" part of the story: She refused to obey. Sure, she did train, and spent nights patrolling for fresh vamps, and plotted against one Big Bad after another. But she made the job her own. Tell no one? As if. Give up her social life? Not without a knock-down-drag-out. Avoid romance? Unlikely, what with broody, dreamy Angel lurking just outside her window.

When I saw Buffy, stake in hand, bantering with a vampire atop a tombstone, it was not so much my understanding of the image—I knew the toy surprise would be watching the pint-sized blonde kick Fangboy's ass—that excited me. It was the banter. Every quip was a reminder that Buffy was playing through the pain, fighting to keep feeling, keep living, keep making her own choices. The flying kicks and quarter-to battles were fun, but it was Buffy's resolve, not the Slayer's might, that vaulted her into the girl-power firmament.

The Third Wave: Enter Veronica

Signature series: *Veronica Mars*

Signature character: Veronica Mars

What makes her special? She takes a licking but keeps on ticking.

Emblematic struggles: Solving the mysteries of her best friend's murder and her mother's disappearance. Taking Dad's side against an angry town, even though it made her a social pariah.

Key physical transformation: She was raped while unconscious at a high school party.

Behind-the-scenes quote: "I thought, well, wouldn't it be interesting if somebody had gotten so far down that she just didn't give a fuck anymore, that [high school] pressure didn't mean much to her?"
—Creator Rob Thomas (Havrilesky)

Inciting incident: Dead friend, missing mom, unsolved rape, a new school year—take your pick.

I believe Rob Thomas when he says, in interview after interview, that he did not model Veronica after Buffy and had only seen a handful of Sunnydale episodes at the time he created his teen noir. Yet I still can't resist connecting dot after dot. There are just too many parallels between these deceptively packaged, pint-sized blondes, too many echoes and riffs—and, frankly, too much cross-casting—to ignore. Buffy walked dark streets hunting for vamps; Veronica stakes out the seedy Camelot motel. Buffy's dad left the family; Lianne Mars abandoned Veronica *and* stole her college money. Buffy learned monster history from Giles, her watcher and fatherly stand-in; Veronica gets her sleuthing shortcuts from Dad Keith, a sheriff turned private investigator. I could go on, but, heck, you probably have your own annotated list.

On first glance, the series's big pictures match as well as the details. Both Whedon and Thomas introduced their heroines with happy, innocent befores (when both girls wore their hair long and straight, like children) and dark, lonely aftermaths. And I mean *dark*: One leaned gothic, one leans noir, but both scribes pile on the hurts to make their outsiders that much more sympathetic—and to make the rare moments of happiness and recognition that much grander. Think of Buffy's tearjerker prom scene, when Jonathan surprised her with the Class Protector award; all the toil, all the life-saving...her classmates had noticed, after all. (Even Giles was impressed.) In a kind of call-and-response move—I don't care what Thomas says, this had to be a shout-out to the Slayer—classmates gave Veronica some love as she accepted her diploma at the end of season two. It was no ninety-second standing ovation, mind you, but there were distinct cheers for the girl who'd introduced herself to viewers as the pariah of Neptune High. And the scene was made more interesting because we can't be sure why people applauded for Veronica. They could have been satisfied clients of our teen P.I. or just classmates made generous by the pomp, circumstance, and freedom of leaving high school behind. On *Veronica Mars*, even the happy surprises produce more questions than answers, and the world never stops to devote its attention—whether evil or benign—on one teen girl.

At this point the Buffy parallel breaks down, because, season-long mysteries notwithstanding, there's no Big Bad (er, except the writers) orchestrating our heroine's every battle from behind the scenes. Rather, Veronica's rape was revealed as a cosmic joke brought on by circumstance and foolish pride: Veronica crashed that party in defiance of the 09er crowd, Madison didn't know the drink she handed Veronica was laced with anything more than spit, and Beaver assaulted her in an attempt to conquer his mixed-up psyche. She wasn't chosen or targeted; she was unlucky. She was spot-on, then, in likening tragedy to "a tornado, uprooting everything, creating chaos" ("Meet John Smith," 1-3). Life is messy, unfathomable—but most of all impersonal. As Veronica is not special, her misfortunes make her the Anygirl to *My So-Called Life*'s Everygirl: Things that could have happened to anyone just happen to happen to her.

The Veronica we meet is a survivor, a kind of second draft cobbled together in the aftermath of losing Lilly, her mom, and control over her own body. But she's also a rebuilt Angela Chase. In the show's hazy, overexposed flashbacks, we saw that Angela and Veronica began their high school years on similar terms: both had two parents at home and spent their days chasing after a wild, exciting best friend. Of course we're meant to feel for Veronica during these glimpses of what used to be and what might have been, but for me the melancholy stretches beyond the realm of Neptune. Veronica's trajectory mimics that of teen girl dramas as a whole, with the average girl now reduced to fleshing out backstory and prologue, little more than a ghostly reminder of happiness past.

Thomas wants it that way. He has said that what he likes about Veronica is that she's beyond the typical teen girl insecurities about having the right look and the right friends, that she's been knocked so low that high school pressure no longer means anything to her (Havrilesky). His protagonist is "over" the high school story, and his series is, too. And so, despite its many echoes of Angela and Buffy, *Veronica Mars* is no hybrid of its predecessors. In this new, third wave of teen girl drama, the heroine ventures into the wider world...and risks getting lost in the process.

Veronica's misfortunes have taught her that everyone is dangerous, and anyone can hurt you—if you let them. So she vows she won't be fooled again. Her investigative work for Dad is a kind of training, a steady inoculation against weakening her resolve. Waiting to snap proof of a spouse's affair, she vowed she'd never marry because, "sooner or later, the people you love let you down" ("Pilot," 1-1). While her sleuthing presents opportunities for insight into our heroine, it also limits our access to her. *Veronica Mars* is a detective series, after all, which means large chunks of episodes are devoted to suspicious characters, wild-goose chases, red herrings, and the genre's other tropes. This heavy emphasis on the seedy underbelly sometimes feels uncomfortably like assimilation into TV's crime-obsessed mainstream. With its complicated, run-time-sapping murder mysteries and hard-boiled, hard-to-know heroine, the show wouldn't need much tweaking to pass for *CSI: Neptune*. Post-Angela, girl-centric, high school-set series have always relied on a hook, but Thomas appears to have unwittingly reversed the phenomenon. The show has morphed into a detective story, first and foremost; this time the teen protagonist is just the hook.

Scratch that: The teen *girl* is the hook. Here's Thomas recounting the origin of his series:

> This idea that I was attracted to, and had been thinking about since I taught high school, was this vague notion about teenagers being desensitized and jaded and sexualized so much earlier than I feel like even my generation fifteen, twenty years before had been. That seemed like a perfect thing to try to shine a spotlight on. [That concept] was interesting to me when the protagonist was a boy, but when I started thinking in terms of a girl who had seen too much and experienced too much at too young of an age, it became even more potent to me. It just seemed that much edgier and more difficult to swallow, in a good way. (Havrilesky)

This is outside-in storytelling: What kind of protagonist will make the genre more interesting, and with what can she be saddled (rape! a dead best friend!) to make it edgier still? The answer, of course, was a scarred Angela, an un-super Buffy, driven to solve a familiar kind of murder mystery. Though I, too, held my breath waiting to learn who killed Lilly Kane, the very question dug up old hurts from 1995, when ABC replaced *My So-Called Life* the following season with *Murder One*, a legal noir revolving around the murder of a teen girl. ("I guess ABC is more comfortable with a dead girl than a live one," Holzman remarked at the time [Chambers].) With Lilly and Veronica, teen girl drama both doubles back to that time and tiptoes forward—here's another dead girl, yes, but Thomas also presents a whipsmart live one, and she's the one who cracks the case.

The more I reflect on this evolution from so-called experiment to teen girl as hook, the more Angela, Buffy, and Veronica appear sisters in a decade-spanning trilogy: follow along as television ignores, then indulges, and finally co-opts the female adolescent experience! *My So-Called Life* and *Buffy* indulged and awoke our inner teens by putting the feelings of adolescence front and center. They taught us the teen girl story, the recurring beats, milestones, and conflicts, and we bring that understanding and its related assumptions to our experience of Veronica. We fill in the blanks as we want to, seeing Buffy parallels, sensing Angela's ghost just outside the room. Meanwhile, the story moves on, dancing from one Neptune intrigue to the next. In shifting much of its attention away from Veronica in favor of typical TV mysteries of the week and season, the third wave and its Anygirl offer the final lesson of adolescence: Out in the big, bad, messy world, nothing is ever all about *you*.

SAMANTHA BORNEMANN has written about film and television for Playboy.com, PopMatters, and ShinyGun. com, the magazine she founded with fellow Northwestern grads in 2000. She lives in Chicago and is at work on a novel about Everygirls (and boys) grown up.

References

Chambers, Bill. "Film Freak Central DVD Review: My So-Called Life (Volume One)." *Film Freak Central.* Aug. 2000. <http://www.filmfreakcentral. net/dvdreviews/mysocalledlife.htm>.

Gross, Edward, ed. "Buffy Meets the Press." *Vampires & Slayers.* <http:// www.vampiresandslayers.com/buffy.htm>.

Havrilesky, Heather. "The Man Behind Veronica." *Salon.* 29 Mar. 2005. <http://dir.salon.com/story/ent/feature/2005/03/29/rob_thomas/index. html>.

Mendoza, Manuel. "Teen Drama Still Has Impact 10 Years After Cancellation." *The Dallas Morning News*, 26 Mar. 2004.

"Pilot." *My So-Called Life.* Episode 1, Dir. Scott Winant. ABC, 25 Aug. 1994.

I had one "big" idea when I wrote the Veronica Mars pilot.

Executives always tend to ask you the question, "What's it really about?"

Well, it's about a seventeen-year-old girl who happens to be a detective....

"No, what's it about?"

Oh, that. The zeitgest, etc.? It's about this prematurely jaded generation of teenagers who are exposed to too much too soon. They can access anything. They're sexualized too early.

Veronica will be the poster child for loss of innocence.

I went to high school in the early eighties, taught high school in the early nineties and wrote about high school in the early 2000s. Even in the span of those twenty years, the changing expectations of what a typical teenager has experienced, witnessed, googled, understands are radically different. (For a better—certainly scarier—example, see the movie Thirteen.)

Judy Fitzwater

From Golden Girl to Rich Dude Kryptonite

Why Veronica Mars Is in with the Out-Crowd

"WE USED TO be friends," the *Veronica Mars* theme song by the Dandy Warhols reminds us at the beginning of each episode. Sassy "bad-ass" Veronica was once one of Neptune High School's in-crowd, a friend of the powerful elite. She was also innocent and naïve. However, when we first met Veronica in her hometown of Neptune, California, all of that was in the past. Her best friend had been murdered, her mother had abandoned her, she'd lost her virginity under circumstances she couldn't remember, and she was no longer one of the favored. The seventeen-year-old social pariah was a far cry from what she'd been only a year before, when she was a member of the pep squad (for P.E. credit, not to attract boys) and welcome at the best lunch table at school. She was jaded. Her hair was shorter, her clothes edgy, and her attitude—well, authority? What's that?

But Veronica was far more than a girl whose world had been shattered. She'd been fast-tracked to a maturity she might never have experienced if Lilly Kane hadn't been murdered. To understand her transformation, we need to look at what she would have been like if Lilly were still alive. Would she still be one of the in-crowd? And why does she continue to long for the life she believes she's lost?

The writers gave us Veronica's own answer to the first question in the dream sequence in the last episode of season two, "Not Pictured" (2-22). Here we saw Veronica's vision of her ideal life: her loving, intact family preparing for her high school graduation. Her mother is cooking a pancake breakfast and her father is wearing his sheriff's uniform. Veronica is dressed in a sweet floral sundress, something the new Veronica would never wear. (For her real graduation Veronica donned a black halter dress.)

At school searching for her cap and gown, Duncan and Logan pull her leg about Wallace, whom she's never met, and she believes them, something that would never happen with the cynical new Veronica. Logan responds, "...you have to be the most gullible girl I've ever met." And when she meets up with Wallace, she tells him, "High school was a blast." He replies, "Oh, you're one of those."

Obviously Veronica was dreaming, both literally and figuratively. Wishing she were still so "gullible" is a symptom of how truly horrific she's discovered life can be. Neptune High is a minefield of amoral students and faculty to be negotiated carefully. Lilly was about to open Veronica's eyes before her death. Lilly had a secret to share. Promiscuous Lilly, who hid naked photos of a guy she met in Italy in the vent in her room, was sleeping with her boyfriend's father. It would have been interesting to see how Veronica would have reacted to this information. The fact that she never got to has frozen Veronica's image of her ideal life in a time warp, leaving her to yearn for the time before she knew the truth, for a vision of life that effectively never existed. In true childish fashion, not knowing meant it wasn't so. Not knowing was living in an illusion, which is exactly where Veronica wishes she could return.

Sixteen-year-old Veronica questioned very little. She was a true innocent. She was trusting, she was part of what she thought was a loving family, and she believed in the good of humanity. She wore her hair in long, soft curls, chose modest, age-appropriate clothing, and wore lots of pastels. In a flashback where Lilly was going through her closet before the homecoming dance, Lilly exclaimed, "None of this reflects your personality." She pulled out a dress and declared, "You're not a yellow cotton dress." Veronica asked, "What am I?" And Lilly replied, "You're strapless red satin" ("The Wrath of Con," 1-4).

This is an interesting exchange between these two characters, because sixteen-year-old Veronica *was* a yellow cotton dress. Indeed, these two best friends didn't even seem to know one another. And perhaps here is a flaw in the set-up of an otherwise very well thought-out and skillfully executed plot. Lilly and Veronica were so different it's hard to believe they could have been best friends.

Since our glimpses into their friendship are restricted to Veronica's memory and dream sequences, the viewer can only speculate that, as different as they were, Veronica and Lilly connected on some gut level, as friends often do. They simply liked each other, despite their disparities. Lilly had a certain charm about her, a zest for life we saw demonstrated in the clips Logan put together for the dedication of her memorial fountain at Neptune High. In the film of their homecoming date, she stood in the limo with her head and shoulders through the sunroof, wind blowing through her hair, and declared, "You love me, don't you," as she smiled into the camera ("The Wrath of Con"). We're convinced that Veronica and Logan do love her. And we, as viewers, can't help but love Lilly a little, too. It's this Lilly that Veronica misses so desperately, the exciting, fun-loving, go-for-broke gal who was always pushing the envelope. What Veronica failed to see was Lilly's dark side and the consequences of her actions.

While Veronica and Lilly may have been opposites, Duncan and Veronica were perfectly suited to one another at that point. Both were sweet, sensitive, and moral (note Duncan's throwaway inclusion of an outsider at the lunch table in one of the flashbacks).

We learn that both were virgins in the homecoming memory sequence. Veronica was exactly what she wore: a modest, light-pink formal intended for a dance she had no idea she wouldn't attend. Contrast Veronica's dress to Lilly's, a seductive, glittery metallic gown with a neckline that plunged almost to her waist, a dress far more appropriate for a woman in her thirties.

Veronica's memories of that night are glorified. What the viewer sees when Lilly, Logan, Duncan, and Veronica party in the limo and never make it to the dance is not what most would consider the perfect date. "I've already lived the dream," she thought when Troy invited her to homecoming. "Everything else seems like a cheap reminder"

("The Wrath of Con"). Which may lead the viewer to question: Was Veronica on the same date as the one depicted in the episode? She remembers the events but sees no harm in Lilly kissing her on the lips or the potential danger in the worlds Lilly might introduce her to. For Veronica, it all seemed innocent. The only danger she perceived was her father's anger when she got home after being out all night. The world Lilly lived in and the dangers it posed simply didn't exist for Veronica.

But it did for Duncan. He knew Lilly and what she was capable of well. Towards the end of the first season, Veronica knew much more about her, too. When Duncan was suspected of killing Lilly, she defended him to herself by thinking, "Duncan and Lilly were so different. They didn't always like each other, but they always loved each other" ("Kanes and Abel's," 1-17). She could have been talking about herself, for Veronica continues to love Lilly unquestioningly. Whether or not she continues to like her is never addressed.

As viewers we can only conclude that Veronica's innocence precluded her from processing Lilly's immorality and that the strange tricks played on us by time have kept her from reevaluating those memories. Whatever emotions she experienced at the time seem to have been fixed firmly in her brain along with the sequence of events.

So what did Lilly see in Veronica? Did she see Veronica's potential to become what she is now? Could she have actually seen Veronica as "strapless red satin"? She saw Veronica's potential strength and daring, but she couldn't have envisioned the transformation that would ultimately take place. She could have predicted Veronica's disillusionment, but not as a result of her own death.

Did Veronica have any idea what Lilly was capable of? No. She had no idea that Lilly had a relationship with Weevil and certainly no clue that she was sleeping with Aaron Echolls, despite repeated references to Lilly's numerous lovers. But none of that can touch Veronica's love for Lilly.

On her homecoming date with Troy—wearing strapless red satin—Veronica had the limo stop while she went skinny dipping—alone—in tribute to Lilly. From Lilly she had taken two things: daring and courage. But she directed them toward a two-fold goal: supporting her father and finding Lilly's killer.

Duncan, despite the devils that tormented him following Lilly's death and his horror at the realization that in sleeping with Veronica at Shelly Pomroy's party he may have slept with his own sister, seemed somehow less changed, at least during season one, than Veronica. He remained one of the in-crowd, and his idealism, for lack of a better word, remained intact. Note that when he was elected class president, he extended the coveted Pirate points program to include everyone ("Return of the Kane," 1-6). Veronica has no use for Pirate points, period. Or for politics. Or for working through the system. She now sees life differently. She believes to get respect one must demand it and in the first season repeatedly pushed revenge as the only answer to bullying. Her reputation is, perhaps, the best weapon in her arsenal.

Yet, throughout all this, Veronica, reborn through her friend's murder, her mother's abandonment, and her decision to stand by her father, continues to yearn for a fantasy past that never really existed. She desperately wants her old life back. But even if she could have it, she'd no longer fit into it—especially as it was all a creation within her own mind. Even her home life was a sham. Her mother, who has a serious problem with alcohol, had been having an affair with Jake Kane, bringing Veronica's own parentage into question. At this point, everything she thought she knew has been proved wrong, and her eyes are now wide open. She's fearless, both book and street smart, and incredibly savvy, strong enough to stand on her own. And the part of the in-crowd she mourns and wishes to be a part of likely never even existed. She's changed, not them, and she can no longer pretend they're worthy of her attention.

The in-crowd at Neptune High consists of wealthy (mostly nouveau riche) 09ers. Madison Sinclair's birthday celebration, laughably complete with string quartet and a catered cake during school lunch and a huge invitation-only party later at her home, probably best demonstrated the contrast between the haves and have-nots. The gap is made ironic by the fact that Mac was switched with Madison at birth, for birth is Madison's only claim to status.

In-crowd people like Madison are in the minority, yet they run the school, continually shoving their perceived superiority in the faces of the out-crowd. They know no morality, something Veronica, despite her flirtations with breaking both rules and laws, knows well.

At Gia Goodman's slumber party in "Nobody Puts Baby in a Corner" (2-7), Veronica obviously did not belong, nor did she want to. She was only there to gain information. Around the pool, all of the girls were dressed in scanty bathing suits, while Veronica was clad in a long-sleeved top and jeans. Attendee Madison declared that *Pretty Woman* was her favorite movie, and stated, "Vivian is like my hero." To which Veronica replied, "She's a *hooker*," not once, but twice. When Beaver and Dick showed up for a panty raid, she'd had enough and left. The partygoers are all portrayed as shallow, immature, and immoral. Veronica had no time to waste on any of them.

Veronica stated in the pilot that her fall from grace came about because of her decision to stand by her father, that she was forced to choose between him and the in-crowd. That choice, however, was not her sin. Her sin was in thinking for herself, for questioning the judgment of the teens in power (who deemed her father unworthy)—because admission to the in-crowd means giving up autonomy, or in the case of maturing teenagers, never achieving it.

Hopefully Veronica's naïveté would have soon evaporated with or without Lilly's death. Lilly told Veronica she had a secret. It would have only been a matter of time before she'd confessed her affair to Veronica. Then Veronica would have had to make a choice. She might well have chosen to stand by Lilly, as evidenced by her visit to Shelly's party. The lure to belong, especially in high school, is strong. But the knowledge of what was really happening with Lilly and the in-crowd was soon to be revealed. Once it was, there would have been no putting the genie back into the bottle. Part of her innocence would have been gone.

And if she'd stood by Lilly unquestioningly, what kind of person would she have become? Just another spineless in-crowder, certainly not someone worthy of our admiration. Interestingly enough, it was imperative that Lilly die first—before Veronica found out her secret—or her love for Lilly might have been destroyed.

Veronica never got the opportunity to choose. With Lilly's death and her mother's departure, Veronica lost her emotional and intellectual innocence. With the loss of her virginity, she lost her physical innocence as well, allowing for her complete transformation. It was at this pivotal point that Veronica became the girl we love: the avenger.

The "rape" that turned out not to have been a rape (at least until the end of season two) was a really interesting and effective addition to the plot during the first season, and one that the viewer might have questioned when originally watching the series. Did we really have to go there? But by the end of the first season, it became obvious that yes, we did. Lilly's death and her mother's disappearance were not sufficient to bring about the change we see in Veronica. If they had been, she would never have gone to Shelly's party. She went to the party in a last-ditch effort to prove that she was still the girl she had been, that she could still fit in without Lilly and Duncan (who, at that point, was convinced he'd been having a romance with his half-sister). And it was here that she had to lose the last of her innocence. She met with one betrayal after another. She was drugged, and, despite numerous opportunities for her classmates to rescue her from the inevitable, she ultimately had sex and was labeled a slut. (Considering the amount of bed-hopping going on in Neptune, such an appellation hardly seems relevant. It's an example of what's allowed by the in-crowd and forbidden to the out-crowd.)

After realizing what had happened to her, Veronica went to Sheriff Lamb to report her rape. He scoffed at her situation and sent her away in shame. Her last shred of respect for authority was destroyed.

Through unraveling the mystery of the "rape," however, the writers ultimately redeemed her, at least until season two, from that horrible experience. In good romantic fashion, Veronica was not actually raped. Instead she slept, albeit unknowingly, with her one true love, Duncan. For Duncan, this was a horrific, incestuous event, but one that served a dual purpose. His horror at what he'd done created an insurmountable rift between him and Veronica, and allowed him to find a new love.

Meg Manning, who bore a striking resemblance to the sweet innocent that Veronica had once been, was a logical substitute for Duncan's affection. And Meg and Duncan's relationship laid the foundation for the undoing of the once-again budding relationship between Veronica and Duncan at the beginning of season two. Both wanted to recapture what they once had, but couldn't.

Although Duncan will always be Veronica's one true love (and she his), they are no longer suited to share a happily ever after. By the end of season two, Duncan had put out a hit on Aaron Echolls, bringing his moral suitability for our heroine into question. There's no easy path for these two lovers. They can never have the ideal life that Veronica and Duncan once envisioned at sixteen. Duncan's perceived obstacle to their union—incest—was replaced by obstacles he created himself. He's a father now, he's had another love, and he's a kidnapper on the run from the law. Actually, in many ways he's becoming, once again, far more suited to Veronica and far more interesting to the viewer. True love, especially unchallenged, makes for boring TV.

But Veronica's love life is destined to be intermittent at best, for she has work to do. Dick proclaimed her to be "rich dude kryptonite" ("Versatile Toppings," 2-14), and that's exactly what she is. Fall for Veronica Mars and she'll find every skeleton in your closet, or at least every bag of weed in your locker.

It's here that the revelation in season two that Veronica was actually raped at Shelly's party by Beaver should be addressed. Veronica's chlamydia becomes an important clue in unraveling the mystery of the school bus deaths. Taking away the "save" we thought we'd been given in season one concerning the rape emphasized once more that nasty people populate the city of Neptune and Neptune High. Her STD became one more physical trial for a young woman who will be hit by many more.

Veronica yearns to go back to her quiet life, but there's no going back. That life doesn't exist anymore, not that it ever did. She is now the problem solver, the righter of wrongs, the one they—both in-crowd and out—turned to when they found themselves threatened in the dangerous world that was Neptune High. One assumes she'll be doing the same at Hearst College.

Most significant in her transformation from innocence to strength is her heeding the call to solve the mystery of Lilly's death. Neither Logan nor Duncan nor Lilly's parents took on that challenge. Sheriff Lamb is totally incompetent and swallowed the whole Abel Koontz confession without question. And while her father Keith did pursue the case, he came to the wrong conclusion with disastrous consequences. It was Veronica's determination that ultimately solved the case. It was her wit, her courage, her character, and her tenacity that allowed her to avenge Lilly.

Veronica struggles with her fears and her dreams of what might have been. Yet she forges ahead, knowing there's no turning back, no second-guessing her commitment. She discovered Lilly's murderer and the killer of a busload of Neptune students. Along the way, she helped numerous individuals caught in their own crises. While she remains, at least to some extent, a social pariah, her abilities are well-established and respected by all, even those in authority. She's courageous, single-minded, and, at times, ruthless. She's not above blackmail, raiding police and school files, or even tampering with police evidence. And, ultimately, she is triumphant. She brings the murderers to justice, even when the justice system lets her down, as with the Aaron Echolls "not guilty" verdict. She does what she does because it's the right thing to do and because there's no one else to do it. At graduation, the crowd, despite a few boos, cheered her success and acknowledged her value to them.

So, would Veronica's innocence have died on its own without the events set in motion by Lilly's death? Most definitely. With murderers and rapists, thieves and drug dealers, blackmailers and thugs roaming the halls of Neptune High, Veronica was bound to notice eventually. Would she have done anything about it? Probably not. She had to lose most of what she held dear before choosing to turn and fight.

Why does she yearn for the past? Because it was a time when she didn't know the truth, and the truth, as far as she's concerned, ruined her life. But Veronica's a smart girl; she couldn't stay sixteen forever. Fortunately for us viewers, she hasn't.

> **JUDY FITZWATER** is the author of the Jennifer Marsh mystery series, published by Ballantine Books, and the suspense novel, *No Safe Place*, a May 2006 release from Silhouette Bombshell. A former journalist and an Air Force brat, she now lives in the Washington, D.C., area with her husband, where she writes novels filled with mystery, humor, and suspense.

And here's me *in fanboy mode.*

When Heather Havrilesky wrote a big, effusive review/think-piece about Veronica Mars *for Salon.com, it made my week, possibly my month.*

I felt like Warren Beatty must've felt like when he read Pauline Kael's review of Bonnie and Clyde. *I felt like I'd arrived. I mean, it's nice if* People *makes you a "pick" rather than a "pan," but Heather writing such glowing things in* Salon? *I was positively giddy. It meant the show was cool. This was even a bigger coup than the positive mention in* The Onion. *In the contingent of I-only-watch-quality-TV people, Heather's say-so is pretty much holy writ.*

Now that I know she lives in Los Angeles, I want Heather and her husband and her new daughter and two dogs to come over for a barbecue with my wife and daughter and two dogs. Can someone arrange that?

Heather Havrilesky

The Importance
of Not Being Earnest

"SOONER OR LATER, the people you love let you down." This is what Veronica Mars wants us to know first and foremost, in the first scene of the first episode of the first season of the show. Before she tells us a thing about herself, before she lays out all she's been through in the past year, she wants to issue a warning to the naïve idealists and wide-eyed optimists out there, to prepare us for the disappointments to come. "Sooner or later" (maybe this week, maybe next month, maybe ten years from now) "the people you love" (your mom, your dad, your boyfriend, your so-called best friend) will "let you down" (break your heart, disappoint you, dump you like a bad habit, or have an affair with your boyfriend's dad, skip town, and neglect to call or write).

Coming from an adult, such a sweeping statement would sound far too cynical and world-weary to bear. It would hint at a predisposition to blame, to hold grudges, to live in the past, and it would suggest an inability to get over it, to grow up, to move forward. The kind of grown-up who walks around spewing fatalistic truisms about the inevitability of being let down by the ones you love also typically wears lint-covered Cosby sweaters, eats at the same really bad diner three nights a week, and says things like, "Why get married when you can have a pet? Pets are much easier to live with—and a lot less expensive! Bahahaha!"

But coming from a high school student, such a statement sounds breathtakingly—no, inspiringly—jaded. Because in high school, nothing is better than being world-weary. World-weary is the state that all high school students aspire to, the ultimate achievement on the emotional battlefield of the teenage years, and the natural ending point to the high school trajectory. Because even when you enter high school as a freshman, full of hope and romantic visions of big football games, winning the lead role in the fall musical, or getting noticed by some hot senior with a Mustang convertible and parents with a stocked liquor cabinet who leave town a lot, even then, you know where you're headed. You know that you'll have to savor the excitement and the novelty while you can, because by the time you're a senior, nothing about high school should seem remotely dramatic or even worthwhile. By senior year, the only real choice, the only clear solution to the sticky trap of leaving those teenage years behind, is to be totally over high school—and everything else in the world, too, if you can manage it.

But Veronica takes it a step further. To be totally over not just high school, but totally over the people you love? To recognize, with an exhausted, eye-rolling certainty, that your loved ones are destined to let you down? To know, beyond a shadow of a doubt, that even if they haven't let you down yet, they're sure to do it sooner or later? That's pretty heady stuff. That's the holy grail.

Because being a teenager is all about taking all the things you cared about as a kid and smashing them to tiny little bits. Suddenly, there is no Santa Claus, your teddy bear is banished to a lonely box in the attic, and the advice "Just be yourself and they'll love you" is revealed to be a complete crock of shit. On top of all that, almost everything you ever cared about is "totally gay," and not only aren't your parents all that lovable or cool, they're also old and lame and they smell like blue cheese.

Considering these recent revelations, it's not a big stretch to think that those you love will disappoint you. Your mom disappoints you every time she puts on that idiotic reindeer sweatshirt with the sequins and the felt on it, even though it's the middle of February and it makes her look like she belongs in an insane asylum. Your best friend disappoints you regularly, like that time she drank four fuzzy navels, stuck her tongue in your crush's ear, then threw up in the hot tub at beach week.

Veronica's statement makes perfect sense. But to utter those words so calmly? To let such a big assessment slip, matter-of-factly, as opposed to, say, screaming it at your mom as you run to your room and hurl yourself onto your bed face-first? That's power. To feel that resolved about your alienation, to be that sure of the total hopelessness of it all? That's freedom. That's better than reading the complete works of Rimbaud, learning to play the Cure's "Pictures of You" on electric guitar, and getting away with growing marijuana in the closet of your room by telling your mom it's part of a biology project.

My glorious salvation from naïveté and innocence came, like Veronica's, early in my high school tenure, about halfway through my sophomore year. I didn't achieve Veronica's world-weary calm or her enviably blasé state of mind until years later, but I did take those first delectable steps towards disillusionment and despair, and it was every bit as tragic and heart-stopping as any teenager could hope for.

During a summer of working at an ice cream store and eating bowls of ice cream the size of my head, I gained ten pounds, and they must've been the good kind of pounds, because after years of being flatly ignored by the opposite sex, a senior—let's call him "Mark"— suddenly took notice of me.

By "took notice" I mean he decided I looked like just the sort of sophomore girl to save him from his romantically uneventful high school existence. I was a cheerleader, and probably had that young, slightly bovine look that made me an easy mark. Plus, I was easy enough to find in the high school gym that summer, weaseling my way out of pyramids of questionable structural integrity, thereby hoping to avoid being involved in the type of catastrophic cheerleading accidents notorious in the South for transforming peppy little ponytailed girls into sullen, drooling paraplegics overnight.

After looming around the gym and the ice cream place for a few weeks, Mark asked me out, and soon, it was completely obvious we were meant to be together. We had so much in common! We laughed at the same jokes—his jokes, mostly—and we both really liked dogs, pizza, and Duke basketball. What's more (as if we needed more!), we both hated UNC basketball. But the most amazing thing was that we both totally loved Rush. If that wasn't a sign that we were star-crossed, I didn't know what was.

After three glorious months together, just as I was starting to pick out names for our offspring, Mark's best friend, who happened to be a blue-eyed, blonde-haired, six-foot-tall senior named Tammy, started to notice Mark's potential. Mark had always longed for Tammy, of course, but Tammy had always dated much more sophisticated, older guys—guys with apartments of their own, guys with mustaches, for Christ's sake. Tammy was totally over high school, and had been for years. She was as world-weary as they came.

But thanks to me, Mark was starting to look like a lot of fun. Like the star of a mediocre sitcom, he didn't seem all that charming or funny until you threw in a laugh track, cued to guffaw loudly at every single thing that came out of his mouth. My days as a wide-eyed optimist were numbered.

Sadly, the fall from grace of the soon-to-be-world-weary high school girl isn't quite as speedy as Veronica Mars makes it seem when she's having a flashback of a long-haired, more innocent Veronica. What we don't see are those long nights she spent face-down on her bed, crying her eyes out, or calling Duncan and whining, "Why? Whyyy?!!!" We don't see her gazing longingly out the window of her chemistry class, like I did, seeing Mark and Tammy strolling by, hand in hand, her puffy blonde head of hair looming a full foot above his. I still remember that jittery, heavy feeling in my chest, like my heart was a coffee tin filled with nails. "How could he have turned his back on me like this?" I wondered, tears welling up in my eyes. It didn't make sense, even though Tammy was tall and blonde and had probably learned a great deal about sex from those men and their mustaches. "Could she possibly love Rush half as much as I do? Does she know every word to 'Tom Sawyer' and 'Red Barchetta'? There's no way she does! It's just not possible!"

But little did I know, I was beginning a very important journey, and without this first crucial step down the path to alienation and disillusionment, I would never get all of the deeply cynical outlooks and dysfunctional tics and bitter perspectives that I so richly deserved.

Some kids skipped this step. They entered high school full of skepticism and anger. Instead of leaping head-long into the arms of a senior (a senior who drove a Pinto, for God's sake) only to be dropped on their asses, they side-stepped the whole heartbreaking stunt, choosing to linger angrily in the parking lot smoking Marlboro Reds instead. I considered this a cheat. You can't just skip to the end! You have to chase all the lame, shallow stuff everyone else is chasing! Even if it's all empty and stupid and pointless and you just get dumped or end up with a roofie in your drink or all of the above, you're in high school. You have to join the herd, possibly getting stampeded to death along the way. You'll have plenty of time to pout and roll your eyes at the sad little conformist chumps when you're old and crusty and your pathetic offspring trundle off to high school.

Veronica didn't take any shortcuts to world-weariness, either. She didn't leave school one day a typical girl, and then show up the next day with a pierced tongue and a Sex Pistols T-shirt, her mind blown by having read *Catcher in the Rye* for the first time. She was once just as clueless as the rest of us were, which makes her all the more likeable and heroic. The long-haired, sweet-faced Veronica of the flashbacks, the one who was in love with the cutest guy in school, Duncan Kane, and friends with the coolest girl, his sister Lilly? She was everything our naïve high school freshmen selves wanted to be: pretty, popular, and thrilled about every second of it. She climbed the mountain, and saw what was on the other side: cool parties at really big, expensive houses where they served kegs of beer and elaborate fruit punches and really tasty peach wine coolers.

If Veronica had skipped straight to the jaded stage, she'd be about as cool as that skinny, geeky kid who you never noticed until he showed up to school one day with a two-foot-high purple Mohawk, mumbling about how he doesn't care what anyone thinks of him because everyone is full of crap, they're all just conformist automatons who'll end up as bankers and lawyers and dumb housewives some day. He was right, of course, but it was tough to respect his superior attitude when he'd been rejected or teased or roundly ignored by those future bankers and lawyers and dumb housewives for years. In high school, everyone knows you can't make a really tasty peach wine cooler from sour grapes.

It wasn't years of rejection, but a succession of tragedies—boyfriend Duncan dumped her, best friend Lilly was murdered by Aaron Echolls, Mommy bedded Mr. Kane then disappeared, Daddy lost his job as sheriff—that forced Veronica to face the ugly fact that life is filled with sadness, loss, and disappointments, and that it's pure foolishness to trust anyone, ever.

Of course, this disillusionment is exactly what gives Veronica her power. Sure, she's a million things that every high school kid aspires to be: smart and scholarly but not overly concerned about grades, socially smooth but completely bored by the high school social scene, pretty in a completely unassailable way, effortlessly stylish, funny but never by pandering for laughs or attention, and openly scornful toward the popular kids but nice to the underdog. Her real appeal, though, comes from being totally over high school, because that offers her immunity from what everyone else thinks of her. Not only is she herself utterly without shame—you can only sink so low, after all, before you have to give up on dignity entirely—but she's armed with a heavy arsenal of witty retorts ready to launch at the slightest provocation. Considering the fact that the petty little skirmishes of the high school battlefield hinge on wisecracks and an ability to quickly shame your opponent into submission, Veronica's shamelessness and way with a comeback give her a major advantage over any and all opponents.

Shame is kryptonite to the high school kid, which is why the shameless fare so well in that environment. Those with the most power are always shameless: the kids who are totally over high school and therefore care the least about whether or not they're perceived badly, the kids who know how to appear unconcerned, and the kids who are far too dumb to have extra brain cells to devote to figuring out what anyone thinks of them.

That's why overconfident jerks, fakers, sociopaths, and morons do so well in high school; it's a bizarre microcosm that's extremely forgiving to the shameless. Not surprisingly, it's extremely unforgiving to those who are earnest, genuine, brainy, sensitive, and/or neurotic. Smart kids have the hardest time of all, of course: painfully aware of how they're perceived, prone to overthinking the most insignificant situation or conversation, likely to obsess or become neurotic over nothing, and worst of all, vulnerable to self-consciousness, second-guessing, and deep bouts of shame.

Veronica combines the intelligence and wit and wiles of the latter group with the shamelessness of the former, except her shamelessness arises from her world-weariness and alienation. And unlike the overconfident morons like Dick, who rule the school with their blunt weapons of blind aggression, selfishness, and disdain for all things humble and genuine, Veronica is aware of the disapproval of others, but remains immune to it.

After my heartbreak over Mark, the petty squabbles and power plays between kids my age seemed silly and insignificant. I had been involved in a tragic story of love and loss, after all, which everyone in school knew about. They probably couldn't have cared less, of course, but that's not how it seemed at the time. At the time, it was like Romeo suddenly dumped Juliet for some fair-skinned tart down the lane, even though Juliet was really nice and clearly loved Rush way more than that flaxen-haired trollop! At the time, it was a tale of woe, and I was the victim, the sorry, sobbing wench left behind, clutching my hand to my heart. I was just like Veronica, walking in her white party dress to the police station to report being date raped—you know, except for the fact that Mark and I merely ate at McDonald's and made out on his parents' couch; I didn't lose my virginity until years later. But that's how I felt, just like Veronica did! Soiled, ashamed, besotted, befouled, adrift! A wanton woman, used up and cast aside like yesterday's flavor of wine cooler!

I had been so publicly rejected that, in order to survive, I had to forget what anyone thought. But who cared anyway? Once Mark and Tammy graduated and promptly broke up, the main players in my drama were gone. All that were left were just sophomores and juniors. What did I care what a bunch of second-ran Mercutios and Benvolios thought of my tragic plight?

But thankfully, as the years pass, that recklessness and world-weary angst give way to a more optimistic perspective—it really has to, unless you want to end up covered in lint, proselytizing about how pets are better than spouses. At some point, Veronica will be forced to move past it, too; she'll gather up her resources, reassess the events of the past, and get over it. Even after her best friend's murder, even after the roofie and the rape and the very public rejections, even after her dad lost his position as sheriff and her mom skipped town, even after the nasty stand-off with Aaron Echolls and that terrible moment on the rooftop when she thought her dad was dead, we trust that, as an adult, Veronica will be fine. Sure, she'll spend a few more years in this jaded state, rolling her eyes at the patheticness of belligerent frat boys and drunken sorority girls. And maybe it'll take a few years of therapy, in which she'll chuckle that Duncan Kane was kind of a bore anyway, or marvel at how ridiculous it was that she ever could have been attracted to a total jerk like Logan Echolls in the first place. Maybe it'll require Veronica to make some good, trustworthy friends who aren't likely to succumb to the charms of wealthy Neanderthals like the ones who ruled Neptune High. Maybe she'll have to fall in love with a really nice, generous guy—someone sweet and earnest, like Deputy Leo, but without the unsavory ties to the Neptune police department.

But for now? Veronica is astonishingly world-weary, and we love her dearly for it.

HEATHER HAVRILESKY grew up in Durham, North Carolina, and graduated from Duke University. In 1996, she and illustrator Terry Colon created "Filler," a popular cartoon that ran for five years on *Suck.com*, one of the Web's first pop culture magazines. She's written for the *LA Times*, the *Washington Post*, *New York*, *Spin*, *BookForum*, and NPR's *All Things Considered*. She is currently a TV critic for *Salon. com* and maintains the Rabbit Blog. She lives in Los Angeles with her husband Bill and their two dogs.

Acknowledgments

The publisher thanks Abigail Allen, Josette Covington, Meadow Fallon-Dora, Debra Holliman, Wai-Yin Kwan, Adam Levine, Sunil Patel, Carolyn Paterson, Christer Vindberg, and the rest of the staff of Mars Investigations: The (In)Complete Guide to Veronica Mars (www.marsinvestigations.net) for their assistance in reviewing the manuscript.